Henry W. Longfellow.
1879.

THE

COMPLETE PROSE WORKS

OF

HENRY WADSWORTH LONGFELLOW

WITH

His Later Poems

ILLUSTRATED

WITH A BIOGRAPHICAL SKETCH

BY

OCTAVIUS B. FROTHINGHAM

BOSTON

HOUGHTON, MIFFLIN AND COMPANY

New York : 11 East Seventeenth Street

The Riverside Press, Cambridge

The Riverside Press, Cambridge:

Electrotyped and Printed by H. O. Houghton & Co.

CONTENTS OF VOLUME III.

LIST OF ILLUSTRATIONS.

NOTE. — The numerous borders, tail-pieces, and ornaments used in the half-titles, illustrated headings, and at the end of chapters were chiefly designed, when not otherwise indicated in the above list, by L. S. IPSEN, S. L. SMITH, and LOUIS RITTER.

IN THE HARBOR

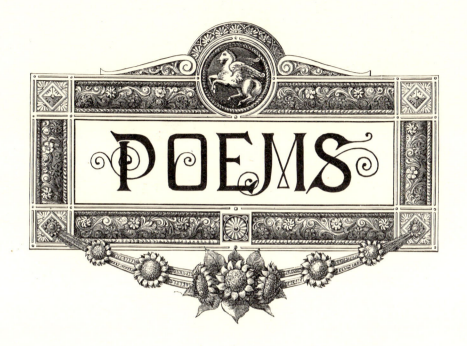

POEMS

BECALMED.

Becalmed upon the sea of Thought,
Still unattained the land it sought,
My mind, with loosely-hanging sails,
Lies waiting the auspicious gales.

On either side, behind, before,
The ocean stretches like a floor, —
A level floor of amethyst,
Crowned by a golden dome of mist.

Blow, breath of inspiration, blow!
Shake and uplift this golden glow!
And fill the canvas of the mind
With wafts of thy celestial wind.

Blow, breath of song! until I feel
The straining sail, the lifting keel,
The life of the awakening sea,
Its motion and its mystery!

HERMES TRISMEGISTUS.

As Seleucus narrates, Hermes describes the principles that rank as wholes in two myriads of books; or, as we are informed by Manetho, he perfectly unfolded these principles in three myriads six thousand five hundred and twenty-five volumes. . . . .

. . . Our ancestors dedicated the inventions of their wisdom to this deity, inscribing all their own writings with the name of Hermes. — IAMBLICUS.

STILL through Egypt's desert places
    Flows the lordly Nile,
From its banks the great stone faces
    Gaze with patient smile.

Still the pyramids imperious
    Pierce the cloudless skies,
And the Sphinx stares with mysterious,
    Solemn, stony eyes.

But where are the old Egyptian
    Demi-gods and kings?
Nothing left but an inscription
    Graven on stones and rings.
Where are Helios and Hephæstus,
    Gods of eldest eld?
Where is Hermes Trismegistus,
    Who their secrets held?

Where are now the many hundred
    Thousand books he wrote?
By the Thaumaturgists plundered,
    Lost in lands remote;
In oblivion sunk forever,
    As when o'er the land
Blows a storm-wind, in the river
    Sinks the scattered sand.

Something unsubstantial, ghostly,
  Seems this Theurgist,
In deep meditation mostly
  Wrapped, as in a mist.
Vague, phantasmal, and unreal
  To our thought he seems,
Walking in a world ideal,
  In a land of dreams.

Was he one, or many, merging
  Name and fame in one,
Like a stream, to which, converging,
  Many streamlets run?
Till, with gathered power proceeding,
  Ampler sweep it takes,
Downward the sweet waters leading
  From unnumbered lakes.

By the Nile I see him wandering,
  Pausing now and then,
On the mystic union pondering
  Between gods and men;
Half believing, wholly feeling,
  With supreme delight,
How the gods, themselves concealing,
  Lift men to their height.

Or in Thebes, the hundred-gated,
  In the thoroughfare
Breathing, as if consecrated,
  A diviner air;

And amid discordant noises,
  In the jostling throng,
Hearing far, celestial voices
  Of Olympian song.

Who shall call his dreams fallacious?
  Who has searched or sought
All the unexplored and spacious
  Universe of thought?
Who, in his own skill confiding,
  Shall with rule and line
Mark the border-land dividing
  Human and divine?

Trismegistus! three times greatest!
  How thy name sublime
Has descended to this latest
  Progeny of time!
Happy they whose written pages
  Perish with their lives,
If amid the rumbling ages
  Still their name survives!

Thine, O priest of Egypt, lately
  Found I in the vast,
Weed-encumbered, sombre, stately,
  Grave-yard of the Past;
And a presence moved before me
  On that gloomy shore,
As a waft of wind, that o'er me
  Breathed, and was no more.

THE POET'S CALENDAR.

JANUARY.

I.

JANUS am I; oldest of potentates;
  Forward I look, and backward, and below
I count, as god of avenues and gates,
  The years that through my portals come
    and go.

II.

I block the roads, and drift the fields with snow;
  I chase the wild-fowl from the frozen fen;
My frosts congeal the rivers in their flow,
  My fires light up the hearths and hearts of
    men.

FEBRUARY.

I am lustration; and the sea is mine!
  I wash the sands and headlands with my
    tide;
My brow is crowned with branches of the
    pine;
  Before my chariot-wheels the fishes glide.
By me all things unclean are purified,
  By me the souls of men washed white
    again;
E'en the unlovely tombs of those who died
  Without a dirge, I cleanse from every
    stain.

MARCH.

I Martius am! Once first, and now the third!
 To lead the Year was my appointed place;
A mortal dispossessed me by a word,
 And set there Janus with the double face.
Hence I make war on all the human race;
 I shake the cities with my hurricanes;
I flood the rivers and their banks efface,
 And drown the farms and hamlets with my
   rains.

APRIL.

I open wide the portals of the Spring
 To welcome the procession of the flowers.
With their gay banners, and the birds that
   sing
 Their song of songs from their aerial towers,
I soften with my sunshine and my showers
 The heart of earth; with thoughts of love
   I glide
Into the hearts of men; and with the Hours
 Upon the Bull with wreathèd horns I ride.

MAY.

Hark! The sea-faring wild-fowl loud proclaim
 My coming, and the swarming of the bees.
These are my heralds, and behold! my name
 Is written in blossoms on the hawthorn-
   trees.
I tell the mariner when to sail the seas;
 I waft o'er all the land from far away
The breath and bloom of the Hesperides,
 My birthplace. I am Maia. I am May.

JUNE.

Mine is the Month of Roses; yes, and mine
 The Month of Marriages! All pleasant sights
And scents, the fragrance of the blossoming
   vine,
 The foliage of the valleys and the heights.
Mine are the longest days, the loveliest nights;
 The mower's scythe makes music to my ear;
I am the mother of all dear delights;
 I am the fairest daughter of the year.

JULY.

My emblem is the Lion, and I breathe
  The breath of Libyan deserts o'er the land;
My sickle as a sabre I unsheathe,
  And bent before me the pale harvests stand.
The lakes and rivers shrink at my command,
  And there is thirst and fever in the air;
The sky is changed to brass, the earth to sand;
  I am the Emperor whose name I bear.

AUGUST.

The Emperor Octavian, called the August,
  I being his favorite, bestowed his name
Upon me, and I hold it still in trust,
  In memory of him and of his fame.
I am the Virgin, and my vestal flame
  Burns less intensely than the Lion's rage;
Sheaves are my only garlands, and I claim
  The golden Harvests as my heritage.

SEPTEMBER.

I bear the Scales, where hang in equipoise
  The night and day; and when unto my lips
I put my trumpet, with its stress and noise
  Fly the white clouds like tattered sails of
    ships;
The tree-tops lash the air with sounding whips;
  Southward the clamorous sea-fowl wing their
    flight;
The hedges are all red with haws and hips,
  The Hunter's Moon reigns empress of the
    night.

OCTOBER.

My ornaments are fruits; my garments leaves,
  Woven like cloth of gold, and crimson dyed;
I do not boast the harvesting of sheaves,
  O'er orchards and o'er vineyards I preside.
Though on the frigid Scorpion I ride,
The dreamy air is full, and overflows
With tender memories of the summer-tide,
  And mingled voices of the doves and crows.

NOVEMBER.

The Centaur, Sagittarius, am I,
  Born of Ixion's and the cloud's embrace;
With sounding hoofs across the earth I fly,
  A steed Thessalian with a human face.
Sharp winds the arrows are with which I
    chase
  The leaves, half dead already with affright;
I shroud myself in gloom; and to the race
  Of mortals bring nor comfort nor delight.

DECEMBER.

Riding upon the Goat, with snow-white hair,
  I come, the last of all. This crown of mine
Is of the holly; in my hand I bear
  The thyrsus, tipped with fragrant cones of
    pine.
I celebrate the birth of the Divine,
  And the return of the Saturnian reign;—
My songs are carols sung at every shrine,
  Proclaiming " Peace on earth, good will to
    men."

MAD RIVER,

IN THE WHITE MOUNTAINS.

TRAVELLER.

WHY dost thou wildly rush and roar,
  Mad River, O Mad River?
Wilt thou not pause and cease to pour
Thy hurrying, headlong waters o'er
  This rocky shelf forever?

What secret trouble stirs thy breast?
  Why all this fret and flurry?
Dost thou not know that what is best
In this too restless world is rest
  From over-work and worry?

THE RIVER.

What wouldst thou in these mountains
    seek,
  O stranger from the city?

Is it perhaps some foolish freak
Of thine, to put the words I speak
  Into a plaintive ditty?

TRAVELLER.

Yes; I would learn of thee thy song,
  With all its flowing numbers,
And in a voice as fresh and strong
As thine is, sing it all day long,
  And hear it in my slumbers.

THE RIVER.

A brooklet nameless and unknown
  Was I at first, resembling
A little child, that all alone
Comes venturing down the stairs of stone,
  Irresolute and trembling.

Later, by wayward fancies led,
    For the wide world I panted;
Out of the forest, dark and dread,
Across the open fields I fled,
    Like one pursued and haunted.

I tossed my arms, I sang aloud,
    My voice exultant blending
With thunder from the passing cloud,
The wind, the forest bent and bowed,
    The rush of rain descending.

I heard the distant ocean call,
    Imploring and entreating;
Drawn onward, o'er this rocky wall
I plunged, and the loud waterfall
    .Made answer to the greeting.

And now, beset with many ills,
    A toilsome life I follow;
Compelled to carry from the hills

These logs to the impatient mills
    Below there in the hollow.

Yet something ever cheers and charms
    The rudeness of my labors;
Daily I water with these arms
The cattle of a hundred farms,
    And have the birds for neighbors.

Men call me Mad, and well they may,
    When, full of rage and trouble,
I burst my banks of sand and clay,
And sweep their wooden bridge away,
    Like withered reeds or stubble.

Now go and write thy little rhyme,
    As of thine own creating.
Thou seest the day is past its prime;
I can no longer waste my time;
    The mills are tired of waiting.

AUF WIEDERSEHEN.

IN MEMORY OF J. T. F.

UNTIL we meet again! That is the meaning
Of the familiar words, that men repeat
   At parting in the street.
Ah yes, till then! but when death intervening
Rends us asunder, with what ceaseless pain
   We wait for the Again!

The friends who leave us do not feel the
   sorrow
Of parting, as we feel it, who must stay
   Lamenting day by day,
And knowing, when we wake upon the mor-
   row,
We shall not find in its accustomed place
   The one beloved face.

It were a double grief, if the departed,
Being released from earth, should still retain
   A sense of earthly pain;
It were a double grief, if the true-hearted,
Who loved us here, should on the farther shore
   Remember us no more.

Believing, in the midst of our afflictions,
That death is a beginning, not an end,
   We cry to them, and send
Farewells, that better might be called predic-
   tions,
Being fore-shadowings of the future, thrown
   Into the vast Unknown.

Faith overleaps the confines of our reason,
And if by faith, as in old times was said,
   Women received their dead
Raised up to life, then only for a season
Our partings are, nor shall we wait in vain
   Until we meet again!

THE CHILDREN'S CRUSADE.

[A FRAGMENT.]

"The Children's Crusade" was left unfinished by Mr. Longfellow. It is founded upon an event which occurred in the year 1212. An army of twenty thousand children, mostly boys, under the lead of a boy of ten years, named Nicolas, set out from Cologne for the Holy Land. When they reached Genoa only seven thousand remained. There, as the sea did not divide to allow them to march dry-shod to the East, they broke up. Some got as far as Rome; two ship-loads sailed from Pisa, and were not heard of again; the rest straggled back to Germany.

I.

WHAT is this I read in history,
Full of marvel, full of mystery,
Difficult to understand?
Is it fiction, is it truth?
Children in the flower of youth,
Heart in heart, and hand in hand,
Ignorant of what helps or harms,
Without armor, without arms,
Journeying to the Holy Land!

Who shall answer or divine?
Never since the world was made
Such a wonderful crusade
Started forth for Palestine.
Never while the world shall last

Will it reproduce the past;
Never will it see again
Such an army, such a band,
Over mountain, over main,
Journeying to the Holy Land.

Like a shower of blossoms blown
From the parent trees were they;
Like a flock of birds that fly
Through the unfrequented sky,
Holding nothing as their own,
Passed they into lands unknown,
Passed to suffer and to die.

O the simple, child-like trust!
O the faith that could believe
What the harnessed, iron-mailed
Knights of Christendom had failed,
By their prowess, to achieve,
They, the children, could and must!

Little thought the Hermit, preaching
Holy Wars to knight and baron,
That the words dropped in his teaching,
His entreaty, his beseeching,
Would by children's hands be gleaned,
And the staff on which he leaned
Blossom like the rod of Aaron.

As a summer wind upheaves
The innumerable leaves
In the bosom of a wood, —
Not as separate leaves, but massed
All together by the blast, —
So for evil or for good
His resistless breath upheaved
All at once the many-leaved,
Many-thoughted multitude.

In the tumult of the air
Rock the boughs with all the nests
Cradled on their tossing crests;
By the fervor of his prayer
Troubled hearts were everywhere
Rocked and tossed in human breasts.

For a century, at least,
His prophetic voice had ceased;
But the air was heated still
By his lurid words and will,

As from fires in far-off woods,
In the autumn of the year,
An unwonted fever broods
In the sultry atmosphere.

II.

In Cologne the bells were ringing,
In Cologne the nuns were singing
Hymns and canticles divine;
Loud the monks sang in their stalls,
And the thronging streets were loud
With the voices of the crowd; —
Underneath the city walls
Silent flowed the river Rhine.

From the gates, that summer day,
Clad in robes of hodden gray,
With the red cross on the breast,
Azure-eyed and golden-haired,
Forth the young crusaders fared;
While above the band devoted
Consecrated banners floated,
Fluttered many a flag and streamer,
And the cross o'er all the rest!
Singing lowly, meekly, slowly,
" Give us, give us back the holy
Sepulchre of the Redeemer!"
On the vast procession pressed,
Youths and maidens. . . .

III.

Ah! what master hand shall paint
How they journeyed on their way,
How the days grew long and dreary,
How their little feet grew weary,
How their little hearts grew faint!

Ever swifter day by day
Flowed the homeward river; ever
More and more its whitening current
Broke and scattered into spray,
Till the calmly-flowing river
Changed into a mountain torrent,
Rushing from its glacier green
Down through chasm and black ravine.
Like a phœnix in its nest,
Burned the red sun in the West,
Sinking in an ashen cloud;
In the East, above the crest
Of the sea-like mountain chain,

Like a phœnix from its shroud,
Came the red sun back again.

Now around them, white with snow,
Closed the mountain peaks. Below,
Headlong from the precipice
Down into the dark abyss,
Plunged the cataract, white with foam;
And it said, or seemed to say:
"Oh return, while yet you may,
Foolish children, to your home,
There the Holy City is!"

But the dauntless leader said:
"Faint not, though your bleeding feet
O'er these slippery paths of sleet
Move but painfully and slowly;
Other feet than yours have bled;

Other tears than yours been shed.
Courage! lose not heart or hope;
On the mountains' southern slope
Lies Jerusalem the Holy!"
As a white rose in its pride,
By the wind in summer-tide
Tossed and loosened from the branch,
Showers its petals o'er the ground,
From the distant mountain's side,
Scattering all its snows around,
With mysterious, muffled sound,
Loosened, fell the avalanche.
Voices, echoes far and near,
Roar of winds and waters blending,
Mists uprising, clouds impending,
Filled them with a sense of fear,
Formless, nameless, never ending.

.   .   .   .

THE CITY AND THE SEA.

THE panting City cried to the Sea,
"I am faint with heat,—O breathe on me!"

And the Sea said, "Lo, I breathe! but my breath
To some will be life, to others death!"

As to Prometheus, bringing ease
In pain, come the Oceanides,

So to the City, hot with the flame
Of the pitiless sun, the east wind came.

It came from the heaving breast of the deep,
Silent as dreams are, and sudden as sleep.

Life-giving, death-giving, which will it be;
O breath of the merciful, merciless Sea?

SUNDOWN.

THE summer sun is sinking low;
Only the tree-tops redden and glow:
Only the weathercock on the spire
Of the neighboring church is a flame of fire;
    All is in shadow below.

O beautiful, awful summer day,
What hast thou given, what taken away?
Life and death, and love and hate,

Homes made happy or desolate,
    Hearts made sad or gay!

On the road of life one mile-stone more!
In the book of life one leaf turned o'er!
Like a red seal is the setting sun
On the good and the evil men have done, —
    Naught can to-day restore!

July 24, 1879.

PRESIDENT GARFIELD.

" E VENNI DAL MARTIRIO A QUESTA PACE."

THESE words the poet heard in Paradise,
  Uttered by one who, bravely dying here,
  In the true faith was living in that sphere
  Where the celestial cross of sacrifice
Spread its protecting arms athwart the skies;
  And set thereon, like jewels crystal clear,
  The souls magnanimous, that knew not fear,
  Flashed their effulgence on his dazzled eyes.

Ah me! how dark the discipline of pain,
  Were not the suffering followed by the
    sense
  Of infinite rest and infinite release!
This is our consolation; and again
  A great soul cries to us in our suspense,
  " I came from martyrdom unto this peace!"

DECORATION DAY.

SLEEP, comrades, sleep and rest
  On this Field of the Grounded Arms,
Where foes no more molest,
  Nor sentry's shot alarms!

Ye have slept on the ground before,
  And started to your feet
At the cannon's sudden roar,
  Or the drum's redoubling beat.

But in this camp of Death
  No sound your slumber breaks;
Here is no fevered breath,
  No wound that bleeds and aches.

All is repose and peace,
  Untrampled lies the sod;
The shouts of battle cease,
  It is the truce of God!

Rest, comrades, rest and sleep!
  The thoughts of men shall be
As sentinels to keep
  Your rest from danger free.

Your silent tents of green
  We deck with fragrant flowers;
Yours has the suffering been,
  The memory shall be ours.

February 3, 1882.

CHIMES.

Sweet chimes! that in the loneliness of night
　Salute the passing hour, and in the dark
　And silent chambers of the household mark
　The movements of the myriad orbs of light!
Through my closed eyelids, by the inner sight,
　I see the constellations in the arc
　Of their great circles moving on, and hark!

I almost hear them singing in their flight.
Better than sleep it is to lie awake,
　O'er-canopied by the vast starry dome
　Of the immeasurable sky; to feel
The slumbering world sink under us, and make
　Hardly an eddy,—a mere rush of foam
　On the great sea beneath a sinking keel.

August 28, 1879.

FOUR BY THE CLOCK.

Four by the clock! and yet not day;
But the great world rolls and wheels away,
With its cities on land, and its ships at sea,
Into the dawn that is to be!

Only the lamp in the anchored bark
Sends its glimmer across the dark,
And the heavy breathing of the sea
Is the only sound that comes to me.

Nahant, *September* 8, 1880,
Four o'clock in the morning.

THE FOUR LAKES OF MADISON.

Four limpid lakes,—four Naiades
Or sylvan deities are these,
　In flowing robes of azure dressed;
Four lovely handmaids, that uphold
Their shining mirrors, rimmed with gold,
　To the fair city in the West.

By day the coursers of the sun
Drink of these waters as they run
　Their swift diurnal round on high;

By night the constellations glow
Far down the hollow deeps below,
　And glimmer in another sky.

Fair lakes, serene and full of light,
Fair town, arrayed in robes of white,
　How visionary ye appear!
All like a floating landscape seems
In cloud-land or the land of dreams,
　Bathed in a golden atmosphere!

MOONLIGHT.

As a pale phantom with a lamp
　Ascends some ruin's haunted stair,
So glides the moon along the damp
　Mysterious chambers of the air.

Now hidden in cloud, and now revealed,
　As if this phantom, full of pain,
Were by the crumbling walls concealed,
　And at the windows seen again.

Until at last, serene and proud
  In all the splendor of her light,
She walks the terraces of cloud,
  Supreme as Empress of the Night.

I look, but recognize no more
  Objects familiar to my view;
The very pathway to my door
  Is an enchanted avenue.

All things are changed. One mass of shade,
  The elm-trees drop their curtains down;
By palace, park, and colonnade
  I walk as in a foreign town.

The very ground beneath my feet
  Is clothed with a diviner air;
While marble paves the silent street
  And glimmers in the empty square.

Illusion! Underneath there lies
  The common life of every day;
Only the spirit glorifies
  With its own tints the sober gray.

In vain we look, in vain uplift
  Our eyes to heaven, if we are blind;
We see but what we have the gift
  Of seeing; what we bring we find.

December 20, 1878.

TO THE AVON.

FLOW on, sweet river! like his verse
Who lies beneath this sculptured hearse;
Nor wait beside the churchyard wall
For him who cannot hear thy call.

Thy playmate once; I see him now
A boy with sunshine on his brow,
And hear in Stratford's quiet street
The patter of his little feet.

I see him by thy shallow edge
Wading knee-deep amid the sedge;

And lost in thought, as if thy stream
Were the swift river of a dream.

He wonders whitherward it flows;
And fain would follow where it goes,
To the wide world, that shall erelong
Be filled with his melodious song.

Flow on, fair stream! That dream is o'er;
He stands upon another shore;
A vaster river near him flows,
And still he follows where it goes.

ELEGIAC VERSE.

I.

PERADVENTURE of old, some bard in Ionian
    Islands,
    Walking alone by the sea, hearing the wash
      of the waves,
Learned the secret from them of the beauti-
    ful verse elegiac,
    Breathing into his song motion and sound
      of the sea.

For as the wave of the sea, upheaving in long
    undulations,
    Plunges loud on the sands, pauses, and
      turns, and retreats,
So the Hexameter, rising and singing, with
    cadence sonorous,
    Falls; and in refluent rhythm back the
      Pentameter flows.[1]

II.

Not in his youth alone, but in age, may the
    heart of the poet
    Bloom into song, as the gorse blossoms in
      autumn and spring.

[1] Compare Schiller.

    In Hexameter steigt des Springquells flüssige Säule;
      Im Pentameter drauf fällt sie melodisch herab.

See also Coleridge's translation.

III.

Not in tenderness wanting, yet rough are the
    rhymes of our poet;
    Though it be Jacob's voice, Esau's, alas! are
      the hands.

IV.

Let us be grateful to writers for what is left
    in the inkstand;
    When to leave off is an art only attained
      by the few.

V.

How can the Three be One? you ask me; I
    answer by asking,
    Hail and snow and rain, are they not three,
      and yet one?

VI.

By the mirage uplifted the land floats vague
    in the ether,
    Ships and the shadows of ships hang in the
      motionless air;
So by the art of the poet our common life is
    uplifted,
    So, transfigured, the world floats in a lumi-
      nous haze.

VII.

Like a French poem is Life; being only perfect in structure
When with the masculine rhymes mingled
the feminine are.

VIII.

Down from the mountain descends the brooklet, rejoicing in freedom;
Little it dreams of the mill hid in the valley below;
Glad with the joy of existence, the child goes
singing and laughing,
Little dreaming what toils lie in the future
concealed.

IX.

As the ink from our pen, so flow our thoughts
and our feelings
When we begin to write, however sluggish
before.

X.

Like the Kingdom of Heaven, the Fountain
of Youth is within us;
If we seek it elsewhere, old shall we grow
in the search.

XI.

If you would hit the mark, you must aim a
little above it;
Every arrow that flies feels the attraction
of earth.

XII.

Wisely the Hebrews admit no Present tense
in their language;
While we are speaking the word, it is already the Past.

XIII.

In the twilight of age all things seem strange
and phantasmal,
As between daylight and dark ghost-like the
landscape appears.

XIV.

Great is the art of beginning, but greater the
art is of ending;
Many a poem is marred by a superfluous
verse.

1881.

THE BELLS OF SAN BLAS.[1]

WHAT say the Bells of San Blas
To the ships that southward pass
    From the harbor of Mazatlan?
To them it is nothing more
Than the sound of surf on the shore, —
    Nothing more to master or man.

But to me, a dreamer of dreams,
To whom what is and what seems
    Are often one and the same, —
The Bells of San Blas to me
Have a strange, wild melody,
    And are something more than a name.

For bells are the voice of the church;
They have tones that touch and search
    The hearts of young and old;
One sound to all, yet each
Lends a meaning to their speech,
    And the meaning is manifold.

They are a voice of the Past,
Of an age that is fading fast,
    Of a power austere and grand;
When the flag of Spain unfurled
Its folds o'er this western world,
    And the Priest was lord of the land.

The chapel that once looked down
On the little seaport town
    Has crumbled into the dust;
And on oaken beams below
The bells swing to and fro,
    And are green with mould and rust.

"Is, then, the old faith dead,"
They say, "and in its stead
    Is some new faith proclaimed,
That we are forced to remain
Naked to sun and rain,
    Unsheltered and ashamed?

[1] The last poem written by Mr. Longfellow.

"Once in our tower aloof
We rang over wall and roof
    Our warnings and our complaints;
And round about us there
The white doves filled the air,
    Like the white souls of the saints.

"The saints! Ah, have they grown
Forgetful of their own?
    Are they asleep, or dead,
That open to the sky
Their ruined Missions lie,
    No longer tenanted?

"Oh, bring us back once more
The vanished days of yore,
    When the world with faith was filled;

Bring back the fervid zeal,
The hearts of fire and steel,
    The hands that believe and build.

"Then from our tower again
We will send over land and main
    Our voices of command,
Like exiled kings who return
To their thrones, and the people learn
    That the Priest is lord of the land!"

O Bells of San Blas, in vain
Ye call back the Past again!
    The Past is deaf to your prayer;
Out of the shadows of night
The world rolls into light;
    It is daybreak everywhere.

March 15, 1882.

A FRAGMENT.

AWAKE! arise! the hour is late!
    Angels are knocking at thy door!
They are in haste and cannot wait,
    And once departed come no more.

Awake! arise! the athlete's arm
    Loses its strength by too much rest;
The fallow land, the untilled farm
    Produces only weeds at best.

PRELUDE.

As treasures that men seek,
  Deep-buried in sea-sands,
Vanish if they but speak,
  And elude their eager hands,

So ye escape and slip,
  O songs, and fade away,
When the word is on my lip
  To interpret what ye say.

Were it not better, then,
  To let the treasures rest
Hid from the eyes of men,
  Locked in their iron chest?

I have but marked the place,
  But half the secret told,
That, following this slight trace,
  Others may find the gold.

FROM THE FRENCH.

WILL ever the dear days come back again,
  Those days of June, when lilacs were in
    bloom,
  And bluebirds sang their sonnets in the
    gloom
  Of leaves that roofed them in from sun or
    rain?
I know not; but a presence will remain
  Forever and forever in this room,

Formless, diffused in air, like a perfume,—
  A phantom of the heart, and not the brain.
Delicious days! when every spoken word
  Was like a foot-fall nearer and more near,
  And a mysterious knocking at the gate
Of the heart's secret places, and we heard
  In the sweet tumult of delight and fear
  A voice that whispered, "Open, I cannot
    wait!"

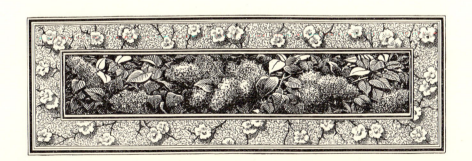

AT LA CHAUDEAU.

FROM THE FRENCH OF XAVIER MARMIER.

AT La Chaudeau, — 't is long since then:
I was young, — my years twice ten;
All things smiled on the happy boy,
Dreams of love and songs of joy,
Azure of heaven and wave below,
  At La Chaudeau.

To La Chaudeau I come back old:
My head is gray, my blood is cold;
Seeking along the meadow ooze,
Seeking beside the river Seymouse,
The days of my spring-time of long ago
  At La Chaudeau.

At La Chaudeau nor heart nor brain
Ever grows old with grief and pain;
A sweet remembrance keeps off age;

A tender friendship doth still assuage
The burden of sorrow that one may know
  At La Chaudeau.

At La Chaudeau, had fate decreed
To limit the wandering life I lead,
Peradventure I still, forsooth,
Should have preserved my fresh green youth
Under the shadows the hill-tops throw
  At La Chaudeau.

At La Chaudeau, live on, my friends,
Happy to be where God intends;
And sometimes, by the evening fire,
Think of him whose sole desire
Is again to sit in the old château
  At La Chaudeau.

A QUIET LIFE.

FROM THE FRENCH.

LET him who will, by force or fraud innate,
 Of courtly grandeurs gain the slippery
  height;
 I, leaving not the home of my delight,
 Far from the world and noise will meditate.
Then, without pomps or perils of the great,
 I shall behold the day succeed the night;
 Behold the alternate seasons take their flight,
 And in serene repose old age await.

And so, whenever Death shall come to close
 The happy moments that my days compose,
 I, full of years, shall die, obscure, alone!
How wretched is the man, with honors
  crowned,
 Who, having not the one thing needful
  found,
 Dies, known to all, but to himself unknown.
      September 11, 1879.

THE WINE OF JURANÇON.

FROM THE FRENCH OF CHARLES CORAN.

LITTLE sweet wine of Jurançon,
  You are dear to my memory still!
With mine host and his merry song,
  Under the rose-tree I drank my fill.

Twenty years after, passing that way,
  Under the trellis I found again
Mine host still sitting there *au frais*,
  And singing still the same refrain.

The Jurançon, so fresh and bold,
  Treats me as one it used to know,

Souvenirs of the days of old
  Already from the bottle flow.

With glass in hand our glances met;
  We pledge, we drink. How sour it is!
Never Argenteuil piquette
  Was to my palate sour as this!

And yet the vintage was good, in sooth;
  The self-same juice, the self-same cask!
It was you, O gayety of my youth,
  That failed in the autumnal flask!

PERSONAL POEMS

LOSS AND GAIN.

WHEN I compare
What I have lost with what I have gained,
What I have missed with what attained,
Little room do I find for pride.

I am aware
How many days have been idly spent;

How like an arrow the good intent
Has fallen short or been turned aside.

But who shall dare
To measure loss and gain in this wise?
Defeat may be victory in disguise;
The lowest ebb is the turn of the tide.

AUTUMN WITHIN.

IT is autumn; not without,
But within me is the cold.
Youth and spring are all about;
It is I that have grown old.

Birds are darting through the air,
Singing, building without rest;

Life is stirring everywhere,
Save within my lonely breast.

There is silence: the dead leaves
Fall and rustle and are still;
Beats no flail upon the sheaves,
Comes no murmur from the mill.

April 9, 1874.

VICTOR AND VANQUISHED.

As one who long hath fled with panting breath
Before his foe, bleeding and near to fall,
I turn and set my back against the wall,
And look thee in the face, triumphant Death,
I call for aid, and no one answereth;
I am alone with thee, who conquerest all;
Yet me thy threatening form doth not appall,

For thou art but a phantom and a wraith.
Wounded and weak, sword broken at the hilt,
With armor shattered, and without a shield,
I stand unmoved; do with me what thou wilt;
I can resist no more, but will not yield.
This is no tournament where cowards tilt;
The vanquished here is victor of the field.

April 4, 1876.

MEMORIES.

Oft I remember those whom I have known
  In other days, to whom my heart was led
  As by a magnet, and who are not dead,
  But absent, and their memories overgrown
With other thoughts and troubles of my own,
  As graves with grasses are, and at their
    head
  The stone with moss and lichens so o'er-
    spread,

Nothing is legible but the name alone.
And is it so with them? After long years,
  Do they remember me in the same way,
  And is the memory pleasant as to me?
I fear to ask; yet wherefore are my fears?
  Pleasures, like flowers, may wither and
    decay,
  And yet the root perennial may be.

September 23, 1881.

MY BOOKS.

Sadly as some old mediæval knight
  Gazed at the arms he could no longer wield,
  The sword two-handed and the shining shield
  Suspended in the hall, and full in sight,
While secret longings for the lost delight
  Of tourney or adventure in the field
  Came over him, and tears but half con-
    cealed

Trembled and fell upon his beard of white,
So I behold these books upon their shelf,
  My ornaments and arms of other days;
  Not wholly useless, though no longer used,
For they remind me of my other self,
  Younger and stronger, and the pleasant ways
  In which I walked, now clouded and con-
    fused.

December 27, 1881.

L'ENVOI

POSSIBILITIES.

Where are the Poets, unto whom belong
  The Olympian heights; whose singing shafts
    were sent
  Straight to the mark, and not from bows
    half bent,
  But with the utmost tension of the thong?
Where are the stately argosies of song,
  Whose rushing keels made music as they
    went
  Sailing in search of some new continent,

With all sail set, and steady winds and
    strong?
Perhaps there lives some dreamy boy, untaught
  In schools, some graduate of the field or
    street,
  Who shall become a master of the art,
An admiral sailing the high seas of thought,
  Fearless and first, and steering with his fleet
  For lands not yet laid down in any chart.

January 17, 1882.

ENGRAVED BY G. KRUELL.

MICHAEL ANGELO.

MICHAEL ANGELO

Michel più che mortal, Angel divino.

ARIOSTO.

Similamente operando all' artista
Ch' a l'abito dell' arte e man che trema.

DANTE, *Par.* xiii. *st.* 77.

MICHAEL·ANGELO
·DEDICATION·

Nothing that is shall perish utterly,
  But perish only to revive again
  In other forms, as clouds restore in rain
  The exhalations of the land and sea.
Men build their houses from the masonry
  Of ruined tombs; the passion and the pain
  Of hearts, that long have ceased to beat, remain
  To throb in hearts that are, or are to be.
So from old chronicles, where sleep in dust
  Names that once filled the world with trumpet tones,
  I build this verse; and flowers of song have thrust
Their roots among the loose disjointed stones,
  Which to this end I fashion as I must.
  Quickened are they that touch the Prophet's bones.

MICHAEL ANGELO

PART FIRST

I.

PROLOGUE AT ISCHIA.

The Castle Terrace. VITTORIA COLONNA *and* JULIA GONZAGA.

VITTORIA.

Will you then leave me, Julia, and so soon,
To pace alone this terrace like a ghost?

JULIA.

To-morrow, dearest.

VITTORIA.

     Do not say to-morrow.
A whole month of to-morrows were too soon.
You must not go. You are a part of me.

JULIA.

I must return to Fondi.

VITTORIA.

     The old castle
Needs not your presence. No one waits for
  you.
Stay one day longer with me. They who go
Feel not the pain of parting; it is they
Who stay behind that suffer. I was thinking
But yesterday how like and how unlike
Have been, and are, our destinies. Your hus-
  band,

The good Vespasian, an old man, who seemed
A father to you rather than a husband,
Died in your arms; but mine, in all the flower
And promise of his youth, was taken from
  me
As by a rushing wind. The breath of battle
Breathed on him, and I saw his face no more,
Save as in dreams it haunts me. As our love
Was for these men, so is our sorrow for them.
Yours a child's sorrow, smiling through its
  tears;
But mine the grief of an impassioned woman,
Who drank her life up in one draught of love.

JULIA.

Behold this locket. This is the white hair
Of my Vespasian. This is the flower-of-love,
This amaranth, and beneath it the device
Non moritura. Thus my heart remains
True to his memory; and the ancient castle,
Where we have lived together, where he died,
Is dear to me as Ischia is to you.

VITTORIA.

I did not mean to chide you.

JULIA.

     Let your heart
Find, if it can, some poor apology
For one who is too young, and feels too keenly

The joy of life, to give up all her days
To sorrow for the dead. While I am true
To the remembrance of the man I loved
And mourn for still, I do not make a show
Of all the grief I feel, nor live secluded
And, like Veronica da Gámbara,
Drape my whole house in mourning, and drive
    forth
In coach of sable drawn by sable horses,
As if I were a corpse. Ah, one to-day
Is worth for me a thousand yesterdays.

VITTORIA.

Dear Julia! Friendship has its jealousies
As well as love. Who waits for you at Fondi?

JULIA.

A friend of mine and yours; a friend and
    friar.
You have at Naples your Fra Bernardino;
And I at Fondi have my Fra Bastiano,
The famous artist, who has come from Rome
To paint my portrait. That is not a sin.

VITTORIA.

Only a vanity.

JULIA.

        He painted yours.

VITTORIA.

Do not call up to me those days departed,
When I was young, and all was bright about
    me,
And the vicissitudes of life were things
But to be read of in old histories,
Though as pertaining unto me or mine
Impossible. Ah, then I dreamed your dreams,
And now, grown older, I look back and see
They were illusions.

JULIA.

            Yet without illusions
What would our lives become, what we our-
    selves?
Dreams or illusions, call them what you will,
They lift us from the commonplace of life
To better things.

VITTORIA.

                    Are there no brighter dreams,
No higher aspirations, than the wish
To please and to be pleased?

JULIA.

                    For you there are:
I am no saint; I feel the world we live in
Comes before that which is to be hereafter,
And must be dealt with first.

VITTORIA.

                    But in what way?

JULIA.

Let the soft wind that wafts to us the odor
Of orange blossoms, let the laughing sea
And the bright sunshine bathing all the
          world,
Answer the question.

VITTORIA.

                    And for whom is meant
This portrait that you speak of?

JULIA.

                    For my friend
The Cardinal Ippolito.

VITTORIA.

                    For him?

JULIA.

Yes, for Ippolito the Magnificent.
'T is always flattering to a woman's pride
To be admired by one whom all admire.

VITTORIA.

Ah, Julia, she that makes herself a dove
Is eaten by the hawk. Be on your guard.
He is a Cardinal; and his adoration
Should be elsewhere directed.

JULIA.

                    You forget
The horror of that night, when Barbarossa,
The Moorish corsair, landed on our coast
To seize me for the Sultan Soliman;
How in the dead of night, when all were sleep-
          ing,

He scaled the castle wall; how I escaped,
And in my night-dress, mounting a swift
          steed,
Fled to the mountains, and took refuge there
Among the brigands. Then of all my friends
The Cardinal Ippolito was first
To come with his retainers to my rescue.
Could I refuse the only boon he asked
At such a time, my portrait?

VITTORIA.

                    I have heard
Strange stories of the splendors of his pal-
          ace,
And how, apparelled like a Spanish Prince,
He rides through Rome with a long retinue
Of Ethiopians and Numidians
And Turks and Tartars, in fantastic dresses,
Making a gallant show. Is this the way
A Cardinal should live?

JULIA.

                    He is so young;
Hardly of age, or little more than that;
Beautiful, generous, fond of arts and letters,
A poet, a musician, and a scholar;
Master of many languages, and a player
On many instruments. In Rome, his palace
Is the asylum of all men distinguished
In art or science, and all Florentines
Escaping from the tyranny of his cousin,
Duke Alessandro.

VITTORIA.

                    I have seen his portrait,
Painted by Titian. You have painted it
In brighter colors.

JULIA.

                    And my Cardinal,
At Itri, in the courtyard of his palace,
Keeps a tame lion!

VITTORIA.

                    And so counterfeits
St. Mark, the Evangelist!

JULIA.

                    Ah, your tame lion
Is Michael Angelo.

VITTORIA.

            You speak a name
That always thrills me with a noble sound,
As of a trumpet! Michael Angelo!
A lion all men fear and none can tame;
A man that all men honor, and the model
That all should follow; one who works and
      prays,
For work is prayer, and consecrates his life
To the sublime ideal of his art,
Till art and life are one; a man who holds
Such place in all men's thoughts, that when
      they speak
Of great things done, or to be done, his name
Is ever on their lips.

JULIA.

            You too can paint
The portrait of your hero, and in colors
Brighter than Titian's; I might warn you
      also
Against the dangers that beset your path;
But I forbear.

VITTORIA.

         If I were made of marble,
Of Fior di Persico or Pavonazzo,
He might admire me: being but flesh and
      blood,

I am no more to him than other women;
That is, am nothing.

JULIA.

         Does he ride through Rome
Upon his little mule, as he was wont,
With his slouched hat, and boots of Cordovan,
As when I saw him last?

VITTORIA.

           Pray do not jest.
I cannot couple with his noble name
A trivial word! Look, how the setting sun
Lights up Castel-a-mare and Sorrento,
And changes Capri to a purple cloud!
And there Vesuvius with its plume of smoke,
And the great city stretched upon the shore
As in a dream!

JULIA.

        Parthenope the Siren!

VITTORIA.

And yon long line of lights, those sunlit win-
      dows
Blaze like the torches carried in procession
To do her honor! It is beautiful!

JULIA.

I have no heart to feel the beauty of it!
My feet are weary, pacing up and down
These level flags, and wearier still my thoughts
Treading the broken pavement of the Past.
It is too sad. I will go in and rest,
And make me ready for to-morrow's journey.

VITTORIA.

I will go with you; for I would not lose
One hour of your dear presence. 'T is enough
Only to be in the same room with you.
I need not speak to you, nor hear you speak;
If I but see you, I am satisfied.

                  [They go in.

II.

MONOLOGUE.

MICHAEL ANGELO'S *Studio. He is at work on the cartoon
of the Last Judgment.*

MICHAEL ANGELO.

Why did the Pope and his ten Cardinals
Come here to lay this heavy task upon me?

Were not the paintings on the Sistine ceiling
Enough for them? They saw the Hebrew
    leader
Waiting, and clutching his tempestuous beard,
But heeded not. The bones of Julius
Shook in their sepulchre. I heard the sound;
They only heard the sound of their own voices.

Are there no other artists here in Rome
To do this work, that they must needs seek
    me?
Fra Bastian, my Fra Bastian, might have
    done it;
But he is lost to art. The Papal Seals,
Like leaden weights upon a dead man's eyes,
Press down his lids; and so the burden falls
On Michael Angelo, Chief Architect
And Painter of the Apostolic Palace.
That is the title they cajole me with,
To make me do their work and leave my own;
But having once begun, I turn not back.
Blow, ye bright angels, on your golden trum-
    pets
To the four corners of the earth, and wake

The dead to judgment! Ye recording angels,
Open your books and read! Ye dead, awake!
Rise from your graves, drowsy and drugged
    with death,
As men who suddenly aroused from sleep
Look round amazed, and know not where
    they are!

In happy hours, when the imagination
Wakes like a wind at midnight, and the soul
Trembles in all its leaves, it is a joy
To be uplifted on its wings, and listen
To the prophetic voices in the air
That call us onward. Then the work we do
Is a delight, and the obedient hand
Never grows weary. But how different is it
In the disconsolate, discouraged hours,
When all the wisdom of the world appears
As trivial as the gossip of a nurse
In a sick-room, and all our work seems useless.

What is it guides my hand, what thoughts
    possess me,
That I have drawn her face among the angels,

Where she will be hereafter? O sweet dreams,
That through the vacant chambers of my
    heart
Walk in the silence, as familiar phantoms
Frequent an ancient house, what will ye with
    me?
'T is said that Emperors write their names in
    green
When under age, but when of age in purple.
So Love, the greatest Emperor of them all,
Writes his in green at first, but afterwards
In the imperial purple of our blood.
First love or last love, — which of these two
    passions
Is more omnipotent? Which is more fair,
The star of morning or the evening star?
The sunrise or the sunset of the heart?
The hour when we look forth to the unknown,
And the advancing day consumes the shadows,
Or that when all the landscape of our lives
Lies stretched behind us, and familiar places
Gleam in the distance, and sweet memories
Rise like a tender haze, and magnify
The objects we behold, that soon must vanish?

What matters it to me, whose countenance
Is like the Laocoön's, full of pain; whose fore-
    head
Is a ploughed harvest-field, where threescore
    years
Have sown in sorrow and have reaped in an-
    guish;
To me, the artisan, to whom all women
Have been as if they were not, or at most
A sudden rush of pigeons in the air,
A flutter of wings, a sound, and then a si-
    lence?
I am too old for love; I am too old
To flatter and delude myself with visions
Of never-ending friendship with fair women,
Imaginations, fantasies, illusions,
In which the things that cannot be take shape,
And seem to be, and for the moment are.
                        [*Convent bells ring.*

Distant and near and low and loud the bells,
Dominican, Benedictine, and Franciscan,
Jangle and wrangle in their airy towers,
Discordant as the brotherhoods themselves
In their dim cloisters. The descending sun

Seems to caress the city that he loves,
And crowns it with the aureole of a saint.
I will go forth and breathe the air a while.

III.

SAN SILVESTRO.

A Chapel in the Church of San Silvestro on Monte Cavallo.

VITTORIA COLONNA, CLAUDIO TOLOMMEI, *and others.*

VITTORIA.

Here let us rest a while, until the crowd
Has left the church. I have already sent
For Michael Angelo to join us here.

MESSER CLAUDIO.

After Fra Bernardino's wise discourse
On the Pauline Epistles, certainly
Some words of Michael Angelo on Art
Were not amiss, to bring us back to earth.

MICHAEL ANGELO, *at the door.*

How like a Saint or Goddess she appears;
Diana or Madonna, which I know not!
In attitude and aspect formed to be
At once the artist's worship and despair!

VITTORIA.

Welcome, Maestro. We were waiting for you.

MICHAEL ANGELO.

I met your messenger upon the way,
And hastened hither.

VITTORIA.

                It is kind of you
To come to us, who linger here like gossips
Wasting the afternoon in idle talk.
These are all friends of mine and friends of
    yours.

MICHAEL ANGELO.

If friends of yours, then are they friends of
    mine.
Pardon me, gentlemen. But when I entered
I saw but the Marchesa.

VITTORIA.

                    Take this seat
Between me and Ser Claudio Tolommei,
Who still maintains that our Italian tongue

Should be called Tuscan.   But for that of-
    fence
We will not quarrel with him.

MICHAEL ANGELO.

            Eccellenza —

VITTORIA.

Ser Claudio has banished Eccellenza
And all such titles from the Tuscan tongue.

MESSER CLAUDIO.

'T is the abuse of them and not the use
I deprecate.

MICHAEL ANGELO.

        The use or the abuse,
It matters not.   Let them all go together,
As empty phrases and frivolities,
And common as gold-lace upon the collar
Of an obsequious lackey.

VITTORIA.

            That may be,
But something of politeness would go with
    them ;
We should lose something of the stately man-
    ners
Of the old school.

MESSER CLAUDIO.

    Undoubtedly.

VITTORIA.

            But that
Is not what occupies my thoughts at present,
Nor why I sent for you, Messer Michele,
It was to counsel me.   His Holiness
Has granted me permission, long desired,
To build a convent in this neighborhood,
Where the old tower is standing, from whose
    top
Nero looked down upon the burning city.

MICHAEL ANGELO.

It is an inspiration!

VITTORIA.

            I am doubtful
How I shall build; how large to make the
        convent,
And which way fronting.

MICHAEL ANGELO.

                Ah, to build, to build!
That is the noblest art of all the arts,
Painting and sculpture are but images,
Are merely shadows cast by outward things
On stone or canvas, having in themselves
No separate existence. Architecture,
Existing in itself, and not in seeming
A something it is not, surpasses them
As substance shadow. Long, long years ago,
Standing one morning near the Baths of Titus,
I saw the statue of Laocoön
Rise from its grave of centuries, like a ghost
Writhing in pain; and as it tore away
The knotted serpents from its limbs, I heard,
Or seemed to hear, the cry of agony
From its white, parted lips. And still I mar-
        vel
At the three Rhodian artists, by whose hands
This miracle was wrought. Yet he beholds
Far nobler works who looks upon the ruins
Of temples in the Forum here in Rome.
If God should give me power in my old age
To build for Him a temple half as grand
As those were in their glory, I should count
My age more excellent than youth itself,
And all that I have hitherto accomplished
As only vanity.

VITTORIA.

            I understand you.
Art is the gift of God, and must be used
Unto His glory. That in art is highest
Which aims at this. When St. Hilarion blessed
The horses of Italicus, they won
The race at Gaza, for his benediction
O'erpowered all magic; and the people shouted
That Christ had conquered Marnas. So that
        art
Which bears the consecration and the seal
Of holiness upon it will prevail

Over all others. Those few words of yours
Inspire me with new confidence to build.
What think you? The old walls might serve,
        perhaps,
Some purpose still. The tower can hold the
        bells.

MICHAEL ANGELO.

If strong enough.

VITTORIA.

        If not, it can be strengthened.

MICHAEL ANGELO.

I see no bar nor drawback to this building,
And on our homeward way, if it shall please
        you,
We may together view the site.

VITTORIA.

                    I thank you.
I did not venture to request so much.

MICHAEL ANGELO.

Let us now go to the old walls you spake of,
Vossignoria —

VITTORIA.

        What, again, Maestro?

MICHAEL ANGELO.

Pardon me, Messer Claudio, if once more
I use the ancient courtesies of speech.
I am too old to change.

IV.

CARDINAL IPPOLITO.

A richly furnished apartment in the Palace of CARDINAL
IPPOLITO. *Night.*

JACOPO NARDI, *an old man, alone.*

NARDI.

I am bewildered. These Numidian slaves,
In strange attire; these endless antechambers;
This lighted hall, with all its golden splendors,
Pictures, and statues! Can this be the dwell-
        ing
Of a disciple of that lowly Man
Who had not where to lay his head? These
        statues

Are not of Saints; nor is this a Madonna,
This lovely face, that with such tender eyes
Looks down upon me from the painted canvas.
My heart begins to fail me. What can he
Who lives in boundless luxury at Rome
Care for the imperilled liberties of Florence,
Her people, her Republic? Ah, the rich
Feel not the pangs of banishment. All doors
Are open to them, and all hands extended.
The poor alone are outcasts; they who risked
All they possessed for liberty, and lost;
And wander through the world without a
    friend,
Sick, comfortless, distressed, unknown, uncared
    for.

Enter CARDINAL IPPOLITO, *in Spanish cloak and
slouched hat.*

IPPOLITO.

I pray you pardon me that I have kept you
Waiting so long alone.

NARDI.

          I wait to see
The Cardinal.

IPPOLITO.

       I am the Cardinal;
And you?

NARDI.

Jacopo Nardi,

IPPOLITO.

          You are welcome,
I was expecting you. Philippo Strozzi
Had told me of your coming.

NARDI.

          'T was his son
That brought me to your door.

IPPOLITO.

        Pray you, be seated.
You seem astonished at the garb I wear,
But at my time of life, and with my habits,
The petticoats of a Cardinal would be —
Troublesome; I could neither ride nor walk,
Nor do a thousand things, if I were dressed
Like an old dowager. It were putting wine

Young as the young Astyanax into goblets
As old as Priam.

NARDI.

        Oh, your Eminence
Knows best what you should wear.

IPPOLITO.

          Dear Messer Nardi,
You are no stranger to me. I have read
Your excellent translation of the books
Of Titus Livius, the historian
Of Rome, and model of all historians
That shall come after him. It does you honor;
But greater honor still the love you bear
To Florence, our dear country, and whose an-
    nals
I hope your hand will write, in happier days
Than we now see.

NARDI.

       Your Eminence will pardon
The lateness of the hour.

IPPOLITO.

        The hours I count not
As a sun-dial; but am like a clock,
That tells the time as well by night as day.
So, no excuse. I know what brings you here.
You come to speak of Florence.

NARDI.

          And her woes.

IPPOLITO.

The Duke, my cousin, the black Alessandro,
Whose mother was a Moorish slave, that fed
The sheep upon Lorenzo's farm, still lives
And reigns.

NARDI.

       Alas, that such a scourge
Should fall on such a city!

IPPOLITO.

          When he dies,
The Wild Boar in the gardens of Lorenzo,
The beast obscene, should be the monument
Of this bad man.

NARDI.

He walks the streets at night

With revellers, insulting honest men.
No house is sacred from his lusts. The con-
    vents
Are turned by him to brothels, and the honor
Of women and all ancient pious customs
Are quite forgotten now. The offices
Of the Priori and Gonfalonieri
Have been abolished. All the magistrates
Are now his creatures. Liberty is dead.
The very memory of all honest living
Is wiped away, and even our Tuscan tongue
Corrupted to a Lombard dialect.

IPPOLITO.

And worst of all his impious hand has broken
The Martinella, — our great battle bell,
That, sounding through three centuries, has
    led
The Florentines to victory, — lest its voice
Should waken in their souls some memory
Of far-off times of glory.

NARDI.

             What a change
Ten little years have made! We all remem-
    ber
Those better days, when Niccolà Capponi,

The Gonfaloniere, from the windows
Of the Old Palace, with the blast of trumpets,
Proclaimed to the inhabitants that Christ
Was chosen King of Florence; and already
Christ is dethroned, and slain, and in his stead
Reigns Lucifer! Alas, alas, for Florence!

IPPOLITO.

Lilies with lilies, said Savonarola;
Florence and France! But I say Florence
    only,
Or only with the Emperor's hand to help us
In sweeping out the rubbish.

NARDI.

             Little hope
Of help is there from him. He has betrothed
His daughter Margaret to this shameless Duke.
What hope have we from such an Emperor?

IPPOLITO.

Baccio Valori and Philippo Strozzi,
Once the Duke's friends and intimates, are
    with us,
And Cardinals Salvati and Ridolfi.
We shall soon see, then, as Valori says,
Whether the Duke can best spare honest
    men,
Or honest men the Duke.

NARDI.

          We have determined
To send ambassadors to Spain, and lay
Our griefs before the Emperor, though I fear
More than I hope.

IPPOLITO.

          The Emperor is busy
With this new war against the Algerines,
And has no time to listen to complaints
From our ambassadors; nor will I trust them,
But go myself. All is in readiness
For my departure, and to-morrow morning
I shall go down to Itri, where I meet
Dante da Castiglione and some others,
Republicans and fugitives from Florence,
And then take ship at Gaëta, and go
To join the Emperor in his new crusade
Against the Turk. I shall have time enough
And opportunity to plead our cause.

NARDI, *rising.*

It is an inspiration, and I hail it
As of good omen. May the power that
    sends it
Bless our beloved country, and restore
Its banished citizens. The soul of Florence
Is now outside its gates. What lies within
Is but a corpse, corrupted and corrupting.
Heaven help us all. I will not tarry longer,
For you have need of rest. Good-night.

IPPOLITO.

                Good-night!

Enter FRA SEBASTIANO; *Turkish attendants.*

IPPOLITO.

Fra Bastiano, how your portly presence
Contrasts with that of the spare Florentine
Who has just left me!

FRA SEBASTIANO.

         As we passed each other,
I saw that he was weeping.

IPPOLITO.

            Poor old man!

FRA SEBASTIANO.

Who is he?

IPPOLITO.

      Jacopo Nardi. A brave soul;
One of the Fuorusciti, and the best
And noblest of them all; but he has made me
Sad with his sadness. As I look on you
My heart grows lighter. I behold a man
Who lives in an ideal world, apart
From all the rude collisions of our life,
In a calm atmosphere.

FRA SEBASTIANO.

           Your Eminence
Is surely jesting. If you knew the life
Of artists as I know it, you might think
Far otherwise.

IPPOLITO.

        But wherefore should I jest?
The world of art is an ideal world, —
The world I love, and that I fain would live
    in;

So speak to me of artists and of art,
Of all the painters, sculptors, and musicians
That now illustrate Rome.

FRA SEBASTIANO.

            Of the musicians,
I know but Goudimel, the brave maestro
And chapel-master of his Holiness,
Who trains the Papal choir.

IPPOLITO.

          In church this morning,
I listened to a mass of Goudimel,
Divinely chanted. In the Incarnatus,
In lieu of Latin words, the tenor sang
With infinite tenderness, in plain Italian,
A Neapolitan love-song.

FRA SEBASTIANO.

         You amaze me.
Was it a wanton song?

IPPOLITO.

          Not a divine one.
I am not over-scrupulous, as you know,
In word or deed, yet such a song as that,
Sung by the tenor of the Papal choir,
And in a Papal mass, seemed out of place;
There's something wrong in it.

FRA SEBASTIANO.

          There's something wrong
In everything. We cannot make the world
Go right. 'T is not my business to reform
The Papal choir.

IPPOLITO.

         Nor mine, thank Heaven!
Then tell me of the artists.

FRA SEBASTIANO.

          Naming one
I name them all; for there is only one:
His name is Messer Michael Angelo.
All art and artists of the present day
Centre in him.

IPPOLITO.

You count yourself as nothing?

FRA SEBASTIANO.

Or less than nothing, since I am at best
Only a portrait-painter; one who draws
With greater or less skill, as best he may,
The features of a face.

IPPOLITO.

                    And you have had
The honor, nay, the glory, of portraying
Julia Gonzaga! Do you count as nothing
A privilege like that? See there the portrait
Rebuking you with its divine expression.
Are you not penitent? He whose skilful hand
Painted that lovely picture has not right
To vilipend the art of portrait-painting.
But what of Michael Angelo?

FRA SEBASTIANO.

                    But lately
Strolling together down the crowded Corso,
We stopped, well pleased, to see your Emi-
          nence
Pass on an Arab steed, a noble creature,
Which Michael Angelo, who is a lover
Of all things beautiful, especially
When they are Arab horses, much admired,
And could not praise enough.

IPPOLITO, *to an attendant.*

                    Hassan, to-morrow,
When I am gone, but not till I am gone, —
Be careful about that, — take Barbarossa
To Messer Michael Angelo, the sculptor,
Who lives there at Macello dei Corvi,
Near to the Capitol; and take besides
Some ten mule-loads of provender, and say
Your master sends them to him as a present.

FRA SEBASTIANO.

A princely gift. Though Michael Angelo
Refuses presents from his Holiness,
Yours he will not refuse.

IPPOLITO.

                    You think him like
Thymœtes, who received the wooden horse
Into the walls of Troy. That book of Virgil
Have I translated in Italian verse,
And shall, some day, when we have leisure
          for it,

Be pleased to read you. When I speak of
          Troy
I am reminded of another town
And of a lovelier Helen, our dear Countess
Julia Gonzaga. You remember, surely,
The adventure with the corsair Barbarossa,
And all that followed?

FRA SEBASTIANO.

                    A most strange adventure;
A tale as marvellous and full of wonder
As any in Boccaccio or Sacchetti;
Almost incredible!

IPPOLITO.

                    Were I a painter
I should not want a better theme than that:
The lovely lady fleeing through the night
In wild disorder; and the brigands' camp
With the red fire-light on their swarthy
          faces.
Could you not paint it for me?

FRA SEBASTIANO.

                    No, not I.
It is not in my line.

IPPOLITO.

                    Then you shall paint
The portrait of the corsair, when we bring
          him
A prisoner chained to Naples: for I feel
Something like admiration for a man
Who dared this strange adventure.

FRA SEBASTIANO.

                    I will do it.
But catch the corsair first.

IPPOLITO.

                    You may begin
To-morrow with the sword. Hassan, come
          hither;
Bring me the Turkish scimitar that hangs
Beneath the picture yonder. Now unsheathe
          it.
'T is a Damascus blade; you see the inscrip-
          tion
In Arabic: *La Allah illa Allah,* —
There is no God but God.

FRA SEBASTIANO.

        How beautiful
In fashion and in finish! It is perfect.
The Arsenal of Venice cannot boast
A finer sword.

IPPOLITO.

    You like it? It is yours.

FRA SEBASTIANO.

You do not mean it.

IPPOLITO.

      I am not a Spaniard,
To say that it is yours and not to mean it.
I have at Itri a whole armory
Full of such weapons. When you paint the
   portrait
Of Barbarossa, it will be of use.
You have not been rewarded as you should
   be
For painting the Gonzaga. Throw this bauble
Into the scale, and make the balance equal.
Till then suspend it in your studio;
You artists like such trifles.

   122

FRA SEBASTIANO.

       I will keep it
In memory of the donor. Many thanks.

IPPOLITO.

Fra Bastian, I am growing tired of Rome,
The old dead city, with the old dead peo-
   ple;
Priests everywhere, like shadows on a wall,
And morning, noon, and night the ceaseless
   sound
Of convent bells. I must be gone from
   here;
Though Ovid somewhere says that Rome is
   worthy
To be the dwelling-place of all the Gods,
I must be gone from here. To-morrow morn-
   ing
I start for Itri, and go thence by sea
To join the Emperor, who is making war
Upon the Algerines; perhaps to sink
Some Turkish galleys, and bring back in
   chains
The famous corsair. Thus would I avenge
The beautiful Gonzaga.

FRA SEBASTIANO.

     An achievement
Worthy of Charlemagne, or of Orlando.
Berni and Ariosto both shall add
A canto to their poems, and describe you
As Furioso and Innamorato.
Now I must say good-night.

IPPOLITO.

     You must not go;
First you shall sup with me. My seneschal,
Giovan Andrea dal Borgo a San Sepolcro, —
I like to give the whole sonorous name,
It sounds so like a verse of the Æneid, —
Has brought me eels fresh from the Lake of
  Fondi,
And Lucrine oysters cradled in their shells:
These, with red Fondi wine, the Cæcuban
That Horace speaks of, under a hundred keys
Kept safe, until the heir of Posthumus
Shall stain the pavement with it, make a feast
Fit for Lucullus, or Fra Bastian even;
So we will go to supper, and be merry.

FRA SEBASTIANO.

Beware! Remember that Bolsena's eels
And Vernage wine once killed a Pope of
  Rome!

IPPOLITO.

'T was a French Pope; and then so long ago;
Who knows? — perhaps the story is not true.

V.

BORGO DELLE VERGINE AT NAPLES.

Room in the Palace of JULIA GONZAGA.

Night.

JULIA GONZAGA, GIOVANNI VALDESSO.

JULIA.

Do not go yet.

VALDESSO.

    The night is far advanced;
I fear to stay too late, and weary you
With these discussions.

JULIA.

     I have much to say.
I speak to you, Valdesso, with that frank-
  ness
Which is the greatest privilege of friend-
  ship, —
Speak as I hardly would to my confessor,
Such is my confidence in you.

VALDESSO.

     Dear Countess,
If loyalty to friendship be a claim
Upon your confidence, then I may claim it.

JULIA.

Then sit again, and listen unto things
That nearer are to me than life itself.

VALDESSO.

In all things I am happy to obey you,
And happiest then when you command me
  most.

JULIA.

Laying aside all useless rhetoric,
That is superfluous between us two,
I come at once unto the point, and say,
You know my outward life, my rank and for-
  tune;
Countess of Fondi, Duchess of Trajetto,
A widow rich and flattered, for whose hand
In marriage princes ask, and ask it only
To be rejected. All the world can offer
Lies at my feet. If I remind you of it,
It is not in the way of idle boasting,
But only to the better understanding
Of what comes after.

VALDESSO.

    God hath given you also
Beauty and intellect; and the signal grace
To lead a spotless life amid temptations
That others yield to.

JULIA.

    But the inward life, —
That you know not; 't is known but to my-
  self,
And is to me a mystery and a pain.
A soul disquieted, and ill at ease,

A mind perplexed with doubts and apprehen-
    sions,
A heart dissatisfied with all around me,
And with myself, so that sometimes I
    weep,
Discouraged and disgusted with the world.

VALDESSO.

Whene'er we cross a river at a ford,
If we would pass in safety, we must keep
Our eyes fixed steadfast on the shore be-
    yond,
For if we cast them on the flowing stream,
The head swims with it; so if we would
    cross
The running flood of things here in the
    world,
Our souls must not look down, but fix their
    sight
On the firm land beyond.

JULIA.

            I comprehend you.
You think I am too worldly; that my head
Swims with the giddying whirl of life about
    me.
Is that your meaning?

VALDESSO.

           Yes; your meditations
Are more of this world and its vanities
Than of the world to come.

JULIA.

            Between the two
I am confused.

VALDESSO.

          Yet have I seen you listen
Enraptured when Fra Bernardino preached
Of faith and hope and charity.

JULIA.

                              I listen,
But only as to music without meaning.
It moves me for the moment, and I think
How beautiful it is to be a saint,
As dear Vittoria is : but I am weak
And wayward, and I soon fall back again
To my old ways, so very easily.
There are too many week-days for one Sun-
        day.

VALDESSO.

Then take the Sunday with you through the
    — week,
And sweeten with it all the other days.

JULIA.

In part I do so; for to put a stop
To idle tongues, what men might say of me
If I lived all alone here in my palace,
And not from a vocation that I feel
For the monastic life, I now am living
With Sister Caterina at the convent
Of Santa Chiara, and I come here only
On certain days, for my affairs, or visits
Of ceremony, or to be with friends.
For I confess, to live among my friends
Is Paradise to me ; my Purgatory
Is living among people I dislike.
And so I pass my life in these two worlds,
This palace and the convent.

VALDESSO.

                        It was then
The fear of man, and not the love of God,
That led you to this step. Why will you
        not
Give all your heart to God?

JULIA.

                    If God commands it,
Wherefore hath He not made me capable
Of doing for Him what I wish to do
As easily as I could offer Him
This jewel from my hand, this gown I wear,
Or aught else that is mine?

VALDESSO.

                      The hindrance lies
In that original sin, by which all fell.

JULIA.

Ah me, I cannot bring my troubled mind
To wish well to that Adam, our first par-
        ent,
Who by his sin lost Paradise for us,
And brought such ills upon us.

VALDESSO.

                        We ourselves,
When we commit a sin, lose Paradise,
As much as he did. Let us think of this,
And how we may regain it.

JULIA.

                      Teach me, then,
To harmonize the discord of my life,
And stop the painful jangle of these wires.

VALDESSO.

That is a task impossible, until
You tune your heart-strings to a higher key
Than earthly melodies.

JULIA.

                      How shall I do it?
Point out to me the way of this perfection,
And I will follow you ; for you have made
My soul enamored with it, and I cannot
Rest satisfied until I find it out.
But lead me privately, so that the world
Hear not my steps ; I would not give occa-
        sion
For talk among the people.

VALDESSO.

                        Now at last
I understand you fully. Then, what need
Is there for us to beat about the bush?
I know what you desire of me.

JULIA.

                      What rudeness!
If you already know it, why not tell me?

VALDESSO.

Because I rather wait for you to ask it
With your own lips.

JULIA.

Do me the kindness, then,

To speak without reserve; and with all frank-
    ness,
If you divine the truth, will I confess it.

VALDESSO.

I am content.

JULIA.

Then speak.

VALDESSO.

              You would be free
From the vexatious thoughts that come and go
Through your imagination, and would have me
Point out some royal road and lady-like
Which you may walk in, and not wound your
    feet;
You would attain to the divine perfection,
And yet not turn your back upon the world;
You would possess humility within,
But not reveal it in your outward actions;
You would have patience, but without the
    rude
Occasions that require its exercise;
You would despise the world, but in such
    fashion
The world should not despise you in return;
Would clothe the soul with all the Chris-
    tian graces,
Yet not despoil the body of its gauds;
Would feed the soul with spiritual food,
Yet not deprive the body of its feasts;
Would seem angelic in the sight of God,
Yet not too saint-like in the eyes of men;
In short, would lead a holy Christian life
In such a way that even your nearest friend
Would not detect therein one circumstance
To show a change from what it was before.
Have I divined your secret?

JULIA.

              You have drawn
The portrait of my inner self as truly
As the most skilful painter ever painted
A human face.

VALDESSO.

            This warrants me in saying
You think you can win heaven by compro-
    mise,
And not by verdict.

JULIA.

          You have often told me
That a bad compromise was better even
Than a good verdict.

VALDESSO.

             Yes, in suits at law;
Not in religion. With the human soul
There is no compromise. By faith alone
Can man be justified.

JULIA.

            Hush, dear Valdesso;
That is a heresy. Do not, I pray you,
Proclaim it from the house-top, but preserve
    it
As something precious, hidden in your heart,
As I, who half believe and tremble at it.

VALDESSO.

I must proclaim the truth.

JULIA.

             Enthusiast!
Why must you? You imperil both yourself
And friends by your imprudence. Pray, be
    patient.
You have occasion now to show that virtue
Which you lay stress upon. Let us return
To our lost pathway. Show me by what
    steps
I shall walk in it.

              [*Convent bells are heard.*

VALDESSO.

            Hark! the convent bells
Are ringing; it is midnight; I must leave
    you.
And yet I linger. Pardon me, dear Count-
    ess,
Since you to-night have made me your con-
    fessor,
If I so far may venture, I will warn you
Upon one point.

JULIA.

        What is it? Speak, I pray you,
For I have no concealments in my conduct;
All is as open as the light of day.
What is it you would warn me of?

VALDESSO.
                    Your friendship
With Cardinal Ippolito.

JULIA.
                    What is there
To cause suspicion or alarm in that,
More than in friendships that I entertain
With you and others? I ne'er sat with him
Alone at night, as I am sitting now
With you, Valdesso.

VALDESSO.
                    Pardon me; the portrait
That Fra Bastiano painted was for him.
Is that quite prudent?

JULIA.
                    That is the same question
Vittoria put to me, when I last saw her.
I make you the same answer. That was not
A pledge of love, but of pure gratitude.
Recall the adventure of that dreadful night
When Barbarossa with two thousand Moors
Landed upon the coast, and in the darkness
Attacked my castle. Then, without delay,
The Cardinal came hurrying down from Rome
To rescue and protect me. Was it wrong

That in an hour like that I did not weigh
Too nicely this or that, but granted him
A boon that pleased him, and that flattered
    me?

VALDESSO.
Only beware lest, in disguise of friendship
Another corsair, worse than Barbarossa,
Steal in and seize the castle, not by storm
But strategy. And now I take my leave.

JULIA.
Farewell; but ere you go look forth and see
How night hath hushed the clamor and the
    stir
Of the tumultuous streets. The cloudless
    moon
Roofs the whole city as with tiles of silver;
The dim, mysterious sea in silence sleeps;
And straight into the air Vesuvius lifts
His plume of smoke. How beautiful it is!
                    [Voices in the street.

GIOVAN ANDREA.
Poisoned at Itri.

ANOTHER VOICE.
                    Poisoned? Who is poisoned?

GIOVAN ANDREA.

The Cardinal Ippolito, my master.
Call it malaria. It was very sudden.

[*Julia swoons.*

VI.

VITTORIA COLONNA.

A room in the Torre Argentina.

VITTORIA COLONNA *and* JULIA GONZAGA.

VITTORIA.

Come to my arms and to my heart once
    more ;
My soul goes out to meet you and embrace
    you,
For we are of the sisterhood of sorrow.
I know what you have suffered.

JULIA.

               Name it not.
Let me forget it.

VITTORIA.

          I will say no more.
Let me look at you. What a joy it is
To see your face, to hear your voice again !
You bring with you a breath as of the morn,
A memory of the far-off happy days
When we were young. When did you come
    from Fondi ?

JULIA.

I have not been at Fondi since —

VITTORIA.

                Ah me !
You need not speak the word ; I understand
    you.

JULIA.

I came from Naples by the lovely valley,
The Terra di Lavorro.

VITTORIA.

           And you find me
But just returned from a long journey north-
    ward.
I have been staying with that noble woman,
Renée of France, the Duchess of Ferrara.

JULIA.

Oh, tell me of the Duchess. I have heard
Flaminio speak her praises with such warmth
That I am eager to hear more of her
And of her brilliant court.

VITTORIA.

           You shall hear all.
But first sit down and listen patiently
While I confess myself.

JULIA.

             What deadly sin
Have you committed ?

VITTORIA.

          Not a sin ; a folly.
I chid you once at Ischia, when you told me
That brave Fra Bastian was to paint your
    portrait.

JULIA.

Well I remember it.

VITTORIA.

           Then chide me now,
For I confess to something still more strange.
Old as I am, I have at last consented
To the entreaties and the supplications
Of Michael Angelo —

JULIA.

          To marry him ?

VITTORIA.

I pray you, do not jest with me ! You know,
Or you should know, that never such a
    thought
Entered my breast. I am already married.
The Marquis of Pescara is my husband,
And death has not divorced us.

JULIA.

             Pardon me.
Have I offended you ?

VITTORIA.

         No, but have hurt me.
Unto my buried lord I give myself,
Unto my friend the shadow of myself,

My portrait. It is not from vanity,
But for the love I bear him.

JULIA.

                    I rejoice
To hear these words. Oh, this will be a por-
          trait
Worthy of both of you!   [*A knock.*

VITTORIA.

                    Hark! he is coming.

JULIA.

And shall I go or stay?

VITTORIA.

                    By all means, stay.
The drawing will be better for your pres-
          ence;
You will enliven me.

JULIA.

                    I shall not speak;
The presence of great men doth take from
          me
All power of speech. I only gaze at them
In silent wonder, as if they were gods,
Or the inhabitants of some other planet.

Enter MICHAEL ANGELO.

VITTORIA.

Come in.

MICHAEL ANGELO.

          I fear my visit is ill-timed;
I interrupt you.

VITTORIA.

                    No; this is a friend
Of yours as well as mine, — the Lady Julia,
The Duchess of Trajetto.

MICHAEL ANGELO *to* JULIA.

                    I salute you.
'T is long since I have seen your face, my
          lady;
Pardon me if I say that having seen it,
One never can forget it.

JULIA.

                    You are kind
To keep me in your memory.

MICHAEL ANGELO.

                    It is
The privilege of age to speak with frankness.
You will not be offended when I say
That never was your beauty more divine.

JULIA.

When Michael Angelo condescends to flatter
Or praise me, I am proud, and not offended.

VITTORIA.

Now this is gallantry enough for one;
Show me a little.

MICHAEL ANGELO.

                    Ah, my gracious lady,
You know I have not words to speak your
          praise.
I think of you in silence. You conceal
Your manifold perfections from all eyes,
And make yourself more saint-like day by
          day.
And day by day men worship you the more.
But now your hour of martyrdom has come.
You know why I am here.

VITTORIA.

                    Ah yes, I know it;
And meet my fate with fortitude. You find
          me

Surrounded by the labors of your hands:
The Woman of Samaria at the Well,
The Mater Dolorosa, and the Christ
Upon the Cross, beneath which you have
    written
Those memorable words of Alighieri,
"Men have forgotten how much blood it
    costs."

VITTORIA.

I am ashamed to steal the time from you
That should be given to the Sistine Chapel.
How does that work go on?

MICHAEL ANGELO, *drawing*.

                 But tardily.
Old men work slowly.   Brain and hand alike

MICHAEL ANGELO.

And now I come to add one labor more,
If you will call that labor which is pleasure,
And only pleasure.

VITTORIA.

         How shall I be seated?

MICHAEL ANGELO, *opening his portfolio*.

Just as you are.   The light falls well upon
    you.

123

Are dull and torpid.   To die young is best,
And not to be remembered as old men
Tottering about in their decrepitude.

VITTORIA.

My dear Maestro! have you, then, forgot-
    ten
The story of Sophocles in his old age?

MICHAEL ANGELO.

What story is it?

VITTORIA.

When his sons accused him,
Before the Areopagus, of dotage,
For all defence, he read there to his Judges
The Tragedy of Œdipus Coloneus, —
The work of his old age.

MICHAEL ANGELO.

'T is an illusion,
A fabulous story, that will lead old men
Into a thousand follies and conceits.

VITTORIA.

So you may show to cavillers your painting
Of the Last Judgment in the Sistine Chapel.

MICHAEL ANGELO.

Now you and Lady Julia shall resume
The conversation that I interrupted.

VITTORIA.

It was of no great import; nothing more
Nor less than my late visit to Ferrara,
And what I saw there in the ducal palace.
Will it not interrupt you?

MICHAEL ANGELO.

Not the least.

VITTORIA.

Well, first, then, of Duke Ercole: a man
Cold in his manners, and reserved and silent,
And yet magnificent in all his ways;
Not hospitable unto new ideas,
But from state policy, and certain reasons
Concerning the investiture of the duchy,
A partisan of Rome, and consequently
Intolerant of all the new opinions.

JULIA.

I should not like the Duke. These silent men,
Who only look and listen, are like wells
That have no water in them, deep and empty.
How could the daughter of a king of France
Wed such a duke?

MICHAEL ANGELO.

The men that women marry,
And why they marry them, will always be
A marvel and a mystery to the world.

VITTORIA.

And then the Duchess, — how shall I describe her,
Or tell the merits of that happy nature,
Which pleases most when least it thinks of pleasing?
Not beautiful, perhaps, in form and feature,
Yet with an inward beauty, that shines through
Each look and attitude and word and gesture;
A kindly grace of manner and behavior,
A something in her presence and her ways
That makes her beautiful beyond the reach
Of mere external beauty; and in heart
So noble and devoted to the truth,
And so in sympathy with all who strive
After the higher life.

JULIA.

She draws me to her
As much as her Duke Ercole repels me.

VITTORIA.

Then the devout and honorable women
That grace her court, and make it good to be there;
Francesca Bucyronia, the true-hearted,
Lavinia della Rovere and the Orsini,
The Magdalena and the Cherubina,
And Anne de Parthenai, who sings so sweetly;
All lovely women, full of noble thoughts
And aspirations after noble things.

JULIA.

Boccaccio would have envied you such dames.

VITTORIA.

No; his Fiammettas and his Philomenas
Are fitter company for Ser Giovanni;
I fear he hardly would have comprehended
The women that I speak of.

MICHAEL ANGELO.

Yet he wrote
The story of Griselda. That is something
To set down in his favor.

VITTORIA.

With these ladies
Was a young girl, Olympia Morata,
Daughter of Fulvio, the learned scholar,

Famous in all the universities:
A marvellous child, who at the spinning-wheel,
And in the daily round of household cares,
Hath learned both Greek and Latin; and is now
A favorite of the Duchess and companion
Of Princess Anne. This beautiful young Sappho
Sometimes recited to us Grecian odes
That she had written, with a voice whose sadness
Thrilled and o'ermastered me, and made me look
Into the future time, and ask myself
What destiny will be hers.

JULIA.

      A sad one, surely.
Frost kills the flowers that blossom out of season;
And these precocious intellects portend
A life of sorrow or an early death.

VITTORIA.

About the court were many learned men;
Chilian Sinapius from beyond the Alps,
And Celio Curione, and Manzolli,
The Duke's physician; and a pale young man,
Charles d'Espeville of Geneva, whom the Duchess
Doth much delight to talk with and to read,
For he hath written a book of Institutes
The Duchess greatly praises, though some call it
The Koran of the heretics.

JULIA.

      And what poets
Were there to sing you madrigals, and praise
Olympia's eyes and Cherubina's tresses?

VITTORIA.

None; for great Ariosto is no more.

The voice that filled those halls with melody
Has long been hushed in death.

JULIA.

                    You should have made
A pilgrimage unto the poet's tomb,
And laid a wreath upon it, for the words
He spake of you.

VITTORIA.

                    And of yourself no less,
And of our master, Michael Angelo.

MICHAEL ANGELO.

Of me?

VITTORIA.

        Have you forgotten that he calls you
Michael, less man than angel, and divine?
You are ungrateful.

MICHAEL ANGELO.

                    A mere play on words.
That adjective he wanted for a rhyme,
To match with Gian Bellino and Urbino.

VITTORIA.

Bernardo Tasso is no longer there,
Nor the gay troubadour of Gascony,
Clement Marot, surnamed by flatterers
The Prince of Poets and the Poet of Princes,

Who, being looked upon with much disfavor
By the Duke Ercole, has fled to Venice.

MICHAEL ANGELO.

There let him stay with Pietro Aretino,
The Scourge of Princes, also called Divine.
The title is so common in our mouths,
That even the Pifferari of Abruzzi,
Who play their bag-pipes in the streets of
        Rome
At the Epiphany, will bear it soon,
And will deserve it better than some poets.

VITTORIA.

What bee hath stung you?

MICHAEL ANGELO.

                    One that makes no honey;
One that comes buzzing in through every
        window,
And stabs men with his sting. A bitter
        thought
Passed through my mind, but it is gone again;
I spake too hastily.

JULIA.

                    I pray you, show me
What you have done.

MICHAEL ANGELO.

            Not yet; it is not finished.

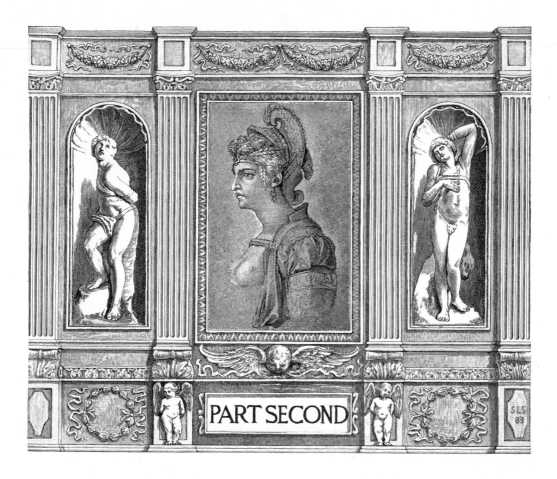

PART SECOND

I.

MONOLOGUE.

A room in MICHAEL ANGELO's *house.*

MICHAEL ANGELO.

FLED to Viterbo, the old Papal city
Where once an Emperor, humbled in his pride,
Held the Pope's stirrup, as his Holiness
Alighted from his mule! A fugitive
From Cardinal Caraffa's hate, who hurls
His thunders at the house of the Colonna,
With endless bitterness! — Among the nuns
In Santa Catarina's convent hidden,
Herself in soul a nun! And now she chides
    me
For my too frequent letters, that disturb
Her meditations, and that hinder me
And keep me from my work; now graciously
She thanks me for the crucifix I sent her,
And says that she will keep it: with one
    hand
Inflicts a wound, and with the other heals it.
                       [Reading.

"Profoundly I believed that God would grant
    you
A supernatural faith to paint this Christ;
I wished for that which now I see fulfilled
So marvellously, exceeding all my wishes.
Nor more could be desired, or even so much.
And greatly I rejoice that you have made
The angel on the right so beautiful;
For the Archangel Michael will place you,
You, Michael Angelo, on that new day,
Upon the Lord's right hand! And waiting
    that,
How can I better serve you than to pray
To this sweet Christ for you, and to beseech
    you
To hold me altogether yours in all things."

Well, I will write less often, or no more,
But wait her coming. No one born in Rome
Can live elsewhere; but he must pine for
    Rome,
And must return to it. I, who am born
And bred a Tuscan and a Florentine,
Feel the attraction, and I linger here
As if I were a pebble in the pavement
Trodden by priestly feet. This I endure,
Because I breathe in Rome an atmosphere
Heavy with odors of the laurel leaves
That crowned great heroes of the sword and
    pen,
In ages past. I feel myself exalted
To walk the streets in which a Virgil walked,
Or Trajan rode in triumph; but far more,
And most of all, because the great Colonna
Breathes the same air I breathe, and is to me
An inspiration. Now that she is gone,
Rome is no longer Rome till she return.
This feeling overmasters me. I know not
If it be love, this strong desire to be
Forever in her presence; but I know
That I, who was the friend of solitude,
And ever was best pleased when most alone,
Now weary grow of my own company.
For the first time old age seems lonely to me.
                    [Opening the Divina Commedia.

I turn for consolation to the leaves
Of the great master of our Tuscan tongue,
Whose words, like colored garnet-shirls in
    lava,
Betray the heat in which they were engen-
    dered.
A mendicant, he ate the bitter bread
Of others, but repaid their meagre gifts
With immortality. In courts of princes
He was a by-word, and in streets of towns
Was mocked by children, like the Hebrew
    prophet,
Himself a prophet. I too know the cry,
Go up, thou bald head! from a generation
That, wanting reverence, wanteth the best
    food
The soul can feed on. There's not room
    enough
For age and youth upon this little planet.
Age must give way. There was not room
    enough
Even for this great poet. In his song

I hear reverberate the gates of Florence,
Closing upon him, never more to open;
But mingled with the sound are melodies
Celestial from the gates of paradise.
He came and he is gone. The people knew
    not
What manner of man was passing by their
    doors,
Until he passed no more; but in his vision
He saw the torments and beatitudes
Of souls condemned or pardoned, and hath
    left
Behind him this sublime Apocalypse.

I strive in vain to draw here on the margin
The face of Beatrice. It is not hers,
But the Colonna's. Each hath his ideal,
The image of some woman excellent,
That is his guide. No Grecian art, nor Ro-
    man,
Hath yet revealed such loveliness as hers.

II.

VITERBO.

VITTORIA COLONNA *at the convent window.*

VITTORIA.

Parting with friends is temporary death,
As all death is. We see no more their faces,
Nor hear their voices, save in memory;
But messages of love give us assurance
That we are not forgotten. Who shall say
That from the world of spirits comes no
    greeting,
No message of remembrance? It may be
The thoughts that visit us, we know not
    whence,
Sudden as inspiration, are the whispers
Of disembodied spirits, speaking to us
As friends, who wait outside a prison wall,
Through the barred windows speak to those
    within.   [A pause.

As quiet as the lake that lies beneath me,
As quiet as the tranquil sky above me,
As quiet as a heart that beats no more,
This convent seems. Above, below, all peace!
Silence and solitude, the soul's best friends,

Are with me here, and the tumultuous world
Makes no more noise than the remotest planet.
O gentle spirit, unto the third circle
Of heaven among the blessed souls ascended,
Who, living in the faith and dying for it,
Have gone to their reward, I do not sigh
For thee as being dead, but for myself
That I am still alive. Turn those dear eyes,
Once so benignant to me, upon mine,
That open to their tears such uncontrolled
And such continual issue. Still awhile
Have patience; I will come to thee at last.
A few more goings in and out these doors,
A few more chimings of these convent bells,
A few more prayers, a few more sighs and
    tears,
And the long agony of this life will end,
And I shall be with thee. If I am wanting
To thy well-being, as thou art to mine,
Have patience; I will come to thee at last.
Ye minds that loiter in these cloister gardens,
Or wander far above the city walls,
Bear unto him this message, that I ever
Or speak or think of him, or weep for him.

By unseen hands uplifted in the light
Of sunset, yonder solitary cloud
Floats, with its white apparel blown abroad,
And wafted up to heaven. It fades away,
And melts into the air. Ah, would that I
Could thus be wafted unto thee, Francesco,
A cloud of white, an incorporeal spirit!

III.

MICHAEL ANGELO AND BENVENUTO CELLINI.

MICHAEL ANGELO, BENVENUTO CELLINI *in gay attire.*

BENVENUTO.

A good day and good year to the divine
Maestro Michael Angelo, the sculptor!

MICHAEL ANGELO.

Welcome, my Benvenuto.

BENVENUTO.

           That is what

My father said, the first time he beheld
This handsome face. But say farewell, not
　　welcome.
I come to take my leave. I start for Flor-
　　ence
As fast as horse can carry me. I long
To set once more upon its level flags
These feet, made sore by your vile Roman
　　pavements.
Come with me; you are wanted there in Flor-
　　ence.
The Sacristy is not finished.

MICHAEL ANGELO.

　　　　　　　　　Speak not of it!
How damp and cold it was! How my bones
　　ached
And my head reeled, when I was working
　　there!
I am too old. I will stay here in Rome,
Where all is old and crumbling, like myself,
To hopeless ruin. All roads lead to Rome.

BENVENUTO.

And all lead out of it.

MICHAEL ANGELO.

　　　　　　　　　There is a charm,
A certain something in the atmosphere,
That all men feel, and no man can describe.

BENVENUTO.

Malaria?

MICHAEL ANGELO.

　　Yes, malaria of the mind,
Out of this tomb of the majestic Past;
The fever to accomplish some great work
That will not let us sleep. I must go on
Until I die.

BENVENUTO.

Do you ne'er think of Florence?

MICHAEL ANGELO.

　　　　　　　　　Yes; whenever
I think of anything beside my work,
I think of Florence. I remember, too,
The bitter days I passed among the quar-
　　ries

Of Seravezza and Pietrasanta;
Road-building in the marshes; stupid peo-
　　ple,
And cold and rain incessant, and mad gusts
Of mountain wind, like howling dervishes,
That spun and whirled the eddying snow
　　about them
As if it were a garment; aye, vexations
And troubles of all kinds, that ended only
In loss of time and money.

BENVENUTO.

　　　　　　　　　True, Maestro;
But that was not in Florence. You should
　　leave
Such work to others. Sweeter memories
Cluster about you, in the pleasant city
Upon the Arno.

MICHAEL ANGELO.

　　　　　　　In my waking dreams
I see the marvellous dome of Brunelleschi,
Ghiberti's gates of bronze, and Giotto's tower;
And Ghirlandajo's lovely Benci glides
With folded hands amid my troubled thoughts,
A splendid vision! Time rides with the old
At a great pace. As travellers on swift steeds
See the near landscape fly and flow behind
　　them,
While the remoter fields and dim horizons
Go with them, and seem wheeling round to
　　meet them,
So in old age things near us slip away,
And distant things go with us. Pleasantly
Come back to me the days when, as a youth,
I walked with Ghirlandajo in the gardens
Of Medici, and saw the antique statues,
The forms august of gods and godlike men,
And the great world of art revealed itself
To my young eyes. Then all that man hath
　　done
Seemed possible to me. Alas! how little
Of all I dreamed of has my hand achieved!

BENVENUTO.

Nay, let the Night and Morning, let Lorenzo
And Julian in the Sacristy at Florence,
Prophets and Sibyls in the Sistine Chapel,
And the Last Judgment answer. Is it fin-
　　ished?

MICHAEL ANGELO.

The work is nearly done. But this Last
    Judgment
Has been the cause of more vexation to me
Than it will be of honor. Ser Biagio,
Master of ceremonies at the Papal court,
A man punctilious and over nice,
Calls it improper ; says that those nude forms,
Showing their nakedness in such shameless
    fashion,
Are better suited to a common bagnio,
Or wayside wine-shop, than a Papal Chapel.
To punish him I painted him as Minos
And leave him there as master of ceremo-
    nies
In the Infernal Regions. What would you
Have done to such a man ?

BENVENUTO.

        I would have killed him.
When any one insults me, if I can
I kill him, kill him.

MICHAEL ANGELO.

        Oh, you gentlemen,
Who dress in silks and velvets, and wear
    swords,
Are ready with your weapons, and have all
A taste for homicide.

124

BENVENUTO.

        I learned that lesson
Under Pope Clement at the siege of Rome,
Some twenty years ago. As I was standing
Upon the ramparts of the Campo Santo
With Alessandro Bene, I beheld
A sea of fog, that covered all the plain,
And hid from us the foe ; when suddenly,
A misty figure, like an apparition,
Rose up above the fog, as if on horseback.
At this I aimed my arquebus, and fired.
The figure vanished ; and there rose a cry
Out of the darkness, long and fierce and loud,
With imprecations in all languages.
It was the Constable of France, the Bourbon,
That I had slain.

MICHAEL ANGELO.

    Rome should be grateful to you.

BENVENUTO.

But has not been ; you shall hear presently.
During the siege I served as bombardier,
There in St. Angelo. His Holiness,
One day, was walking with his Cardinals
On the round bastion, while I stood above
Among my falconets. All thought and feel-
    ing,
All skill in art and all desire of fame,

Were swallowed up in the delightful music
Of that artillery. I saw far off,
Within the enemy's trenches on the Prati,
A Spanish cavalier in scarlet cloak;
And firing at him with due aim and range,
I cut the gay Hidalgo in two pieces.
The eyes are dry that wept for him in Spain.
His Holiness, delighted beyond measure
With such display of gunnery, and amazed
To see the man in scarlet cut in two,
Gave me his benediction, and absolved me
From all the homicides I had committed
In service of the Apostolic Church,
Or should commit thereafter. From that day

BENVENUTO.

              Faith, a pretty artist
To pass his days in stamping leaden seals
On Papal bulls!

MICHAEL ANGELO.

              He has grown fat and lazy,
As if the lead clung to him like a sinker.
He paints no more, since he was sent to
    Fondi
By Cardinal Ippolito to paint
The fair Gonzaga. Ah, you should have
    seen him
As I did, riding through the city gate,

I have not held in very high esteem
The life of man.

MICHAEL ANGELO.

      And who absolved Pope Clement?
Now let us speak of Art.

BENVENUTO.

              Of what you will.

MICHAEL ANGELO.

Say, have you seen our friend Fra Bastian
    lately,
Since by a turn of fortune he became
Friar of the Signet?

In his brown hood, attended by four horse-
    men,
Completely armed, to frighten the banditti.
I think he would have frightened them alone,
For he was rounder than the O of Giotto.

BENVENUTO.

He must have looked more like a sack of
    meal
Than a great painter.

MICHAEL ANGELO.

             Well, he is not great,
But still I like him greatly. Benvenuto,
Have faith in nothing but in industry.

Be at it late and early; persevere,
And work right on through censure and ap-
    plause,
Or else abandon Art.

BENVENUTO.

                No man works harder
Than I do. I am not a moment idle.

MICHAEL ANGELO.

And what have you to show me?

BENVENUTO.

                This gold ring,
Made for his Holiness, — my latest work,
And I am proud of it. A single diamond,
Presented by the Emperor to the Pope.
Targhetta of Venice set and tinted it;
I have reset it, and retinted it
Divinely, as you see. The jewellers
Say I 've surpassed Targhetta.

MICHAEL ANGELO.

                Let me see it.
A pretty jewel.

BENVENUTO.

            That is not the expression.
Pretty is not a very pretty word
To be applied to such a precious stone,
Given by an Emperor to a Pope, and set
By Benvenuto!

MICHAEL ANGELO.

            Messer Benvenuto,
I lose all patience with you; for the gifts
That God hath given you are of such a kind,
They should be put to far more noble uses
Than setting diamonds for the Pope of Rome.
You can do greater things.

BENVENUTO.

            The God who made me
Knows why he made me what I am, — a
    goldsmith,
A mere artificer.

MICHAEL ANGELO.

            Oh no; an artist,
Richly endowed by nature, but who wraps

His talent in a napkin, and consumes
His life in vanities.

BENVENUTO.

            Michael Angelo
May say what Benvenuto would not bear
From any other man. He speaks the truth.
I know my life is wasted and consumed
In vanities; but I have better hours
And higher aspirations than you think.
Once, when a prisoner at St. Angelo,
Fasting and praying in the midnight dark-
    ness,
In a celestial vision I beheld
A crucifix in the sun, of the same substance
As is the sun itself. And since that hour
There is a splendor round about my head,
That may be seen at sunrise and at sunset
Above my shadow on the grass. And now
I know that I am in the grace of God,
And none henceforth can harm me.

MICHAEL ANGELO.

                None but one, —
None but yourself, who are your greatest foe.
He that respects himself is safe from others;
He wears a coat of mail that none can
    pierce.

BENVENUTO.

I always wear one.

MICHAEL ANGELO.

            O incorrigible!
At least, forget not the celestial vision.
Man must have something higher than him-
    self
To think of.

BENVENUTO.

            That I know full well. Now listen.
I have been sent for into France, where grow
The Lilies that illumine heaven and earth,
And carry in mine equipage the model
Of a most marvellous golden salt-cellar
For the king's table; and here in my brain
A statue of Mars Armipotent for the foun-
    tain
Of Fontainebleau, colossal, wonderful.
I go a goldsmith, to return a sculptor.

And so farewell, great Master. Think of me
As one who, in the midst of all his follies,
Had also his ambition, and aspired
To better things.

MICHAEL ANGELO.
                    Do not forget the vision.
[*Sitting down again to the Divina Commedia.*
Now in what circle of his poem sacred
Would the great Florentine have placed this
          man?
Whether in Phlegethon, the river of blood,
Or in the fiery belt of Purgatory,
I know not, but most surely not with those
Who walk in leaden cloaks. Though he is
          one
Whose passions, like a potent alkahest,
Dissolve his better nature, he is not
That despicable thing, a hypocrite;
He doth not cloak his vices, nor deny them.
Come back, my thoughts, from him to Para-
          dise.

IV.

FRA SEBASTIANO DEL PIOMBO.

MICHAEL ANGELO; FRA SEBASTIANO DEL PIOMBO.

MICHAEL ANGELO, *not turning round.*
Who is it?

FRA SEBASTIANO.
          Wait, for I am out of breath
In climbing your steep stairs.

MICHAEL ANGELO.
                    Ah, my Bastiano,
If you went up and down as many stairs
As I do still, and climbed as many ladders,
It would be better for you. Pray sit down.
Your idle and luxurious way of living
Will one day take your breath away entirely,
And you will never find it.

FRA SEBASTIANO.
                    Well, what then?
That would be better, in my apprehension,
Than falling from a scaffold.

MICHAEL ANGELO.
                    That was nothing.

It did not kill me; only lamed me slightly;
I am quite well again.

FRA SEBASTIANO.
                    But why, dear Master,
Why do you live so high up in your house,
When you could live below and have a gar-
          den,
As I do?

MICHAEL ANGELO.
          From this window I can look
On many gardens; o'er the city roofs
See the Campagna and the Alban hills:
And all are mine.

FRA SEBASTIANO.
          Can you sit down in them,
On summer afternoons, and play the lute,
Or sing, or sleep the time away?

MICHAEL ANGELO.
                         I never
Sleep in the day-time; scarcely sleep at night.
I have not time. Did you meet Benvenuto
As you came up the stair?

FRA SEBASTIANO.
                    He ran against me
On the first landing, going at full speed;
Dressed like the Spanish captain in a play,
With his long rapier and his short red cloak.
Why hurry through the world at such a
          pace?
Life will not be too long.

MICHAEL ANGELO.
                    It is his nature,—
A restless spirit, that consumes itself
With useless agitations. He o'erleaps
The goal he aims at. Patience is a plant
That grows not in all gardens. You are
          made
Of quite another clay.

FRA SEBASTIANO.
                    And thank God for it.
And now, being somewhat rested, I will tell
          you
Why I have climbed these formidable stairs.

I have a friend, Francesco Berni, here,
A very charming poet and companion,
Who greatly honors you and all your doings,
And you must sup with us.

MICHAEL ANGELO.

Not I, indeed.
I know too well what artists' suppers are.
You must excuse me.

FRA SEBASTIANO.

I will not excuse you.
You need repose from your incessant work;
Some recreation, some bright hours of pleas-
    ure.

MICHAEL ANGELO.

To me, what you and other men call pleas-
    ure
Is only pain. Work is my recreation,
The play of faculty; a delight like that
Which a bird feels in flying, or a fish
In darting through the water, — nothing more.
I cannot go. The Sibylline leaves of life
Grow precious now, when only few remain.
I cannot go.

FRA SEBASTIANO.

Berni, perhaps, will read
A canto of the Orlando Inamorato.

MICHAEL ANGELO.

That is another reason for not going.
If aught is tedious and intolerable,
It is a poet reading his own verses.

FRA SEBASTIANO.

Berni thinks somewhat better of your verses
Than you of his. He says that you speak
    things,
And other poets words. So, pray you, come.

MICHAEL ANGELO.

If it were now the Improvisatore,
Luigia Pulci, whom I used to hear
With Benvenuto, in the streets of Florence,
I might be tempted. I was younger then,
And singing in the open air was pleasant.

FRA SEBASTIANO.

There is a Frenchman here, named Rabelais,

Once a Franciscan friar, and now a doctor,
And secretary to the embassy:
A learned man, who speaks all languages,
And wittiest of men; who wrote a book
Of the Adventures of Gargantua,
So full of strange conceits one roars with
    laughter
At every page; a jovial boon-companion
And lover of much wine. He too is coming.

MICHAEL ANGELO.

Then you will not want me, who am not
    witty,
And have no sense of mirth, and love not
    wine.
I should be like a dead man at your ban-
    quet.
Why should I seek this Frenchman, Rabe-
    lais?
And wherefore go to hear Francesco Berni,
When I have Dante Alighieri here,
The greatest of all poets?

FRA SEBASTIANO.

And the dullest;
And only to be read in episodes.
His day is past. Petrarca is our poet.

MICHAEL ANGELO.

Petrarca is for women and for lovers,
And for those soft Abati, who delight
To wander down long garden walks in sum-
    mer,
Tinkling their little sonnets all day long,
As lap-dogs do their bells.

FRA SEBASTIANO.

                I love Petrarca.
How sweetly of his absent love he sings,
When journeying in the forest of Ardennes!
."I seem to hear her, hearing the boughs
    and breezes
And leaves and birds lamenting, and the wa-
    ters
Murmuring flee along the verdant herbage."

MICHAEL ANGELO.

Enough. It is all seeming, and no being.
If you would know how a man speaks in
    earnest,
Read here this passage, where St. Peter
    thunders
In Paradise against degenerate Popes
And the corruptions of the church, till all
The heaven about him blushes like a sunset.
I beg you to take note of what he says
About the Papal seals, for that concerns
Your office and yourself.

FRA SEBASTIANO, *reading.*

           Is this the passage?

"Nor I be made the figure of a seal
To privileges venal and mendacious,
Whereat I often redden and flash with
    fire!"—
That is not poetry.

MICHAEL ANGELO.

            What is it, then?

FRA SEBASTIANO.

Vituperation; gall that might have spirted
From Aretino's pen.

MICHAEL ANGELO.

            Name not that man!
A profligate, whom your Francesco Berni
Describes as having one foot in the brothel
And the other in the hospital; who lives
By flattering or maligning, as best serves
His purpose at the time. He writes to me
With easy arrogance of my Last Judgment,
In such familiar tone that one would say
The great event already had occurred,
And he was present, and from observation
Informed me how the picture should be
    painted.

FRA SEBASTIANO.

What unassuming, unobtrusive men
These critics are! Now, to have Aretino
Aiming his shafts at you brings back to
    mind
The Gascon archers in the square of Mi-
    lan,
Shooting their arrows at Duke Sforza's statue,
By Leonardo, and the foolish rabble
Of envious Florentines, that at your David
Threw stones at night. But Aretino praised
    you.

MICHAEL ANGELO.

His praises were ironical. He knows
How to use words as weapons, and to wound
While seeming to defend. But look, Bas-
    tiano,
See how the setting sun lights up that pic-
    ture!

FRA SEBASTIANO.

My portrait of Vittoria Colonna.

MICHAEL ANGELO.

It makes her look as she will look hereafter,
When she becomes a saint!

FRA SEBASTIANO.

A noble woman!

MICHAEL ANGELO.

Ah, these old hands can fashion fairer shapes
In marble, and can paint diviner pictures,
Since I have known her.

FRA SEBASTIANO.

And you like this picture;
And yet it is in oils, which you detest.

FRA SEBASTIANO.

And how soon they fade!
Behold yon line of roofs and belfries painted
Upon the golden background of the sky,
Like a Byzantine picture, or a portrait
Of Cimabue. See how hard the outline,
Sharp - cut and clear, not rounded into
shadow.
Yet that is nature.

MICHAEL ANGELO.

She is always right.
The picture that approaches sculpture near-
est
Is the best picture.

MICHAEL ANGELO.

When that barbarian Jan Van Eyck discov-
ered
The use of oil in painting, he degraded
His art into a handicraft, and made it
Sign-painting, merely, for a country inn
Or wayside wine-shop. 'T is an art for wo-
men,
Or for such leisurely and idle people
As you, Fra Bastiano. Nature paints not
In oils, but frescoes the great dome of heaven
With sunsets, and the lovely forms of clouds
And flying vapors.

FRA SEBASTIANO.

Leonardo thinks
The open air too bright. We ought to paint
As if the sun were shining through a mist.
'T is easier done in oil than in distemper.

MICHAEL ANGELO.

Do not revive again the old dispute;
I have an excellent memory for forgetting,
But I still feel the hurt. Wounds are not
healed
By the unbending of the bow that made
them.

FRA SEBASTIANO.

So say Petrarca and the ancient proverb.

MICHAEL ANGELO.

But that is past. Now I am angry with you,
Not that you paint in oils, but that, grown
 fat
And indolent, you do not paint at all.

FRA SEBASTIANO.

Why should I paint? Why should I toil and
 sweat,
Who now am rich enough to live at ease,
And take my pleasure?

MICHAEL ANGELO.

    When Pope Leo died,
He who had been so lavish of the wealth
His predecessors left him, who received
A basket of gold-pieces every morning,
Which every night was empty, left behind
Hardly enough to pay his funeral.

FRA SEBASTIANO.

I care for banquets, not for funerals,
As did his Holiness. I have forbidden
All tapers at my burial, and procession
Of priests and friars and monks; and have
 provided
The cost thereof be given to the poor!

MICHAEL ANGELO.

You have done wisely, but of that I speak
 not.
Ghiberti left behind him wealth and chil-
 dren;
But who to-day would know that he had
 lived,
If he had never made those gates of bronze
In the old Baptistery, — those gates of bronze,
Worthy to be the gates of Paradise.
His wealth is scattered to the winds; his
 children
Are long since dead; but those celestial gates
Survive, and keep his name and memory
 green.

FRA SEBASTIANO.

But why should I fatigue myself? I think
That all things it is possible to paint

Have been already painted; and if not,
Why, there are painters in the world at pres-
 ent
Who can accomplish more in two short
 months
Than I could in two years; so it is well
That some one is contented to do noth-
 ing,
And leave the field to others.

MICHAEL ANGELO.

     O blasphemer!
Not without reason do the people call you
Sebastian del Piombo, for the lead
Of all the Papal bulls is heavy upon you,
And wraps you like a shroud.

FRA SEBASTIANO.

     Misericordia!
Sharp is the vinegar of sweet wine, and sharp
The words you speak, because the heart
 within you
Is sweet unto the core.

MICHAEL ANGELO.

    How changed you are
From the Sebastiano I once knew,
When poor, laborious, emulous to excel,
You strove in rivalry with Badassare
And Raphael Sanzio.

FRA SEBASTIANO.

    Raphael is dead;
He is but dust and ashes in his grave,
While I am living and enjoying life,
And so am victor. One live Pope is worth
A dozen dead ones.

MICHAEL ANGELO.

    Raphael is not dead;
He doth but sleep; for how can he be dead
Who lives immortal in the hearts of men?
He only drank the precious wine of youth,
The outbreak of the grapes, before the vin-
 tage
Was trodden to bitterness by the feet of
 men.
The gods have given him sleep. We never
 were
Nor could be foes, although our followers,

Who are distorted shadows of ourselves,
Have striven to make us so; but each one
    worked
Unconsciously upon the other's thoughts,
Both giving and receiving. He perchance
Caught strength from me, and I some greater
    sweetness
And tenderness from his more gentle na-
    ture.
I have but words of praise and admiration
For his great genius; and the world is
    fairer
That he lived in it.

FRA SEBASTIANO.

           We at least are friends;
So come with me.

MICHAEL ANGELO.

           No, no; I am best pleased
When I'm not asked to banquets. I have
    reached
A time of life when daily walks are short-
    ened,
And even the houses of our dearest friends,
That used to be so near, seem far away.

FRA SEBASTIANO.

Then we must sup without you. We shall
    laugh
At those who toil for fame, and make their
    lives
A tedious martyrdom, that they may live
A little longer in the mouths of men!
And so, good-night.

MICHAEL ANGELO.

           Good-night, my Fra Bastiano.
           [*Returning to his work.*
How will men speak of me when I am gone,
When all this colorless, sad life is ended,
And I am dust? They will remember only
The wrinkled forehead, the marred counte-
    nance,
The rudeness of my speech, and my rough
    manners,
And never dream that underneath them all
There was a woman's heart of tenderness.
They will not know the secret of my life,
Locked up in silence, or but vaguely hinted
125

In uncouth rhymes, that may perchance sur-
    vive
Some little space in memories of men!
Each one performs his life-work, and then
    leaves it;
Those that come after him will estimate
His influence on the age in which he lived.

V.

MICHAEL ANGELO AND TITIAN: PALAZZO BELVEDERE.

TITIAN'S *studio. A painting of Danaë with a curtain before it.* TITIAN, MICHAEL ANGELO, *and* GIORGIO VASARI.

MICHAEL ANGELO.

So you have left at last your still lagoons,
Your City of Silence floating in the sea,
And come to us in Rome.

TITIAN.

           I come to learn,
But I have come too late. I should have
    seen
Rome in my youth, when all my mind was
    open
To new impressions. Our Vasari here
Leads me about, a blind man, groping darkly
Among the marvels of the past. I touch
    them,
But do not see them.

MICHAEL ANGELO.

           There are things in Rome
That one might walk barefooted here from
    Venice
But to see once, and then to die content.

TITIAN.

I must confess that these majestic ruins
Oppress me with their gloom. I feel as one
Who in the twilight stumbles among tombs,
And cannot read the inscriptions carved upon
    them.

MICHAEL ANGELO.

I felt so once; but I have grown famil-
    iar
With desolation, and it has become
No more a pain to me, but a delight.

TITIAN.

I could not live here. I must have the sea,
And the sea-mist, with sunshine interwoven
Like cloth of gold; must have beneath my
    windows
The laughter of the waves, and at my door
Their pattering footsteps. or I am not happy.

MICHAEL ANGELO.

Then tell me of your city in the sea,
Paved with red basalt of the Paduan hills.
Tell me of art in Venice. Three great
    names,
Giorgione, Titian, and the Tintoretto,

MICHAEL ANGELO.

               When you two
Are gone, who is there that remains behind
To seize the pencil falling from your fingers?

GIORGIO.

Oh there are many hands upraised already
To clutch at such a prize, which hardly
    wait
For death to loose your grasp, — a hundred
    of them:
Schiavone, Bonifazio, Campagnola,
Moretto, and Moroni; who can count them,
Or measure their ambition?

Illustrate your Venetian school, and send
A challenge to the world. The first is dead,
But Tintoretto lives.

TITIAN.

          And paints with fire,
Sudden and splendid, as the lightning paints
The cloudy vault of heaven.

GIORGIO.

          Does he still keep
Above his door the arrogant inscription
That once was painted there, — "The color
    of Titian,
With the design of Michael Angelo"?

TITIAN.

Indeed, I know not. 'Twas a foolish boast,
And does no harm to any but himself.
Perhaps he has grown wiser.

TITIAN.

          When we are gone,
The generation that comes after us
Will have far other thoughts than ours. Our
    ruins
Will serve to build their palaces or tombs.
They will possess the world that we think
    ours,
And fashion it far otherwise.

MICHAEL ANGELO.

            I hear
Your son Orazio and your nephew Marco
Mentioned with honor.

TITIAN.

         Ay, brave lads, brave lads.
But time will show. There is a youth in
    Venice,
One Paul Cagliari, called the Veronese,

ARTIST: WALTER SHIRLAW.

MICHAEL ANGELO'S VISIT TO TITIAN'S STUDIO.

Still a mere stripling, but of such rare prom-
    ise
That we must guard our laurels, or may lose
    them.

MICHAEL ANGELO.

These are good tidings; for I sometimes fear
That, when we die, with us all art will die.
'T is but a fancy. Nature will provide
Others to take our places. I rejoice
To see the young spring forward in the race,
Eager as we were, and as full of hope
And the sublime audacity of youth.

TITIAN.

Men die and are forgotten. The great world
Goes on the same. Among the myriads
Of men that live, or have lived, or shall
    live,
What is a single life, or thine or mine,
That we should think all nature would stand
    still
If we were gone? We must make room for
    others.

MICHAEL ANGELO.

And now, Maestro, pray unveil your picture
Of Danaë, of which I hear such praise.

TITIAN, *drawing back the curtain.*
What think you?

MICHAEL ANGELO.

      That Acrisius did well
To lock such beauty in a brazen tower,
And hide it from all eyes.

TITIAN.

      The model truly
Was beautiful.

MICHAEL ANGELO.

      And more, that you were present,
And saw the showery Jove from high Olym-
    pus
Descend in all his splendor.

TITIAN.

      From your lips
Such words are full of sweetness.

MICHAEL ANGELO.

      You have caught
These golden hues from your Venetian sun-
    sets.

TITIAN.

Possibly.

MICHAEL ANGELO.

      Or from sunshine through a shower
On the lagoons, or the broad Adriatic.
Nature reveals herself in all our arts.
The pavements and the palaces of cities
Hint at the nature of the neighboring hills.
Red lavas from the Euganean quarries
Of Padua pave your streets; your palaces
Are the white stones of Istria, and gleam
Reflected in your waters and your pictures.
And thus the works of every artist show
Something of his surroundings and his hab-
    its.
The uttermost that can be reached by color
Is here accomplished. Warmth and light
    and softness
Mingle together. Never yet was flesh
Painted by hand of artist, dead or living,
With such divine perfection.

TITIAN.

      I am grateful
For so much praise from you, who are a
    master;
While mostly those who praise and those who
    blame
Know nothing of the matter, so that mainly
Their censure sounds like praise, their praise
    like censure.

MICHAEL ANGELO.

Wonderful! wonderful! The charm of color
Fascinates me the more that in myself
The gift is wanting. I am not a painter.

GIORGIO.

Messer Michele, all the arts are yours,
Not one alone; and therefore I may venture
To put a question to you.

MICHAEL ANGELO.

      Well, speak on.

GIORGIO.

Two nephews of the Cardinal Farnese
Have made me umpire in dispute between
    them
Which is the greater of the sister arts,
Painting or sculpture. Solve for me the doubt.

MICHAEL ANGELO.

Sculpture and painting have a common goal,
And whosoever would attain to it,
Whichever path he take, will find that goal
Equally hard to reach.

GIORGIO.

                No doubt, no doubt ;
But you evade the question.

MICHAEL ANGELO.

                When I stand
In presence of this picture, I concede
That painting has attained its uttermost ;
But in the presence of my sculptured fig-
    ures
I feel that my conception soars beyond
All limit I have reached.

GIORGIO.

                You still evade me.

MICHAEL ANGELO.

Giorgio Vasari, I have often said
That I account that painting as the best

Which most resembles sculpture. Here be-
    fore us
We have the proof. Behold those rounded
    limbs !
How from the canvas they detach themselves,
Till they deceive the eye, and one would
    say,
It is a statue with a screen behind it !

TITIAN.

Signori, pardon me ; but all such questions
Seem to me idle.

MICHAEL ANGELO.

                Idle as the wind.
And now, Maestro, I will say once more
How admirable I esteem your work,
And leave you, without further interruption.

TITIAN.

Your friendly visit hath much honored me.

GIORGIO.

Farewell.

MICHAEL ANGELO *to* GIORGIO, *going out.*

        If the Venetian painters knew
But half as much of drawing as of color,
They would indeed work miracles in art,
And the world see what it hath never seen.

VI.

PALAZZO CESARINI.

VITTORIA COLONNA, *seated in an arm-chair ;* JULIA
    GONZAGA, *standing near her.*

JULIA.

It grieves me that I find you still so weak
And suffering.

VITTORIA.

                No, not suffering ; only dying.
Death is the chillness that precedes the dawn ;
We shudder for a moment, then awake
In the broad sunshine of the other life.
I am a shadow, merely, and these hands,
These cheeks, these eyes, these tresses that
    my husband

Once thought so beautiful, and I was proud
    of
Because he thought them so, are faded quite, —
All beauty gone from them.

JULIA.

                Ah, no, not that.
Paler you are, but not less beautiful.

VITTORIA.

Hand me the mirror. I would fain behold
What change comes o'er our features when
    we die.
Thank you. And now sit down beside me
    here.
How glad I am that you have come to-day,
Above all other days, and at the hour
When most I need you

JULIA.

             Do you ever need me?

VITTORIA.

Always, and most of all to-day and now.
Do you remember, Julia, when we walked,
One afternoon, upon the castle terrace
At Ischia, on the day before you left me?

JULIA.

Well I remember; but it seems to me
Something unreal, that has never been, —
Something that I have read of in a book,
Or heard of some one else.

VITTORIA.

          Ten years and more
Have passed since then; and many things
    have happened
In those ten years, and many friends have
    died:
Marco Flaminio, whom we all admired
And loved as our Catullus; dear Valdesso,
The noble champion of free thought and
    speech:
And Cardinal Ippolito, your friend.

JULIA.

Oh, do not speak of him! His sudden death
O'ercomes me now, as it o'ercame me then.
Let me forget it; for my memory

Serves me too often as an unkind friend,
And I remember things I would forget,
While I forget the things I would remember.

VITTORIA.

Forgive me; I will speak of him no more,
The good Fra Bernardino has departed,
Has fled from Italy, and crossed the Alps,
Fearing Caraffa's wrath, because he taught
That He who made us all without our help
Could also save us without aid of ours.
Renée of France, the Duchess of Ferrara,
That Lily of the Loire, is bowed by winds
That blow from Rome; Olympia Morata
Banished from court because of this new
    doctrine.
Therefore be cautious. Keep your secret
    thought
Locked in your breast.

JULIA.

          I will be very prudent.
But speak no more, I pray; it wearies you.

VITTORIA.

Yes, I am very weary. Read to me.

JULIA.

Most willingly. What shall I read?

VITTORIA.

              Petrarca's
Triumph of Death. The book lies on the
    table;
Beside the casket there. Read where you
    find
The leaf turned down. 'T was there I left
    off reading.

JULIA, *reads.*

" Not as a flame that by some force is spent,
    But one that of itself consumeth quite,
    Departed hence in peace the soul content,
In fashion of a soft and lucent light
    Whose nutriment by slow gradation goes,
    Keeping until the end its lustre bright.
Not pale, but whiter than the sheet of snows
    That without wind on some fair hill-top
        lies,
    Her weary body seemed to find repose.

Like a sweet slumber in her lovely eyes,
  When now the spirit was no longer there,
  Was what is dying called by the unwise.
E'en Death itself in her fair face seemed
      fair." —

Is it of Laura that he here is speaking? —
She doth not answer, yet is not asleep;
Her eyes are full of light and fixed on some-
      thing
Above her in the air. I can see naught
Except the painted angels on the ceiling.
Vittoria! speak! What is it? Answer
      me! —
She only smiles, and stretches out her hands.
                    [*The mirror falls and breaks.*

VITTORIA.

Not disobedient to the heavenly vision!
Pescara! my Pescara!   [*Dies.*

JULIA.

              Holy Virgin!
Her body sinks together, — she is dead!
        [*Kneels, and hides her face in Vittoria's lap.*

Enter MICHAEL ANGELO.

JULIA.

Hush! make no noise.

MICHAEL ANGELO.
              How is she?

JULIA.
                    Never better.

MICHAEL ANGELO.

Then she is dead!

JULIA.
            Alas! yes, she is dead!
Even death itself in her fair face seems fair.

MICHAEL ANGELO.

How wonderful! The light upon her face
Shines from the windows of another world.
Saints only have such faces. Holy An-
      gels!
Bear her like sainted Catherine to her rest!
                [*Kisses Vittoria's hand.*

PART THIRD

I.

MONOLOGUE: MACELLO DE' CORVI.

A room in MICHAEL ANGELO'S *house.* MICHAEL ANGELO, *standing before a model of St. Peter's.*

MICHAEL ANGELO.

Better than thou I cannot, Brunelleschi,
And less than thou I will not! If the thought
Could, like a windlass, lift the ponderous
    stones
And swing them to their places; if a breath
Could blow this rounded dome into the air,
As if it were a bubble, and these statues
Spring at a signal to their sacred stations,
As sentinels mount guard upon a wall,
Then were my task completed. Now, alas!
Naught am I but a Saint Sebaldus, holding
Upon his hand the model of a church,
As German artists paint him; and what
    years,
What weary years, must drag themselves
    along,
Ere this be turned to stone! What hin-
    drances
Must block the way; what idle interferences
Of Cardinals and Canons of St. Peter's,
Who nothing know of art beyond the color
Of cloaks and stockings, nor of any building
Save that of their own fortunes! And what
    then?
I must then the short-coming of my means
Piece out by stepping forward, as the Spar-
    tan
Was told to add a step to his short sword.

                 [*A pause.*

And is Fra Bastian dead? Is all that light
Gone out, that sunshine darkened; all that
    music
And merriment, that used to make our lives
Less melancholy, swallowed up in silence
Like madrigals sung in the street at night
By passing revellers? It is strange indeed
That he should die before me. 'T is against
The laws of nature that the young should
    die,
And the old live; unless it be that some
Have long been dead who think themselves
    alive,
Because not buried. Well, what matters it,
Since now that greater light, that was my
    sun,
Is set, and all is darkness, all is darkness!
Death's lightnings strike to right and left of
    me,
And, like a ruined wall, the world around me
Crumbles away, and I am left alone.
I have no friends, and want none. My own
    thoughts
Are now my sole companions, — thoughts of
    her,
That like a benediction from the skies
Come to me in my solitude and soothe me.
When men are old, the incessant thought of
    Death
Follows them like their shadow; sits with
    them
At every meal; sleeps with them when they
    sleep;
And when they wake already is awake,
And standing by their bedside. Then, what
    folly
It is in us to make an enemy
Of this importunate follower, not a friend!
To me a friend, and not an enemy,
Has he become since all my friends are dead.

II.

VIGNA DI PAPA GIULIO.

POPE JULIUS III. *seated by the Fountain of Acqua Vergine,*
surrounded by Cardinals.

JULIUS.

Tell me, why is it ye are discontent,
You, Cardinals Salviati and Marcello,

With Michael Angelo? What has he done,
Or left undone, that ye are set against
    him?
When one Pope dies, another is soon made;
And I can make a dozen Cardinals,
But cannot make one Michael Angelo.

CARDINAL SALVIATI.

Your Holiness, we are not set against him;
We but deplore his incapacity.
He is too old.

JULIUS.

       You, Cardinal Salviati,
Are an old man. Are you incapable?
'T is the old ox that draws the straightest fur-
    row.

CARDINAL MARCELLO.

Your Holiness remembers he was charged
With the repairs upon St. Mary's bridge;
Made cofferdams, and heaped up load on
    load
Of timber and travertine; and yet for years
The bridge remained unfinished, till we gave it
To Baccio Bigio.

JULIUS.

       Always Baccio Bigio!
Is there no other architect on earth?
Was it not he that sometime had in charge
The harbor of Ancona.

CARDINAL MARCELLO.

       Ay, the same.

JULIUS.

Then let me tell you that your Baccio Bigio
Did greater damage in a single day
To that fair harbor than the sea had done
Or would do in ten years. And him you
    think
To put in place of Michael Angelo,
In building the Basilica of St. Peter!
The ass that thinks himself a stag discovers
His error when he comes to leap the ditch.

CARDINAL MARCELLO.

He does not build; he but demolishes
The labors of Bramante and San Gallo.

JULIUS.

Only to build more grandly.

CARDINAL MARCELLO.

But time passes:
Year after year goes by, and yet the work
Is not completed. Michael Angelo
Is a great sculptor, but no architect.
His plans are faulty.

JULIUS.

I have seen his model,
And have approved it. But here comes the
artist.
Beware of him. He may make Persians of
you,
To carry burdens on your backs forever.

The same: MICHAEL ANGELO.

JULIUS.

Come forward, dear Maestro! In these gar-
dens
All ceremonies of our court are banished.
Sit down beside me here.

MICHAEL ANGELO, *sitting down.*

How graciously
Your Holiness commiserates old age
And its infirmities!

JULIUS.

Say its privileges.
Art I respect. The building of this palace
And laying out of these pleasant garden walks
Are my delight, and if I have not asked
Your aid in this, it is that I forbear
To lay new burdens on you at an age
When you need rest. Here I escape from
Rome
To be at peace. The tumult of the city
Scarce reaches here.

MICHAEL ANGELO.

How beautiful it is,
And quiet almost as a hermitage!

JULIUS.

We live as hermits here; and from these
heights

126

O'erlook all Rome and see the yellow Tiber
Cleaving in twain the city, like a sword,
As far below there as St. Mary's bridge.
What think you of that bridge?

MICHAEL ANGELO.

I would advise
Your Holiness not to cross it, or not often;
It is not safe.

JULIUS.

It was repaired of late.

MICHAEL ANGELO.

Some morning you will look for it in vain;
It will be gone. The current of the river
Is undermining it.

JULIUS.

But you repaired it.

MICHAEL ANGELO.

I strengthened all its piers, and paved its
road
With travertine. He who came after me
Removed the stone, and sold it, and filled in
The space with gravel.

JULIUS.

Cardinal Salviati
And Cardinal Marcello, do you listen?
This is your famous Nanni Baccio Bigio.

MICHAEL ANGELO, *aside.*

There is some mystery here. These Cardinals
Stand lowering at me with unfriendly eyes.

JULIUS.

Now let us come to what concerns us more
Than bridge or gardens. Some complaints
are made
Concerning the Three Chapels in St. Peter's;
Certain supposed defects or imperfections,
You doubtless can explain.

MICHAEL ANGELO.

This is no longer
The golden age of art. Men have become
Iconoclasts and critics. They delight not
In what an artist does, but set themselves
To censure what they do not comprehend.

You will not see them bearing a Madonna
Of Cimabue to the church in triumph,
But tearing down the statue of a Pope
To cast it into cannon. Who are they
That bring complaints against me ?

JULIUS.

                Deputies
Of the commissioners ; and they complain
Of insufficient light in the Three Chapels.

CARDINAL MARCELLO.

                We regret
You have departed from Bramante's plan,
And from San Gallo's.

MICHAEL ANGELO.

              Since the ancient time
No greater architect has lived on earth
Than Lazzari Bramante. His design,
Without confusion, simple, clear, well-lighted,

MICHAEL ANGELO.

Your Holiness, the insufficient light
Is somewhere else, and not in the Three
    Chapels.
Who are the deputies that make complaint ?

JULIUS.

The Cardinals Salviati and Marcello,
Here present.

MICHAEL ANGELO, *rising.*

      With permission, Monsignori,
What is it ye complain of ?

Merits all praise, and to depart from it
Would be departing from the truth. San
    Gallo, .
Building about with columns, took all light
Out of this plan ; left in the choir dark cor-
    ners
For infinite ribaldries, and lurking places
For rogues and robbers ; so that when the
    church
Was shut at night, not five and twenty men
Could find them out. It was San Gallo,
    then,
That left the church in darkness, and not I.

CARDINAL MARCELLO.

Excuse me ; but in each of the Three Chapels
Is but a single window.

MICHAEL ANGELO.

Monsignore,
Perhaps you do not know that in the vaulting
Above there are to go three other windows.

CARDINAL SALVIATI.

How should we know ? You never told us
of it.

MICHAEL ANGELO.

I neither am obliged, nor will I be,
To tell your Eminence or any other
What I intend or ought to do. Your office
Is to provide the means, and see that thieves
Do not lay hands upon them. The designs
Must all be left to me.

CARDINAL MARCELLO.

Sir architect,
You do forget yourself, to speak thus rudely
In presence of his Holiness, and to us
Who are his cardinals.

MICHAEL ANGELO, *putting on his hat.*

I do not forget
I am descended from the Counts Canossa,
Linked with the Imperial line, and with Ma-
tilda,
Who gave the Church Saint Peter's Patri-
mony.
I, too, am proud to give unto the Church
The labor of these hands, and what of life
Remains to me. My father Buonarotti
Was Podestà of Chiusi and Caprese.
I am not used to have men speak to me
As if I were a mason, hired to build
A garden wall, and paid on Saturdays
So much an hour.

CARDINAL SALVIATI, *aside.*

No wonder that Pope Clement
Never sat down in presence of this man,
Lest he should do the same ; and always
bade him
Put on his hat, lest he unasked should do
it !

MICHAEL ANGELO.

If any one could die of grief and shame,
I should. This labor was imposed upon me ;
I did not seek it ; and if I assumed it,
'T was not for love of fame or love of
gain,
But for the love of God. Perhaps old age
Deceived me, or self-interest, or ambition ;
I may be doing harm instead of good.
Therefore, I pray your Holiness, release me ;
Take off from me the burden of this work ;
Let me go back to Florence.

JULIUS.

Never, never,
While I am living.

MICHAEL ANGELO.

Doth your Holiness
Remember what the Holy Scriptures say
Of the inevitable time, when those
Who look out of the windows shall be dark-
ened,
And the almond-tree shall flourish ?

JULIUS.

That is in
Ecclesiastes.

MICHAEL ANGELO.

And the grasshopper
Shall be a burden, and desire shall fail,
Because man goeth unto his long home.
Vanity of vanities, saith the Preacher ; all
Is vanity.

JULIUS.

Ah, were to do a thing
As easy as to dream of doing it,
We should not want for artists. But the
men
Who carry out in act their great designs
Are few in number ; ay, they may be
counted
Upon the fingers of this hand. Your place
Is at St. Peter's.

MICHAEL ANGELO.

I have had my dream,
And cannot carry out my great conception,
And put it into act.

JULIUS.

                    Then who can do it?
You would but leave it to some Baccio Bigio
To mangle and deface.

MICHAEL ANGELO.

                    Rather than that,
I will still bear the burden on my shoulders
A little longer. If your Holiness
Will keep the world in order, and will leave
The building of the church to me, the work
Will go on better for it. Holy Father,
If all the labors that I have endured,
And shall endure, advantage not my soul,
I am but losing time.

JULIUS, *laying his hands on* MICHAEL ANGELO'S *shoulders.*
                    You will be gainer
Both for your soul and body.

MICHAEL ANGELO.

                    Not events
Exasperate me, but the purest conclusions
I draw from these events; the sure decline
Of art, and all the meaning of that word;
All that embellishes and sweetens life,
And lifts it from the level of low cares
Into the purer atmosphere of beauty;
The faith in the Ideal; the inspiration
That made the canons in the church of Seville
Say, " Let us build, so that all men hereafter
Will say that we were madmen." Holy
    Father,
I beg permission to retire from here.

JULIUS.

Go; and my benediction be upon you.
                    [*Michael Angelo goes out.*
My Cardinals, this Michael Angelo
Must not be dealt with as a common mason.
He comes of noble blood, and for his crest
Bear two bull's horns; and he has given us
    proof
That he can toss with them. From this day
    forth
Unto the end of time, let no man utter
The name of Baccio Bigio in my presence.
All great achievements are the natural fruits
Of a great character. As trees bear not
Their fruits of the same size and quality,

But each one in its kind with equal ease,
So are great deeds as natural to great men
As mean things are to small ones. By his
    work
We know the master. Let us not perplex him.

III.

BINDO ALTOVITI.

A street in Rome. BINDO ALTOVITI, *standing at the door
of his house.* MICHAEL ANGELO, *passing.*

BINDO.

Good-morning, Messer Michael Angelo!

MICHAEL ANGELO.

Good-morning, Messer Bindo Altoviti!

BINDO.

What brings you forth so early?

MICHAEL ANGELO.

                    The same reason
That keeps you standing sentinel at your
    door, —
The air of this delicious summer morning.
What news have you from Florence?

BINDO.

                    Nothing new;
The same old tale of violence and wrong.
Since the disastrous day at Monte Murlo,
When in procession, through San Gallo's gate,
Bareheaded, clothed in rags, on sorry steeds,
Philippo Strozzi and the good Valori
Were led as prisoners down the streets of
    Florence,
Amid the shouts of an ungrateful people,
Hope is no more, and liberty no more.
Duke Cosimo, the tyrant, reigns supreme.

MICHAEL ANGELO.

Florence is dead: her houses are but tombs;
Silence and solitude are in her streets.

BINDO.

Ah yes; and often I repeat the words
You wrote upon your statue of the Night,
There in the Sacristy of San Lorenzo:

"Grateful to me is sleep; to be of stone
More grateful, while the wrong and shame
    endure;
To see not, feel not, is a benediction;
Therefore awake me not; oh, speak in whis-
    pers."

MICHAEL ANGELO.

        Those are good tidings.
He hath been many years away from us.

BINDO.

Pray you, come in.

MICHAEL ANGELO.

Ah, Messer Bindo, the calamities,
The fallen fortunes, and the desolation
Of Florence are to me tragedy
Deeper than words, and darker than despair.
I, who have worshipped freedom from my
    cradle,
Have loved her with the passion of a lover,
And clothed her with all lovely attributes
That the imagination can conceive,
Or the heart conjure up, now see her dead,
And trodden in the dust beneath the feet
Of an adventurer! It is a grief
Too great for me to bear in my old age.

BINDO.

I say no news from Florence: I am wrong,
For Benvenuto writes that he is coming
To be my guest in Rome.

MICHAEL ANGELO.

        I have not time to stay,
And yet I will. I see from here your house
Is filled with works of art. That bust in
    bronze
Is of yourself. Tell me, who is the master
That works in such an admirable way,
And with such power and feeling?

BINDO.

           Benvenuto.

MICHAEL ANGELO.

Ah? Benvenuto? 'T is a masterpiece!
It pleases me as much, and even more,
Than the antiques about it; and yet they
Are of the best one sees. But you have
    placed it
By far too high. The light comes from below,

And injures the expression. Were these
   windows
Above and not beneath it, then indeed
It would maintain its own among these
   works
Of the old masters, noble as they are.
I will go in and study it more closely.
I always prophesied that Benvenuto,
With all his follies and fantastic ways,
Would show his genius in some work of art
That would amaze the world, and be a chal-
   lenge
Unto all other artists of his time.

                    [*They go in.*

IV.

IN THE COLISEUM.

MICHAEL ANGELO *and* TOMASO DE' CAVALIERI.

CAVALIERI.

What have you here alone, Messer Michele?

MICHAEL ANGELO.

I come to learn.

CAVALIERI.

          You are already master,
And teach all other men.

MICHAEL ANGELO.

             Nay, I know nothing;
Not even my own ignorance, as some
Philosopher hath said. I am a school-boy
Who hath not learned his lesson, and who
   stands
Ashamed and silent in the awful presence
Of the great master of antiquity
Who built these walls cyclopean.

CAVALIERI.

              Gaudentius
His name was, I remember. His reward
Was to be thrown alive to the wild beasts
Here where we now are standing.

MICHAEL ANGELO.

              Idle tales.

CAVALIERI.

But you are greater than Gaudentius was,
And your work nobler.

MICHAEL ANGELO.

       Silence, I beseech you.

CAVALIERI.

Tradition says that fifteen thousand men
Were toiling for ten years incessantly
Upon this amphitheatre.

MICHAEL ANGELO.

        Behold
How wonderful it is! The queen of flowers,
The marble rose of Rome! Its petals torn
By wind and rain of thrice five hundred
   years;
Its mossy sheath half rent away, and sold
To ornament our palaces and churches,
Or to be trodden under feet of man
Upon the Tiber's bank; yet what remains
Still opening its fair bosom to the sun,
And to the constellations that at night
Hang poised above it like a swarm of bees.

CAVALIERI.

The rose of Rome, but not of Paradise;
Not the white rose our Tuscan poet saw,
With saints for petals. When this rose was
   perfect
Its hundred thousand petals were not saints,
But senators in their Thessalian caps,
And all the roaring populace of Rome;
And even an Empress and the Vestal Vir-
   gins,
Who came to see the gladiators die,
Could not give sweetness to a rose like this.

MICHAEL ANGELO.

I spake not of its uses, but its beauty.

CAVALIERI.

The sand beneath our feet is saturate
With blood of martyrs; and these rifted
   stones
Are awful witnesses against a people
Whose pleasure was the pain of dying men.

MICHAEL ANGELO.

Tomaso Cavalieri, on my word,
You should have been a preacher, not a
   painter!
Think you that I approve such cruelties,

Because I marvel at the architects
Who built these walls, and curved these
    noble arches?
Oh, I am put to shame, when I consider
How mean our work is, when compared with
    theirs!
Look at these walls about us and above us!
They have been shaken by earthquakes,
    have been made
A fortress, and been battered by long sieges;
The iron clamps, that held the stones to-
    gether,
Have been wrenched from them; but they
    stand erect
And firm, as if they had been hewn and
    hollowed
Out of the solid rock, and were a part
Of the foundations of the world itself.

CAVALIERI.

Your work, I say again, is nobler work,
In so far as its end and aim are nobler;
And this is but a ruin, like the rest.

Its vaulted passages are made the caverns
Of robbers, and are haunted by the ghosts
Of murdered men.

MICHAEL ANGELO.

        A thousand wild flowers bloom
From every chink, and the birds build their
    nests
Among the ruined arches, and suggest
New thoughts of beauty to the architect.
Now let us climb the broken stairs that lead
Into the corridors above, and study
The marvel and the mystery of that art
In which I am a pupil, not a master.
All things must have an end; the world it-
    self
Must have an end, as in a dream I saw it.
There came a great hand out of heaven, and
    touched
The earth, and stopped it in its course. The
    seas
Leaped, a vast cataract, into the abyss;
The forests and the fields slid off, and floated

Like wooded islands in the air. The dead
Were hurled forth from their sepulchres;
    the living
Were mingled with them, and themselves
    were dead, —
All being dead; and the fair, shining cities
Dropped out like jewels from a broken crown.
Naught but the core of the great globe re-
    mained,
A skeleton of stone. And over it
The wrack of matter drifted like a cloud,
And then recoiled upon itself, and fell
Back on the empty world, that with the
    weight
Reeled, staggered, righted, and then headlong
    plunged
Into the darkness, as a ship, when struck
By a great sea, throws off the waves at
    first
On either side, then settles and goes down
Into the dark abyss, with her dead crew.

CAVALIERI.

But the earth does not move.

MICHAEL ANGELO.

                Who knows? who knows?
There are great truths that pitch their shin-
    ing tents
Outside our walls, and though but dimly seen
In the gray dawn, they will be manifest
When the light widens into perfect day.
A certain man, Copernicus by name,
Sometime professor here in Rome, has whis-
    pered
It is the earth, and not the sun, that moves.
What I beheld was only in a dream,
Yet dreams sometimes anticipate events,
Being unsubstantial images of things
As yet unseen.

V.

BENVENUTO AGAIN : MARCELLO DE' CORVI.

MICHAEL ANGELO, BENVENUTO CELLINI.

MICHAEL ANGELO.

So, Benvenuto, you return once more
To the Eternal City. 'T is the centre
To which all gravitates. One finds no rest

Elsewhere than here.   There may be other
    cities
That please us for a while, but Rome alone
Completely satisfies. It becomes to all
A second native land by predilection,
And not by accident of birth alone.

BENVENUTO.

I am but just arrived, and am now lodging
With Bindo Altoviti. I have been
To kiss the feet of our most Holy Father,
And now am come in haste to kiss the hands
Of my miraculous Master.

MICHAEL ANGELO.

                    And to find him
Grown very old.

BENVENUTO.

            You know that precious stones
Never grow old.

MICHAEL ANGELO.

            Half sunk beneath the horizon,
And yet not gone. Twelve years are a long
    while.
Tell me of France.

BENVENUTO.

                It were too long a tale
To tell you all. Suffice in brief to say
The King received me well, and loved me
    well;
Gave me the annual pension that before me
Our Leonardo had, nor more nor less,
And for my residence the Tour de Nesle,
Upon the river-side.

MICHAEL ANGELO.

            A princely lodging.

BENVENUTO.

What in return I did now matters not,
For there are other things, of greater mo-
    ment,
I wish to speak of. First of all, the letter
You wrote me, not long since, about my
    bust
Of Bindo Altoviti, here in Rome. You said,
" My Benvenuto, I for many years

Have known you as the greatest of all gold-
smiths,
And now I know you as no less a sculptor."
Ah, generous Master! How shall I e'er thank
you
For such kind language?

MICHAEL ANGELO.

By believing it.
I saw the bust at Messer Bindo's house,
And thought it worthy of the ancient mas-
ters,
And said so. That is all.

BENVENUTO.

It is too much;
And I should stand abashed here in your
presence,
Had I done nothing worthier of your praise
Than Bindo's bust.

MICHAEL ANGELO.

What have you done that's better?

BENVENUTO.

When I left Rome for Paris, you remember
I promised you that if I went a goldsmith
I would return a sculptor. I have kept
The promise I then made.

MICHAEL ANGELO.

Dear Benvenuto,
I recognized the latent genius in you,
But feared your vices.

BENVENUTO.

I have turned them all
To virtues. My impatient, wayward nature,
That made me quick in quarrel, now has
served me
Where meekness could not, and where pa-
tience could not,
As you shall hear now. I have cast in bronze
A statue of Perseus, holding thus aloft
In his left hand the head of the Medusa,
And in his right the sword that severed it;
His right foot planted on the lifeless corse;
His face superb and pitiful, with eyes
Down-looking on the victim of his vengeance.

127

MICHAEL ANGELO.

I see it as it should be.

BENVENUTO.

As it will be
When it is placed upon the Ducal Square,
Half-way between your David and the Judith
Of Donatello.

MICHAEL ANGELO.

Rival of them both!

BENVENUTO.

But ah, what infinite trouble have I had
With Bandinello, and that stupid beast,
The major-domo of Duke Cosimo,
Francesco Ricci, and their wretched agent
Gorini, who came crawling round about me
Like a black spider, with his whining voice
That sounded like the buzz of a mosquito!
Oh, I have wept in utter desperation,
And wished a thousand times I had not left
My Tour de Nesle, nor e'er returned to Flor-
ence,
Or thoughts of Perseus. What malignant
falsehoods
They told the Grand Duke, to impede my
work,
And make me desperate!

MICHAEL ANGELO.

The nimble lie
Is like the second-hand upon a clock;
We see it fly; while the hour-hand of truth
Seems to stand still, and yet it moves un-
seen,
And wins at last, for the clock will not
strike
Till it has reached the goal.

BENVENUTO.

My obstinacy
Stood me in stead, and helped me to o'er-
come
The hindrances that envy and ill-will
Put in my way.

MICHAEL ANGELO.

When anything is done
People see not the patient doing of it,

Nor think how great would be the loss to
     man
If it had not been done. As in a building
Stone rests on stone, and wanting the foun-
     dation
All would be wanting, so in human life
Each action rests on the foregone event,
That made it possible, but is forgotten
And buried in the earth.

BENVENUTO.
                    Even Bandinello,
Who never yet spake well of anything,
Speaks well of this; and yet he told the
     Duke
That, though I cast small figures well enough,
I never could cast this.

MICHAEL ANGELO.
                    But you have done it,
And proved Ser Bandinello a false prophet.
That is the wisest way.

BENVENUTO.
                    And ah, that casting!
What a wild scene it was, as late at night,
A night of wind and rain, we heaped the fur-
     nace
With pine of Serristori, till the flames
Caught in the rafters over us, and threatened
To send the burning roof upon our heads;

And from the garden side the wind and rain
Poured in upon us, and half quenched our
     fires.
I was beside myself with desperation.
A shudder came upon me, then a fever;
I thought that I was dying, and was forced
To leave the work-shop, and to throw myself
Upon my bed, as one who has no hope.
And as I lay there, a deformed old man
Appeared before me, and with dismal voice,
Like one who doth exhort a criminal
Led forth to death, exclaimed, " Poor Benve-
     nuto,
Thy work is spoiled! There is no remedy!"
Then, with a cry so loud it might have
     reached
The heaven of fire, I bounded to my feet,
And rushed back to my workmen. They all
     stood
Bewildered and desponding; and I looked
Into the furnace, and beheld the mass
Half molten only, and in my despair
I fed the fire with oak, whose terrible heat
Soon made the sluggish metal shine and
     sparkle.
Then followed a bright flash, and an explo-
     sion,
As if a thunderbolt had fallen among us.
The covering of the furnace had been rent
Asunder, and the bronze was flowing over;
So that I straightway opened all the sluices
To fill the mould. The metal ran like lava,
Sluggish and heavy; and I sent my workmen
To ransack the whole house, and bring to-
     gether
My pewter plates and pans, two hundred of
     them,
And cast them one by one into the furnace
To liquefy the mass, and in a moment
The mould was filled! I fell upon my knees
And thanked the Lord; and then we ate and
     drank
And went to bed, all hearty and contented.
It was two hours before the break of day.
My fever was quite gone.

MICHAEL ANGELO.
                    A strange adventure,
That could have happened to no man alive
But you, my Benvenuto.

CELLINI CASTING THE STATUE. (The Perseus.)

BENVENUTO.

As my workmen said
To major-domo Ricci afterward,
When he inquired of them: "'T was not a
man,
But an express great devil."

MICHAEL ANGELO.

And the statue?

BENVENUTO.

Perfect in every part, save the right foot
Of Perseus, as I had foretold the Duke.
There was just bronze enough to fill the
mould;
Not a drop over, not a drop too little.
I looked upon it as a miracle
Wrought by the hand of God.

MICHAEL ANGELO.

And now I see
How you have turned your vices into virtues.

BENVENUTO.

But wherefore do I prate of this? I came
To speak of other things. Duke Cosimo
Through me invites you to return to Florence,
And offers you great honors, even to make
you
One of the Forty-Eight, his Senators.

MICHAEL ANGELO.

His Senators! That is enough. Since Flor-
ence
Was changed by Clement Seventh from a
Republic
Into a Dukedom, I no longer wish
To be a Florentine. That dream is ended.
The Grand Duke Cosimo now reigns supreme;
All liberty is dead. Ah, woe is me!
I hoped to see my country rise to heights
Of happiness and freedom yet unreached
By other nations, but the climbing wave
Pauses, lets go its hold, and slides again
Back to the common level, with a hoarse
Death-rattle in its throat. I am too old
To hope for better days. I will stay here
And die in Rome. The very weeds, that
grow
Among the broken fragments of her ruins,

Are sweeter to me than the garden flowers
Of other cities; and the desolate ring
Of the Campagna round about her walls
Fairer than all the villas that encircle
The towns of Tuscany.

BENVENUTO.

But your old friends!

MICHAEL ANGELO.

All dead by violence. Baccio Valori
Has been beheaded; Guicciardini poisoned;
Philippo Strozzi strangled in his prison.
Is Florence then a place for honest men
To flourish in? What is there to prevent
My sharing the same fate?

BENVENUTO.

Why, this: if all
Your friends are dead, so are your enemies.

MICHAEL ANGELO.

Is Aretino dead?

BENVENUTO.

He lives in Venice,
And not in Florence.

MICHAEL ANGELO.

'T is the same to me.
This wretched mountebank, whom flatterers
Call the Divine, as if to make the word
Unpleasant in the mouths of those who
speak it
And in the ears of those who hear it, sends
me
A letter written for the public eye,
And with such subtle and infernal malice,
I wonder at his wickedness. 'T is he
Is the express great devil, and not you.
Some years ago he told me how to paint
The scenes of the Last Judgment.

BENVENUTO.

I remember.

MICHAEL ANGELO.

Well, now he writes to me that, as a Christian,
He is ashamed of the unbounded freedom
With which I represent it.

BENVENUTO.

Hypocrite!

MICHAEL ANGELO.

He says I show mankind that I am wanting
In piety and religion, in proportion
As I profess perfection in my art.
Profess perfection? Why, 't is only men
Like Bugiardini who are satisfied
With what they do. I never am content,
But always see the labors of my hand
Fall short of my conception.

BENVENUTO.

I perceive
The malice of this creature. He would
     taint you
With heresy, and in a time like this!
'T is infamous!

MICHAEL ANGELO.

I represent the angels
Without their heavenly glory, and the saints
Without a trace of earthly modesty.

BENVENUTO.

Incredible audacity!

MICHAEL ANGELO.

The heathen
Veiled their Diana with some drapery,
And when they represented Venus naked
They made her by her modest attitude,
Appear half clothed. But I, who am a Chris-
     tian,
Do so subordinate belief to art
That I have made the very violation
Of modesty in martyrs and in virgins
A spectacle at which all men would gaze
With half-averted eyes even in a brothel.

BENVENUTO.

He is at home there, and he ought to
     know
What men avert their eyes from in such
     places;
From the Last Judgment chiefly, I imagine.

MICHAEL ANGELO.

But divine Providence will never leave

The boldness of my marvellous work unpun-
     ished;
And the more marvellous it is, the more
'T is sure to prove the ruin of my fame!
And finally, if in this composition
I had pursued the instructions that he gave
     me
Concerning heaven and hell and paradise,
In that same letter, known to all the world,
Nature would not be forced, as she is now,
To feel ashamed that she invested me
With such great talent; that I stand myself
A very idol in the world of art.
He taunts me also with the Mausoleum
Of Julius, still unfinished, for the reason
That men persuaded the inane old man
It was of evil augury to build
His tomb while he was living; and he speaks
Of heaps of gold this Pope bequeathed to me,
And calls it robbery; — that is what he says.
What prompted such a letter?

BENVENUTO.

Vanity.
He is a clever writer, and he likes
To draw his pen, and flourish it in the face
Of every honest man, as swordsmen do
Their rapiers on occasion, but to show
How skilfully they do it. Had you followed
The advice he gave, or even thanked him
     for it,
You would have seen another style of fence.
'T is but his wounded vanity, and the wish
To see his name in print. So give it not
A moment's thought; it will soon be forgot-
     ten.

MICHAEL ANGELO.

I will not think of it, but let it pass
For a rude speech thrown at me in the
     street,
As boys threw stones at Dante.

BENVENUTO.

And what answer
Shall I take back to Grand Duke Cosimo?
He does not ask your labor or your service;
Only your presence in the city of Florence,
With such advice upon his work in hand
As he may ask, and you may choose to give.

MICHAEL ANGELO.

You have my answer. Nothing he can offer
Shall tempt me to leave Rome. My work
    is here,
And only here, the building of St. Peter's.
What other things I hitherto have done
Have fallen from me, are no longer mine;
I have passed on beyond them, and have left
    them
As milestones on the way. What lies before
    me,
That is still mine, and while it is unfinished
No one shall draw me from it, or persuade
    me,
By promises of ease, or wealth, or honor,
Till I behold the finished dome uprise
Complete, as now I see it in my thought.

BENVENUTO.

And will you paint no more?

MICHAEL ANGELO.

          No more.

BENVENUTO.

             'T is well.
Sculpture is more divine, and more like Na-
    ture,
That fashions all her works in high relief,
And that is sculpture. This vast ball, the
    Earth,
Was moulded out of clay, and baked in
    fire;
Men, women, and all animals that breathe
Are statues and not paintings. Even the
    plants,
The flowers, the fruits, the grasses, were first
    sculptured,
And colored later. Painting is a lie,
A shadow merely.

MICHAEL ANGELO.

         Truly, as you say,
Sculpture is more than painting. It is greater
To raise the dead to life than to create
Phantoms that seem to live. The most ma-
    jestic
Of the three sister arts is that which builds;
The eldest of them all, to whom the others
Are but the hand-maids and the servitors,

Being but imitation, not creation.
Henceforth I dedicate myself to her.

BENVENUTO.

And no more from the marble hew those
    forms
That fill us all with wonder?

MICHAEL ANGELO.

            Many statues
Will there be room for in my work. Their
    station
Already is assigned them in my mind.
But things move slowly. There are hin-
    drances,
Want of material, want of means, delays
And interruptions, endless interference
Of Cardinal Commissioners, and disputes
And jealousies of artists, that annoy me.
But I will persevere until the work
Is wholly finished, or till I sink down
Surprised by death, that unexpected guest,
Who waits for no man's leisure, but steps in,
Unasked and unannounced, to put a stop
To all our occupations and designs.
And then perhaps I may go back to Flor-
    ence;
This is my answer to Duke Cosimo.

VI.

URBINO'S FORTUNE.

MICHAEL ANGELO'S *Studio.* MICHAEL ANGELO *and*
    URBINO.

MICHAEL ANGELO, *pausing in his work.*

Urbino, thou and I are both old men,
My strength begins to fail me.

URBINO.

            Eccellenza,
That is impossible. Do I not see you
Attack the marble blocks with the same fury
As twenty years ago?

MICHAEL ANGELO.

         'T is an old habit.
I must have learned it early from my nurse
At Setignano, the stone-mason's wife;

For the first sounds I heard were of the chisel
Chipping away the stone.

URBINO.

At every stroke
You strike fire with your chisel.

MICHAEL ANGELO.

Ay, because
The marble is too hard.

URBINO.

It is a block
That Topolino sent you from Carrara.
He is a judge of marble.

MICHAEL ANGELO.

I remember.
With it he sent me something of his mak-
    ing, —
A Mercury, with long body and short legs,
As if by any possibility
A messenger of the gods could have short legs.
It was no more like Mercury than you are,
But rather like those little plaster figures
That peddlers hawk about the villages
As images of saints. But luckily
For Topolino, there are many people
Who see no difference between what is best
And what is only good, or not even good;
So that poor artists stand in their esteem
On the same level with the best, or higher.

URBINO.

How Eccellenza laughed!

MICHAEL ANGELO.

Poor Topolino!
All men are not born artists, nor will labor
E'er make them artists.

URBINO.

No, no more
Than Emperors, or Popes, or Cardinals.
One must be chosen for it. I have been
Your color-grinder six and twenty years,
And am not yet an artist.

MICHAEL ANGELO.

Some have eyes

That see not; but in every block of marble
I see a statue, — see it as distinctly
As if it stood before me shaped and perfect
In attitude and action. I have only
To hew away the stone walls that imprison
The lovely apparition, and reveal it
To other eyes as mine already see it.
But I grow old and weak. What wilt thou
    do
When I am dead, Urbino?

URBINO.

Eccellenza,
I must then serve another master.

MICHAEL ANGELO.

Never!
Bitter is servitude at best. Already
So many years hast thou been serving me;
But rather as a friend than as a servant.
We have grown old together. Dost thou
    think
So meanly of this Michael Angelo
As to imagine he would let thee serve,
When he is free from service? Take this
    purse,
Two thousand crowns in gold.

URBINO.

Two thousand crowns!

MICHAEL ANGELO.

Ay, it will make thee rich. Thou shalt not
    die
A beggar in a hospital.

URBINO.

Oh, Master!

MICHAEL ANGELO.

I cannot have them with me on the journey
That I am undertaking. The last garment
That men will make for me will have no
    pockets.

URBINO, *kissing the hand of* MICHAEL ANGELO.
My generous master!

MICHAEL ANGELO.

Hush!

URBINO.

My Providence !

MICHAEL ANGELO.

Not a word more. Go now to bed, old man.
Thou hast served Michael Angelo. Remem-
    ber,
Henceforward thou shalt serve no other mas-
    ter.

VII.

THE OAKS OF MONTE LUCA.

MICHAEL ANGELO, *alone in the woods.*

MICHAEL ANGELO.

How still it is among these ancient oaks !
Surges and undulations of the air
Uplift the leafy boughs, and let them fall
With scarce a sound. Such sylvan quietudes
Become old age. These huge centennial oaks,
That may have heard in infancy the trum-
    pets
Of Barbarossa's cavalry, deride
Man's brief existence, that with all his strength
He cannot stretch beyond the hundredth year.
This little acorn, turbaned like the Turk,

Which with my foot I spurn, may be an oak
Hereafter, feeding with its bitter mast
The fierce wild boar, and tossing in its arms
The cradled nests of birds, when all the men
That now inhabit this vast universe,
They and their children, and their children's
    children,
Shall be but dust and mould, and nothing
    more.
Through openings in the trees I see below
    me
The valley of Clitumnus, with its farms
And snow-white oxen grazing in the shade
Of the tall poplars on the river's brink.
O Nature, gentle mother, tender nurse !
I, who have never loved thee as I ought,
But wasted all my years immured in cities,
And breathed the stifling atmosphere of
    streets,
Now come to thee for refuge. Here is peace.
Yonder I see the little hermitages
Dotting the mountain side with points of
    light,
And here St. Julian's convent, like a nest
Of curlews, clinging to some windy cliff.
Beyond the broad, illimitable plain
Down sinks the sun, red as Apollo's quoit,
That, by the envious Zephyr blown aside,

Struck Hyacinthus dead, and stained the
    earth
With his young blood, that blossomed into
    flowers.
And now, instead of these fair deities,
Dread demons haunt the earth; hermits in-
    habit
The leafy homes of sylvan Hamadryads;
And jovial friars, rotund and rubicund,
Replace the old Silenus with his ass.

Here underneath these venerable oaks,
Wrinkled and brown and gnarled like them
    with age,
A brother of the monastery sits,
Lost in his meditations. What may be
The questions that perplex, the hopes that
    cheer him?
Good-evening, holy father.

MONK.

              God be with you.

MICHAEL ANGELO.

Pardon a stranger if he interrupt
Your meditations.

MONK.

           It was but a dream, —
The old, old dream, that never will come true;
The dream that all my life I have been
    dreaming,
And yet is still a dream.

MICHAEL ANGELO.

           All men have dreams.
I have had mine; but none of them came
    true;
They were but vanity. Sometimes I think
The happiness of man lies in pursuing,
Not in possessing; for the things possessed
Lose half their value. Tell me of your
    dream.

MONK.

The yearning of my heart, my sole desire,
That like the sheaf of Joseph stands upright,
While all the others bend and bow to it;
The passion that torments me, and that
    breathes

New meaning into the dead forms of prayer,
Is that with mortal eyes I may behold
The Eternal City.

MICHAEL ANGELO.

    Rome?

MONK.

             There is but one;
The rest are merely names. I think of it
As the Celestial City, paved with gold,
And sentinelled with angels.

MICHAEL ANGELO.

             Would it were.
I have just fled from it. It is beleaguered
By Spanish troops, led by the Duke of Alva

MONK.

But still for me 't is the Celestial City,
And I would see it once before I die.

MICHAEL ANGELO.

Each one must bear his cross.

MONK.

             Were it a cross
That had been laid upon me, I could bear it,
Or fall with it. It is a crucifix;
I am nailed hand and foot, and I am dying!

MICHAEL ANGELO.

What would you see in Rome?

MONK.

             His Holiness.

MICHAEL ANGELO.

Him that was once the Cardinal Caraffa?
You would but see a man of fourscore years,
With sunken eyes, burning like carbuncles,
Who sits at table with his friends for
    hours,
Cursing the Spaniards as a race of Jews
And miscreant Moors. And with what sol-
    diery
Think you he now defends the Eternal City?

MONK.

With legions of bright angels.

MICHAEL ANGELO.

So he calls them;
And yet in fact these bright angelic legions
Are only German Lutherans.

MONK, *crossing himself*.

Heaven protect us.

MICHAEL ANGELO.

What further would you see?

For he who goes to Rome may see too much.
What would you further?

MONK.

I would see the painting
Of the Last Judgment in the Sistine Chapel.

MICHAEL ANGELO.

The smoke of incense and of altar candles
Has blackened it already.

MONK.

The Cardinals,
Going in their gilt coaches to High Mass.

MICHAEL ANGELO.

Men do not go to Paradise in coaches.

MONK.

The catacombs, the convents, and the
churches;
The ceremonies of the Holy Week
In all their pomp, or, at the Epiphany,
The feast of the Santissima Bambino
At Ara Cœli. But I shall not see them.

MICHAEL ANGELO.

These pompous ceremonies of the Church
Are but an empty show to him who knows
The actors in them. Stay here in your convent,
128

MONK.

Woe is me!
Then I would hear Allegri's Miserere,
Sung by the Papal choir.

MICHAEL ANGELO.

A dismal dirge!
I am an old, old man, and I have lived
In Rome for thirty years and more, and
know
The jarring of the wheels of that great
world,
Its jealousies, its discords, and its strife.
Therefore I say to you, remain content
Here in your convent, here among your
woods,
Where only there is peace. Go not to
Rome.
There was of old a monk of Wittenberg

Who went to Rome; you may have heard
    of him;
His name was Luther; and you know what
    followed.

                [The convent bell rings.

MONK, *rising.*

It is the convent bell; it rings for vespers.
Let us go in; we both will pray for peace.

VIII.

THE DEAD CHRIST.

MICHAEL ANGELO'S *studio.* MICHAEL ANGELO *with a
light, working upon the Dead Christ. Midnight.*

MICHAEL ANGELO.

O Death, why is it I cannot portray
Thy form and features? Do I stand too
    near thee?
Or dost thou hold my hand, and draw me
    back,
As being thy disciple, not thy master?
Let him who knows not what old age is
    like
Have patience till it comes, and he will
    know.
I once had skill to fashion Life and Death
And Sleep, which is the counterfeit of
    Death;
And I remember what Giovanni Strozzi
Wrote underneath my statue of the Night
In San Lorenzo, ah, so long ago!

Grateful to me is sleep! More grateful now
Than it was then; for all my friends are
    dead;
And she is dead, the noblest of them all.
I saw her face, when the great sculptor
    Death,
Whom men should call Divine, had at a
    blow
Stricken her into marble; and I kissed
Her cold white hand. What was it held me
    back
From kissing her fair forehead, and those
    lips,
Those dead, dumb lips? Grateful to me is
    sleep!

Enter GIORGIO VASARI.

GIORGIO.

Good-evening, or good-morning, for I know
    not
Which of the two it is.

MICHAEL ANGELO.

                How came you in?

GIORGIO.

Why, by the door, as all men do.

MICHAEL ANGELO.

                    Ascanio
Must have forgotten to bolt it.

GIORGIO.

                    Probably.
Am I a spirit, or so like a spirit,
That I could slip through bolted door or
    window?
As I was passing down the street, I saw
A glimmer of light, and heard the well-
    known chink
Of chisel upon marble. So I entered,
To see what keeps you from your bed so late.

MICHAEL ANGELO, *coming forward with the lamp.*

You have been revelling with your boon com-
    panions,
Giorgio Vasari, and you come to me
At an untimely hour.

GIORGIO.

           The Pope hath sent me.
His Holiness desires to see again
The drawing you once showed him of the
    dome
Of the Basilica.

MICHAEL ANGELO.

        We will look for it.

GIORGIO.

What is the marble group that glimmers there
Behind you?

MICHAEL ANGELO.

Nothing, and yet everything, —

As one may take it. It is my own tomb,
That I am building.

GIORGIO.

Do not hide it from me.
By our long friendship and the love I bear
you,
Refuse me not!

MICHAEL ANGELO, *letting fall the lamp.*

Life hath become to me
An empty theatre, — its lights extinguished,
The music silent, and the actors gone;
And I alone sit musing on the scenes
That once have been. I am so old that
Death
Oft plucks me by the cloak, to come with
him;
And some day, like this lamp, shall I fall
down,
And my last spark of life will be extin-
guished.
Ah me! ah me! what darkness of despair!
So near to death, and yet so far from God.

Henry W. Longfellow

OUTRE-MER
A PILGRIMAGE
BEYOND THE SEA

I have passed manye landes and manye yles and contrees, and cherched manye fulle straunge places, and have ben in manye a fulle gode honourable companye. Now I am comen home to reste. And thus recordynge the tyme passed, I have fulfilled these thynges and putte hem wryten in this boke, as it woulde come into my mynde.

SIR JOHN MAUNDEVILLE.

THE EPISTLE DEDICATORY.

The cheerful breeze sets fair ; we fill our sail,
And scud before it.   When the critic starts,
And angrily unties his bags of wind,
Then we lay to, and let the blast go by.

HURDIS.

WORTHY AND GENTLE READER, —

I DEDICATE this little book to thee with many fears and misgivings of heart. Being a stranger to thee, and having never administered to thy wants nor to thy pleasures, I can ask nothing at thy hands saving the common courtesies of life. Perchance, too, what I have written will be little to thy taste ; — for it is little in accordance with the stirring spirit of the present age. If so, I crave thy forbearance for having thought that even the busiest mind might not be a stranger to those moments of repose when the clock of time clicks drowsily behind the door, and trifles become the amusement of the wise and great.

Besides, what perils await the adventurous author who launches forth into the uncertain current of public favor in so frail a bark as this ! The very rocking of the tide may overset him ; or peradventure some freebooting critic, prowling about the great ocean of letters, may descry his strange colors, hail him through a gray goose-quill, and perhaps sink him without more ado. Indeed, the success of an unknown author is as uncertain as the wind. " When a book is first to appear in the world," says a celebrated French writer, " one knows not whom to consult to learn its destiny. The stars preside not over its nativity. Their influences have no operation on it ; and the most confident astrologers dare not foretell the diverse risks of fortune it must run."

It is from such considerations, worthy reader, that I would fain bespeak thy friendly offices, at the outset. But in asking these, I would not forestall thy good opinion too far, lest in the sequel I should disappoint thy kind wishes. I ask only a welcome and God-speed ; hoping, that, when thou hast read these pages, thou wilt say to me, in the words of Nick Bottom, the weaver, " I shall desire you of more acquaintance, good Master Cobweb."

Very sincerely thine,

THE AUTHOR.

BRUNSWICK, Maine, 1833.

THE PILGRIM OF OUTRE-MER.

I am a Palmer, as ye se,
Whiche of my lyfe muche part have spent
In many a fayre and farre cuntrie,
As pilgrims do of good intent.

THE FOUR Ps.

"LYSTENYTH, ye godely gentylmen, and all that ben hereyn!" I am a pilgrim benighted on my way, and crave a shelter till the storm is over, and a seat by the fireside in this honorable company. As a stranger I claim this courtesy at your hands; and will repay your hospitable welcome with tales of the countries I have passed through in my pilgrimage.

This is a custom of the olden time. In the days of chivalry and romance, every baron bold, perched aloof in his feudal castle, welcomed the stranger to his halls, and listened with delight to the pilgrim's tale and the song of the troubadour. Both pilgrim and troubadour had their tales of wonder from a distant land, embellished with the magic of Oriental exaggeration. Their salutation was, —

"Lordyng lystnith to my tale,
That is meryer than the nightingale."

The soft luxuriance of the Eastern clime bloomed in the song of the bard; and the wild and romantic tales of regions so far off as to be regarded as almost a fairy land were well suited to the childish credulity of an age when what is now called the Old World was in its childhood. Those times have passed away. The world has grown wiser and less credulous; and the tales which then delighted delight no longer. But man has not changed his nature. He still retains the same curiosity, the same love of novelty, the same fondness for romance and tales by the chimney-corner, and the same desire of wearing out the rainy day and the long winter evening with the illusions of fancy and the fairy sketches of the poet's imagination. It is as true now as ever, that

"Off talys, and tryfulles, many man tellys;
Sume byn trew, and sume byn ellis;
A man may dryfe forthe the day that long tyme dwellis

Wyth harpyng, and pipyng, and other mery spellis,
Wyth gle, and wyth game."

The Pays d'Outre-Mer, or the Land beyond the Sea, is a name by which the pilgrims and crusaders of old usually designated the Holy Land. I, too, in a certain sense, have been a pilgrim of Outre-Mer; for to my youthful imagination the Old World was a kind of Holy Land, lying afar off beyond the blue horizon of the ocean; and when its shores first rose upon my sight, looming through the hazy atmosphere of the sea, my heart swelled with the deep emotions of the pilgrim, when he sees afar the spire which rises above the shrine of his devotion.

In this my pilgrimage, "I have passed many lands and countries, and searched many full strange places." I have traversed France from Normandy to Navarre; smoked my pipe in a Flemish inn; floated through Holland in a Trekschuit; trimmed my midnight lamp in a German university; wandered and mused amid the classic scenes of Italy; and listened to the gay guitar and merry castanet on the borders of the blue Guadalquivir. The recollection of many of the scenes I have passed through is still fresh in my mind; while the memory of others is fast fading away, or is blotted out forever. But now I will stay the too busy hand of time, and call back the shadowy past. Perchance the old and the wise may accuse me of frivolity; but I see in this fair company the bright eye and listening ear of youth, — an age less rigid in its censure and more willing to be pleased. "To gentlewomen and their loves is consecrated all the wooing language, allusions to love-passions, and sweet embracements feigned by the Muse 'mongst hills and rivers; whatsoever tastes of description, battel, story, abstruse antiquity, and law of the kingdome, to the more severe critic. To the one be contenting enjoyment of their auspicious desires; to the other, a happy attendance of their chosen Muses." [1]

And now, fair dames and courteous gentlemen, give me attentive audience : —

> " Lordyng lystnith to my tale,
> That is meryer than the nightingale."

THE NORMAN DILIGENCE.

The French guides, otherwise called the postilians, have one most diabolicall custome in their travelling upon the wayes. Diabolicall it may be well called; for whensoever their horses doe a little anger them, they will say in their fury, Allons, diable, — that is, Go, thou divel. This I know by mine own experience. Coryat's *Crudities.*

It was early in the " leafy month of June " that I travelled through the beautiful province of Normandy. As France was the first foreign country I visited, everything wore an air of freshness and novelty, which pleased my eye, and kept my fancy constantly busy. Life was like a dream. It was a luxury to breathe again the free air, after having been so long cooped up at sea; and, like a long-imprisoned bird let loose from its cage, I revelled in the freshness and sunshine of the morning landscape.

On every side, valley and hill were covered with a carpet of soft velvet green. The birds were singing merrily in the trees, and the landscape wore that look of gayety so well described in the quaint language of an old romance, making the " sad, pensive, and aching heart to rejoice, and to throw off mourning and sadness." Here and there a cluster of chestnut-trees shaded a thatched-roofed cottage, and little patches of vineyard were scattered on the slope of the hills, mingling their delicate green with the deep hues of the early summer grain. The whole landscape had a fresh, breezy look. It was not hedged in from the highways, but lay open to the eye of the traveller, and seemed to welcome him with open arms. I felt less a stranger in the land; and as my eye traced the dusty road winding along through a rich cultivated country, skirted on either side with blossoming fruit-trees, and occasionally caught glimpses of a little farm-house resting in a green hollow and lapped in the bosom of plenty, I felt that I was in a prosperous, hospitable, and happy land.

I had taken my seat on top of the diligence,

in order to have a better view of the country. It was one of those ponderous vehicles which totter slowly along the paved roads of France, laboring beneath a mountain of trunks and bales of all descriptions; and, like the Trojan horse, bearing a groaning multitude within it. It was a curious and cumbersome machine, resembling the bodies of three coaches placed upon one carriage, with a cabriolet on top for outside passengers. On the panels of each door were painted the fleurs-de-lis of France, and upon the side of the coach, emblazoned in golden characters, " *Exploitation Générale des Messageries Royales des Diligences pour le Havre, Rouen, et Paris.*"

It would be useless to describe the motley groups that filled the four quarters of this little world. There was the dusty tradesman, with green coat and cotton umbrella; the sallow invalid, in skull-cap and cloth shoes; the priest in his cassock; the peasant in his frock; and a whole family of squalling children. My fellow-travellers on top were a gay subaltern, with fierce mustache, and a nut-brown village beauty of sweet sixteen. The subaltern wore a military undress, and a little blue cloth cap, in the shape of a cow-bell, trimmed smartly with silver lace, and cocked on one side of his head. The brunette was decked out with a staid white Norman cap, nicely starched and plaited, and nearly three feet high, a rosary and cross about her neck, a linsey-woolsey gown, and wooden shoes.

The personage who seemed to rule this little world with absolute sway was a short, pursy man, with a busy, self-satisfied air, and the sonorous title of *Monsieur le Conducteur.* As insignia of office, he wore a little round fur cap

---

[1] Selden's Prefatory Discourse to the Notes in Drayton's *Poly-Olbion.*

and fur-trimmed jacket; and carried in his hand a small leathern portfolio, containing his way-bill. He sat with us on top of the diligence, and with comic gravity issued his mandates to the postilion below, like some petty monarch speaking from his throne. In every dingy village we thundered through, he had a thousand commissions to execute and to receive; a package to throw out on this side, and another to take in on that; a whisper for the landlady at the inn; a love-letter and a kiss for her daughter; and a wink or a snap of his fingers for the chambermaid at the window. Then there were so many questions to be asked and answered, while changing horses! Everybody had a word to say. It was *Monsieur le Conducteur!* here; *Monsieur le Conducteur!* there. He was in complete bustle; till at length crying, *En route!* he ascended the dizzy height, and we lumbered away in a cloud of dust.

But what most attracted my attention was the grotesque appearance of the postilion and the horses. He was a comical-looking little fellow, already past the heyday of life, with a thin, sharp countenance, to which the smoke of tobacco and the fumes of wine had given the dusty look of parchment. He was equipped in a short jacket of purple velvet, set off with a red collar, and adorned with silken cord. Tight breeches of bright yellow leather arrayed his pipe-stem legs, which were swallowed up in a huge pair of wooden boots, iron-fastened, and armed with long, rattling spurs. His shirt-collar was of vast dimensions, and between it and the broad brim of his high, bell-crowned, varnished hat, projected an eel-skin queue, with a little tuft of frizzled hair, like a powder-puff, at the end, bobbing up and down with the motion of the rider, and scattering a white cloud around him.

The horses which drew the diligence were harnessed to it with ropes and leather thongs, in the most uncouth manner imaginable. They were five in number, black, white, and gray, — as various in size as in color. Their tails were braided and tied up with wisps of straw; and when the postilion mounted and cracked his heavy whip, off they started: one pulling this way, another that, — one on the gallop, another trotting, and the rest dragging along at a scram-

bling pace, between a trot and a walk. No sooner did the vehicle get comfortably in motion, than the postilion, throwing the reins upon his horse's neck, and drawing a flint and steel from one pocket and a short-stemmed pipe from another, leisurely struck fire, and began to smoke. Ever and anon some part of the rope-harness would give way; *Monsieur le Conducteur* from on high would thunder forth an oath or two; a head would be popped out at every window; half a dozen voices exclaim at once, "What's the matter?" and the postilion, apostrophizing the *diable* as usual, would thrust his long whip into the leg of his boot, leisurely dismount, and, drawing a handful of packthread from his pocket, quietly set himself to mend matters in the best way possible.

In this manner we toiled slowly along the dusty highway. Occasionally the scene was enlivened by a group of peasants, driving before them a little ass, laden with vegetables for a neighboring market. Then we would pass a solitary shepherd, sitting by the road-side, with a shaggy dog at his feet, guarding his flock, and making his scanty meal on the contents of his wallet; or perchance a little peasant girl, in wooden shoes, leading a cow by a cord attached to her horns, to browse along the side of the ditch. Then we would all alight to ascend some formidable hill on foot, and be escorted up by a clamorous group of sturdy mendicants, — annoyed by the ceaseless importunity of worthless beggary, or moved to pity by the palsied limbs of the aged, and the sightless eyeballs of the blind.

Occasionally, too, the postilion drew up in front of a dingy little cabaret, completely overshadowed by wide-spreading trees. A lusty grape-vine clambered up beside the door; and a pine-bough was thrust out from a hole in the wall, by way of tavern-bush. Upon the front of the house was generally inscribed in large black letters, "ICI ON DONNE A BOIRE ET A MANGER; ON LOGE A PIED ET A CHEVAL"; a sign which may be thus paraphrased, — "Good entertainment for man and beast"; but which was once translated by a foreigner, "Here they give to eat and drink; they lodge on foot and on horseback!"

Thus one object of curiosity succeeded another; hill, valley, stream, and woodland flitted by me like the shifting scenes of a magic lantern, and one train of thought gave place to another; till at length, in the after part of the day, we entered the broad and shady avenue of fine old trees which leads to the western gate of Rouen, and a few moments afterward were lost in the crowds and confusion of its narrow streets.

THE GOLDEN LION INN.

Monsieur Vinot. Je veux absolument un Lion d'Or; parce qu'on dit. Où allez-vous? Au Lion d'Or! — D'où venez-vous? Du Lion d'Or! — Où irons-nous? Au Lion d'Or! — Où y a-t-il de bon vin? Au Lion d'Or!

La Rose Rouge.

THIS answer of Monsieur Vinot must have been running in my head as the diligence stopped at the Messagerie; for when the porter, who took my luggage, said: —

"*Où allez-vous, Monsieur?*"

I answered, without reflection (for, be it said with all the veracity of a traveller, at that time I did not know there was a Golden Lion in the city), —

"*Au Lion d' Or.*"

And so to the Lion d'Or we went.

The hostess of the Golden Lion received me with a courtesy and a smile, rang the house-bell for a servant, and told him to take the gentleman's things to number thirty-five. I followed him up-stairs. One, two, three, four, five, six, seven! Seven stories high, by Our Lady! — I counted them every one; and when I went down to remonstrate, I counted them again; so that there was no possibility of a mistake. When I asked for a lower room, the hostess told me the house was full; and when I spoke of going to another hotel, she said she should be so very sorry, so *désolée*, to have Monsieur leave her, that I marched up again to number thirty-five.

After finding all the fault I could with the chamber, I ended, as is generally the case with most men on such occasions, by being very well pleased with it. The only thing I could possibly complain of was my being lodged in the seventh story, and in the immediate neighborhood of a gentleman who was learning to play the French horn. But to remunerate me for these disadvantages, my window looked down into a market-place, and gave me a distant view of the towers of the cathedral, and the ruins of the church and abbey of St. Ouen.

When I had fully prepared myself for a ramble through the city, it was already sunset; and after the heat and dust of the day, the freshness of the long evening twilight was delightful. When I enter a new city, I cannot rest till I have satisfied the first cravings of curiosity by rambling through its streets. Nor can I endure a cicerone, with his eternal "This way, Sir." I never desire to be led directly to an object worthy of a traveller's notice, but prefer a thousand times to find my own way, and come upon it by surprise. This was particularly the case at Rouen. It was the first European city of importance that I visited. There was an air of antiquity about the whole city that breathed of the Middle Ages; and so strong and delightful was the impression that it made upon my youthful imagination, that nothing which I afterward saw could either equal or efface it. I have since passed through that city, but I did not stop. I was unwilling to destroy an impression which, even at this distant day, is as fresh upon my mind as if it were of yesterday.

With these delightful feelings I rambled on from street to street, till at length, after threading a narrow alley, I unexpectedly came out in front of the magnificent cathedral. If it had suddenly risen from the earth the effect could not have been more powerful and instantaneous. It completely overwhelmed my imagination; and I stood for a long time motionless, gazing entranced upon the stupendous edifice. I had before seen no specimen of Gothic architecture; and the massive towers before me, the lofty windows of stained glass, the low portal, with its receding arches and rude statues, all produced upon my untravelled mind an im-

pression of awful sublimity. When I entered the church, the impression was still more deep and solemn. It was the hour of vespers. The religious twilight of the place, the lamps that burned on the distant altar, the kneeling crowd, the tinkling bell, and the chant of the evening service that rolled along the vaulted roof in broken and repeated echoes, filled me with new and intense emotions. When I gazed on the stupendous architecture of the church, the huge columns that the eye followed up till they were lost in the gathering dusk of the arches above, the long and shadowy aisles, the statues of saints and martyrs that stood in every recess, the figures of armed knights upon the tombs, the uncertain light that stole through the painted windows of each little chapel, and the form of the cowled and solitary monk, kneeling at the shrine of his favorite saint, or passing between the lofty columns of the church, — all I had read of, but had not seen, — I was transported back to the Dark Ages, and felt as I can never feel again.

On the following day, I visited the remains of an old palace, built by Edward the Third, now occupied as the Palais de Justice, and the ruins of the church and monastery of Saint Antoine. I saw the hole in the tower where the ponderous bell of the abbey fell through; and took a peep at the curious illuminated manuscript of Daniel d'Aubonne in the public library. The remainder of the morning was spent in visiting the ruins of the ancient abbey of St. Ouen, which is now transformed into the Hotel de Ville, and in strolling through its beautiful gardens, dreaming of the present and the past, and given up to "a melancholy of my own."

At the *table d'hôte* of the Golden Lion, I fell into conversation with an elderly gentleman, who proved to be a great antiquarian, and thoroughly read in all the forgotten lore of the city. As our tastes were somewhat similar, we were soon upon very friendly terms; and after dinner we strolled out to visit some remarkable localities, and took the *gloria* together at the Chevalier Bayard.

When we returned to the Golden Lion, he entertained me with many curious stories of the spots we had been visiting. Among others, he related the following singular adventure of a monk of the abbey of St. Antoine, which amused me so much that I cannot refrain from presenting it to my readers. I will not, however, vouch for the truth of the story; for that the antiquarian himself would not do. He said he found it in an ancient manuscript of the Middle Ages, in the archives of the public library; and I give it as it was told me, without note or comment.

MARTIN FRANC AND THE MONK OF SAINT ANTHONY.[1]

> Seignor, oiez une merveille,
> C'onques n'oïstes sa pareille,
> Que je vos vueil dire et conter ;
> Or metez cuer a l'escouter.
>   FABLIAU DU BOUCHIER D'ABBEVILLE.

> Lystyn Lordyngs to my tale,
>   And ye shall here of one story,
> Is better than any wyne or ale,
>   That ever was made in this cuntry.
>   ANCIENT METRICAL ROMANCE.

IN times of old, there lived in the city of Rouen a tradesman named Martin Franc, who, by a series of misfortunes, had been reduced from opulence to poverty. But poverty, which generally makes men humble and laborious, only served to make him proud and lazy; and in proportion as he grew poorer and poorer, he grew also prouder and lazier. He contrived, however, to live along from day to day, by now and then pawning a silken robe of his wife, or selling a silver spoon, or some other trifle, saved from the wreck of his better fortunes; and passed his time pleasantly enough in loitering about the market-place, and walking up and down on the sunny side of the street.

The fair Marguerite, his wife, was celebrated through the whole city for her beauty, her wit, and her virtue. She was a brunette, with the blackest eye, the whitest teeth, and the ripest nut-brown cheek in all Normandy ; her figure was tall and stately, her hands and feet most delicately moulded, and her swimming gait like the motion of a swan. In happier days she had been the delight of the richest tradesmen in the city, and the envy of the fairest dames.

The friends of Martin Franc, like the friends of many a ruined man before and since, deserted him in the day of adversity. Of all that had eaten his dinners, and drunk his wine, and flattered his wife, none sought the narrow alley and humble dwelling of the broken tradesman save one, and that one was Friar Gui, the sacristan of the abbey of St. Anthony. He was a little, jolly, red-faced friar, with a leer in his eye, and rather a doubtful reputation; but as he was a kind of travelling gazette, and always brought the latest news and gossip of the city, and besides was the only person that condescended to visit the house of Martin Franc, — in fine, for the want of a better, he was considered in the light of a friend.

In these constant assiduities, Friar Gui had his secret motives, of which the single heart of Martin Franc was entirely unsuspicious. The keener eye of his wife, however, soon discovered two faces under the hood; but she persevered in misconstruing the friar's intentions, and in dexterously turning aside any expressions of gallantry that fell from his lips. In this way Friar Gui was for a long time kept at bay; and Martin Franc preserved in the day of poverty and distress that consolation of all this world's afflictions, — a friend. But, finally, things came to such a pass, that the honest tradesman opened his eyes, and wondered he had been asleep so long. Whereupon he was irreverent enough to thrust Friar Gui into the street by the shoulders.

Meanwhile the times grew worse and worse. One family relic followed another, — the last silken robe was pawned, the last silver spoon

---

[1] The outlines of the following tale were taken from a Norman Fabliau of the thirteenth century, entitled *Le Segretain Moine.* To judge by the numerous imitations of this story which still exist in old Norman poetry, it seems to have been a prodigious favorite of its day, and to have passed through as many hands as did the body of Friar Gui. It probably had its origin in " The Story of the Little Hunchback," a tale of the Arabian Nights ; and in modern times has been imitated in the poetic tale of " The Knight and the Friar," by George Colman.

sold; until at length poor Martin Franc was forced to "drag the devil by the tail"; in other words, beggary stared him full in the face. But the fair Marguerite did not even then despair. In those days a belief in the immediate guardianship of the saints was much more strong and prevalent than in these lewd and degenerate times; and as there seemed no great probability of improving their condition by any lucky change which could be brought about by mere human agency, she determined to try what could be done by intercession with the patron saint of her husband. Accordingly she repaired one evening to the abbey of St. Anthony, to place a votive candle and offer her prayer at the altar, which stood in the little chapel dedicated to St. Martin.

It was already sunset when she reached the church, and the evening service of the Virgin had commenced. A cloud of incense floated before the altar of the Madonna, and the organ rolled its deep melody along the dim arches of the church. Marguerite mingled with the kneeling crowd, and repeated the responses in Latin, with as much devotion as the most learned clerk of the convent. When the service was over, she repaired to the chapel of St. Martin, and, lighting her votive taper at the silver lamp which burned before his altar, knelt down in a retired part of the chapel, and, with tears in her eyes, besought the saint for aid and protection. While she was thus engaged, the church became gradually deserted, till she was left, as she thought, alone. But in this she was mistaken; for, when she arose to depart, the portly figure of Friar Gui was standing close at her elbow!

"Good evening, fair Marguerite," said he. "St. Martin has heard your prayer, and sent me to relieve your poverty."

"Then," replied she, "the good saint is not very fastidious in the choice of his messengers."

"Nay, goodwife," answered the friar, not at all abashed by this ungracious reply, "if the tidings are good, what matters it who the messenger may be? And how does Martin Franc these days?"

"He is well," replied Marguerite; "and were he present, I doubt not would thank you heartily for the interest you still take in him and his poor wife."

"He has done me wrong," continued the friar. "But it is our duty to forgive our enemies; and so let the past be forgotten. I know that he is in want. Here, take this to him, and tell him I am still his friend."

So saying, he drew a small purse from the sleeve of his habit, and proffered it to his companion. I know not whether it were a suggestion of St. Martin, but true it is that the fair wife of Martin Franc seemed to lend a more willing ear to the earnest whispers of the friar. At length she said, —

"Put up your purse; to-day I can neither deliver your gift nor your message. Martin Franc has gone from home."

"Then keep it for yourself."

"Nay," replied Marguerite, casting down her eyes; "I can take no bribes here in the church, and in the very chapel of my husband's patron saint. You shall bring it to me at my house, if you will."

The friar put up the purse, and the conversation which followed was in a low and indistinct undertone, audible only to the ears for which it was intended. At length the interview ceased; and — O woman! — the last words that the virtuous Marguerite uttered, as she glided from the church, were, —

"To-night; — when the abbey-clock strikes twelve; — remember!"

It would be useless to relate how impatiently the friar counted the hours and the quarters as they chimed from the ancient tower of the abbey, while he paced to and fro along the gloomy cloister. At length the appointed hour approached; and just before the convent-bell sent forth its summons to call the friars of St. Anthony to their midnight devotions, a figure, with a cowl, stole out of a postern-gate, and passing silently along the deserted streets, soon turned into the little alley which led to the dwelling of Martin Franc. It was none other than Friar Gui. He rapped softly at the tradesman's door, and casting a look up and down the street, as if to assure himself that his motions were unobserved, slipped into the house.

"Has Martin Franc returned?" inquired he in a whisper.

"No," answered the sweet voice of his wife; "he will not be back to-night."

"Then all good angels befriend us!" continued the monk, endeavoring to take her hand.

"Not so, good monk," said she, disengaging herself. "You forget the conditions of our meeting."

The friar paused a moment; and then, drawing a heavy leathern purse from his girdle, he threw it upon the table; at the same moment a footstep was heard behind him, and a heavy blow from a club threw him prostrate upon the floor. It came from the strong arm of Martin Franc himself!

It is hardly necessary to say that his absence was feigned. His wife had invented the story to decoy the monk, and thereby to keep her husband from beggary, and to relieve herself, once for all, from the importunities of a false friend. At first Martin Franc would not listen to the proposition; but at length he yielded to the urgent entreaties of his wife; and the plan finally agreed upon was, that Friar Gui, after leaving his purse behind him, should be sent back to the convent with a severer discipline than his shoulders had ever received from any penitence of his own.

The affair, however, took a more serious turn than was intended; for, when they tried to raise the friar from the ground, — he was dead. The blow aimed at his shoulders fell upon his shaven crown; and, in the excitement of the moment, Martin Franc had dealt a heavier stroke than he intended. Amid the grief and consternation which followed this discovery, the quick imagination of his wife suggested an expedient of safety. A bunch of keys at the friar's girdle caught her eye. Hastily unfastening the ring, she gave the keys to her husband, exclaiming, —

"For the holy Virgin's sake, be quick! One of these keys doubtless unlocks the gate of the convent-garden. Carry the body thither, and leave it among the trees!"

Martin Franc threw the dead body of the monk across his shoulders, and with a heavy heart took the way to the abbey. It was a clear, starry night; and though the moon had not yet risen, her light was in the sky, and came reflected down in a soft twilight upon earth. Not a sound was heard through all the long and solitary streets, save at intervals the distant crowing of a cock, or the melancholy hoot of an owl from the lofty tower of the abbey. The silence weighed like an accusing spirit upon the guilty conscience of Martin Franc. He started at the sound of his own breathing, as he panted under the heavy burden of the monk's body; and if, perchance, a bat flitted near him on drowsy wings, he paused, and his heart beat audibly with terror. At length he reached the garden-wall of the abbey, opened the postern-gate with the key, and bearing the monk into the garden, seated him upon a stone bench by the edge of the fountain, with his head resting against a column, upon which was sculptured an image of the Madonna. He then replaced the bunch of keys at the monk's girdle, and returned home with hasty steps.

When the prior of the convent, to whom the repeated delinquencies of Friar Gui were but too well known, observed that he was again absent from his post at midnight prayers, he waxed exceedingly angry; and no sooner were the duties of the chapel finished, than he sent a monk in pursuit of the truant sacristan, summoning him to appear immediately at his cell. By chance it happened that the monk chosen for this duty was an enemy of Friar Gui; and very shrewdly supposing that the sacristan had stolen out of the garden-gate on some midnight adventure, he took that direction in pursuit. The moon was just climbing the convent-wall, and threw its silvery light through the trees of the garden, and on the sparkling waters of the fountain, that fell with a soft lulling sound into the deep basin below. As the monk passed on his way, he stopped to quench his thirst with a draught of the cool water, and was turning to depart, when his eye caught the motionless form of the sacristan, sitting erect in the shadow of the stone column.

"How is this, Friar Gui?" quoth the monk. "Is this a place to be sleeping at midnight, when the brotherhood are all at their prayers?"

Friar Gui made no answer.

"Up, up! thou eternal sleeper, and do pen-

ARTIST: ALFRED PARSONS.

THE MONK OF ST. ANTHONY.

ance for thy negligence. The prior calls for thee at his cell!" continued the monk, growing angry, and shaking the sacristan by the shoulder.

But still no answer.

"Then, by Saint Anthony, I'll wake thee!"

And saying this, he dealt the sacristan a heavy box on the ear. The body bent slowly forward from its erect position, and, giving a headlong plunge, sank with a heavy splash into the basin of the fountain. The monk waited a few moments in expectation of seeing Friar Gui rise dripping from his cold bath; but he waited in vain; for he lay motionless at the bottom of the basin, — his eyes open, and his ghastly face distorted by the ripples of the water. With a beating heart the monk stooped down, and, grasping the skirt of the sacristan's habit, at length succeeded in drawing him from the water. All efforts, however, to resuscitate him were unavailing. The monk was filled with terror, not doubting that the friar had died untimely by his hand; and as the animosity between them was no secret in the convent, he feared that, when the deed was known, he should be accused of murder. He therefore looked round for an expedient to relieve himself from the dead body; and the well-known character of the sacristan soon suggested one. He determined to carry the body to the house of the most noted beauty of Rouen, and leave it on the door-step; so that all suspicion of the murder might fall upon the shoulders of some jealous husband. The beauty of Martin Franc's wife had penetrated even the thick walls of the convent, and there was not a friar in the whole abbey of Saint Anthony who had not done penance for his truant imagination. Accordingly, the dead body of Friar Gui was laid upon the monk's brawny shoulders, carried back to the house of Martin Franc, and placed in an erect position against the door. The monk knocked loud and long; and then, gliding through a by-lane, stole back to the convent.

A troubled conscience would not suffer Martin Franc and his wife to close their eyes; but they lay awake lamenting the doleful events of the night. The knock at the door sounded like a death-knell in their ears. It still continued at intervals, rap — rap — rap! — with a dull, low sound, as if something heavy were swinging against the panel; for the wind had risen during the night, and every angry gust that swept down the alley swung the arms of the lifeless sacristan against the door. At length Martin Franc mustered courage enough to dress himself and go down, while his wife followed him with a lamp in her hand: but no sooner had he lifted the latch, than the ponderous body of Friar Gui fell stark and heavy into his arms.

"Jesu Maria!" exclaimed Marguerite, crossing herself; "here is the monk again!"

"Yes, and dripping wet, as if he had just been dragged out of the river!"

"Oh, we are betrayed!" exclaimed Marguerite in agony.

"Then the Devil himself has betrayed us," replied Martin Franc, disengaging himself from the embrace of the sacristan; "for I met not a living being; the whole city was as silent as the grave."

"Saint Martin defend us!" continued his terrified wife. "Here, take this scapulary to guard you from the Evil One; and lose no time. You must throw the body into the river, or we are lost! Holy Virgin! How bright the moon shines!"

Saying this, she threw round his neck a scapulary, with the figure of a cross on one end, and an image of the Virgin on the other; and Martin Franc again took the dead friar upon his shoulders, and with fearful misgivings departed on his dismal errand. He kept as much as possible in the shadow of the houses, and had nearly reached the quay, when suddenly he thought he heard footsteps behind him. He stopped to listen; it was no vain imagination; they came along the pavement, tramp, tramp! and every step grew louder and nearer. Martin Franc tried to quicken his pace, — but in vain: his knees smote together and he staggered against the wall. His hand relaxed its grasp, and the monk slid from his back and stood ghastly and straight beside him, supported by chance against the shoulder of his bearer. At that moment a man came round the corner, tottering beneath the weight of a huge sack. As his head was bent downwards, he did not perceive Martin Franc till he was close upon him; and when, on looking up, he saw two figures standing motionless in the shadow of the wall, he thought himself waylaid, and, without waiting to be assaulted, dropped the sack from his shoulders and ran off at full speed. The sack fell heavily on the pavement, and directly at the feet of Martin Franc. In the fall the string was broken; and out came the bloody head, not of a dead monk, as it first seemed to the excited imagination of Martin Franc, but of a dead hog! When the terror and surprise caused by this singular event had a little subsided, an idea came into the mind of Martin Franc, very similar to what would have come into the mind of almost any person in similar circumstances. He took the hog out of the sack, and putting the body of the monk into its place, secured it well with the remnants of the broken string, and then hurried homeward with the animal upon his shoulders.

He was hardly out of sight when the man with the sack returned, accompanied by two others. They were surprised to find the sack still lying on the ground, with no one near it, and began to jeer the former bearer, telling him he had been frightened at his own shadow on the wall. Then one of them took the sack upon his shoulders without the least suspicion of the change that had been made in its contents, and all three disappeared.

Now it happened that the city of Rouen was at that time infested by three street robbers, who walked in darkness like the pestilence, and always carried the plunder of their midnight marauding to the Tête-de-Bœuf, a little tavern in one of the darkest and narrowest lanes of the city. The host of the Tête-de-Bœuf was privy to all their schemes, and had an equal share in the profits of their nightly excursions. He gave a helping hand, too, by the length of his bills, and by plundering the pockets of any chance traveller that was luckless enough to sleep under his roof.

On the night of the disastrous adventure of Friar Gui, this little marauding party had been prowling about the city until a late hour, without finding anything to reward their labors. At length, however, they chanced to spy a hog, hanging under a shed in a butcher's yard, in readiness for the next day's market; and as they were not very fastidious in selecting their plunder, but, on the contrary, rather addicted to taking whatever they could lay their hands on, the hog was straightway purloined, thrust into a large sack, and sent to the Tête-de-Bœuf on the shoulders of one of the party, while the other two continued their nocturnal excursion. It was this person who had been so terrified at the appearance of Martin Franc and the dead monk; and as this encounter had interrupted any further operations of the party, the dawn of day being now near at hand they all repaired to their gloomy den in the Tête-de-Bœuf. The host was impatiently waiting their return; and, asking what plunder they had brought with them, proceeded without delay to remove it from the sack. The first thing that presented itself, on untying the string, was the monk's hood.

"The devil take the devil!" cried the host, as he opened the neck of the sack; "what's this? Your hog wears a cowl!"

"The poor fellow has become disgusted with the world, and turned monk!" said he who held the light, a little surprised at seeing the head covered with a coarse gray cloth.

"Sure enough he has," exclaimed another, starting back in dismay, as the shaven crown and ghastly face of the friar appeared. "Holy St. Benedict be with us! It is a monk stark dead!"

"A dead monk, indeed!" said a third, with an incredulous shake of the head; "how could a dead monk get into this sack? No, no; there is some sorcery in this. I have heard it said that Satan can take any shape he pleases; and you may rely upon it this is Satan himself, who has taken the shape of a monk to get us all hanged."

"Then we had better kill the devil than have the devil kill us!" replied the host, crossing himself; "and the sooner we do it the better; for it is now daylight, and the people will soon be passing in the street."

"So say I," rejoined the man of magic; "and my advice is, to take him to the butcher's yard, and hang him up in the place where we found the hog."

This proposition so pleased the others that it was executed without delay. They carried the friar to the butcher's house, and, passing a strong cord round his neck, suspended him to a beam in the shed, and there left him.

When the night was at length past, and daylight began to peep into the eastern windows of the city, the butcher arose, and prepared himself for market. He was casting up in his mind what the hog would bring in his stall, when, looking upward, lo! in its place he recognized the dead body of Friar Gui.

"By St. Denis!" quoth the butcher. "I always feared that this friar would not die quietly in his cell; but I never thought I should find him hanging under my own roof. This must not be; it will be said that I murdered him, and I shall pay for it with my life. I must contrive some way to get rid of him."

So saying, he called his man, and, showing him what had been done, asked him how he should dispose of the body so that he might not be accused of murder. The man, who was of a ready wit, reflected a moment, and then answered, —

"This is indeed a difficult matter; but there is no evil without its remedy. We will place the friar on horseback " —

"What! a dead man on horseback? — impossible!" interrupted the butcher. "Who ever heard of a dead man on horseback!"

"Hear me out, and then judge. We must place the body on horseback as well as we may, and bind it fast with cords; and then set the horse loose in the street, and pursue him, crying out that the monk has stolen the horse. Thus all who meet him will strike him with their staves as he passes, and it will be thought that he came to his death in that way."

Though this seemed to the butcher rather a mad project, yet, as no better one offered itself at the moment, and there was no time for reflection, mad as the project was, they determined to put it into execution. Accordingly the butcher's horse was brought out, and the friar was bound upon his back, and with much difficulty fixed in an upright position. The butcher then gave the horse a blow upon the crupper with his staff, which set him into a smart gallop down the street, and he and his man joined in pursuit, crying, —

"Stop thief! Stop thief! The friar has stolen my horse!"

As it was now sunrise, the streets were full of people, — peasants driving their goods to market, and citizens going to their daily avo-

cations. When they saw the friar dashing at full speed down the street, they joined in the cry of "Stop thief! — Stop thief!" and many who endeavored to seize the bridle, as the friar passed them at full speed, were thrown upon the pavement, and trampled under foot; others joined in the halloo and the pursuit; but this only served to quicken the gallop of the frightened steed, who dashed down one street and up another like the wind, with two or three mounted citizens clattering in full cry at his heels. At length they reached the market-place. The people scattered right and left in dismay; and the steed and rider dashed onward, overthrowing in their course men and women, and stalls, and piles of merchandise, and sweeping away like a whirlwind. Tramp — tramp — tramp! they clattered on; they had distanced all pursuit. They reached the quay; the wide pavement was cleared at a bound, — one more wild leap, — and splash! — both horse and rider sank into the rapid current of the river, — swept down the stream, — and were seen no more!

THE VILLAGE OF AUTEUIL.

Il n'est tel plaisir
Que d'estre à gésir
Parmy les beaux champs,
L'herbe verde choisir,
Et prendre bon temps.
MARTIAL D'AUVERGNE.

THE sultry heat of summer always brings with it, to the idler and the man of leisure, a longing for the leafy shade and the green luxuriance of the country. It is pleasant to interchange the din of the city, the movement of the crowd, and the gossip of society, with the silence of the hamlet, the quiet seclusion of the grove, and the gossip of a woodland brook. As is sung in the old ballad of Robin Hood, —

> " In somer, when the shawes be sheyn,
>   And leves be large and long,
>   Hit is full mery in feyre foreste,
>   To here the foulys song;
>   To se the dere draw to the dale
>   And leve the hilles hee,
>   And shadow hem in the leves grene,
>   Vnder the grene wode tre."

It was a feeling of this kind that prompted me, during my residence in the North of France, to pass one of the summer months at Auteuil, the pleasantest of the many little villages that lie in the immediate vicinity of the metropolis. It is situated on the outskirts of the Bois de Boulogne, a wood of some extent, in whose green alleys the dusty cit enjoys the luxury of an evening drive, and gentlemen meet in the morning to give each other satisfaction in the usual way. A cross-road, skirted with green hedge-rows, and overshadowed by tall poplars, leads you from the noisy highway of St. Cloud and Versailles to the still retirement of this suburban hamlet. On either side the eye discovers old châteaux amid the trees, and green parks, whose pleasant shades recall a thousand images of La Fontaine, Racine, and Molière; and on an eminence, overlooking the windings of the Seine, and giving a beautiful though distant view of the domes and gardens of Paris, rises the village of Passy, long the residence of our countrymen Franklin and Count Rumford.

I took up my abode at a *maison de santé;* not that I was a valetudinarian, but because I there found some one to whom I could whisper, "How sweet is solitude!" Behind the house was a garden filled with fruit-trees of various kinds, and adorned with gravel-walks and green arbors, furnished with tables and rustic seats, for the repose of the invalid and the sleep of the indolent. Here the inmates of the rural hospital met on common ground, to breathe the invigorating air of morning, and while away the lazy noon or vacant evening with tales of the sick-chamber.

The establishment was kept by Dr. Dentdelion, a dried-up little fellow, with red hair, a sandy complexion, and the physiognomy and gestures of a monkey. His character corresponded to his outward lineaments; for he had all a monkey's busy and curious impertinence. Nevertheless, such as he was, the village Æsculapius strutted forth the little great man of Auteuil. The peasants looked up to him as to an oracle; he contrived to be at the head of everything, and laid claim to the credit of all public improvements in the village; in fine, he was a great man on a small scale.

It was within the dingy walls of this little potentate's imperial palace that I chose my country residence. I had a chamber in the second story, with a solitary window, which looked upon the street, and gave me a peep into a neighbor's garden. This I esteemed a great privilege; for, as a stranger, I desired to see all that was passing out of doors; and the sight of green trees, though growing on another's ground, is always a blessing. Within doors — had I been disposed to quarrel with my household gods — I might have taken some objection to my neighborhood; for on one side of me was a consumptive patient, whose graveyard cough drove me from my chamber by day; and on the other, an English colonel, whose incoherent ravings, in the delirium of a high and obstinate fever, often broke my slumbers by night; but I found ample amends for these inconveniences in the society of those who were so little indisposed as hardly to know what ailed them, and those who, in health themselves, had accompanied a friend or relative to the shades of the country in pursuit of it. To these I am indebted for much courtesy; and particularly to one who, if these pages should ever meet her eye, will not, I hope, be unwilling to accept this slight memorial of a former friendship.

It was, however, to the Bois de Boulogne that I looked for my principal recreation. There I took my solitary walk, morning and evening; or, mounted on a little mouse-colored donkey, paced demurely along the woodland pathway. I had a favorite seat beneath the shadow of a venerable oak, one of the few hoary patriarchs of the wood which had survived the bivouacs of the allied armies. It stood upon the brink of a little glassy pool, whose tranquil bosom was the image of a quiet and secluded life, and stretched its parental arms over a rustic bench, that had been constructed beneath it for the accommodation of the foot-traveller, or, perchance, some idle dreamer like myself. It seemed to look round with a lordly air upon its old hereditary domain, whose stillness was no longer broken by the tap of the martial drum, nor the discordant clang of arms; and, as the breeze whispered among its branches, it seemed to be holding friendly colloquies with a few of its venerable contemporaries, who stooped from the opposite bank of the pool, nodding gravely now and then, and gazing at themselves, with a sigh, in the mirror below.

In this quiet haunt of rural repose I used to sit at noon, hear the birds sing, and "possess myself in much quietness." Just at my feet lay the little silver pool, with the sky and the woods painted in its mimic vault, and occasionally the image of a bird, or the soft, watery outline of a cloud, floating silently through its sunny hollows. The water-lily spread its broad, green leaves on the surface, and rocked to sleep a little world of insect life in its golden cradle. Sometimes a wandering leaf came floating and wavering downward, and settled on the water; then a vagabond insect would break the smooth surface into a thousand ripples, or a green-coated frog slide from the bank, and, plump! dive headlong to the bottom.

I entered, too, with some enthusiasm, into all the rural sports and merrimakes of the village. The holidays were so many little eras of mirth and good feeling; for the French have that happy and sunshiny temperament — that merry-go-mad character — which renders all their social meetings scenes of enjoyment and hilarity. I made it a point never to miss any of the *fêtes champêtres*, or rural dances, at the wood of Boulogne; though I confess it sometimes gave me a momentary uneasiness to see my rustic throne beneath the oak usurped by a noisy group of girls, the silence and decorum of my imaginary realm broken by music and laughter, and, in a word, my whole kingdom turned topsy-turvy with romping, fiddling, and dancing. But I am naturally, and from principle, too, a lover of all those innocent amusements which cheer the laborer's toil, and, as it were, put their shoulders to the wheel of life, and help the poor man along with his load of cares. Hence I saw with no small delight the rustic swain astride the wooden horse of the *carrousel*, and the village maiden whirling round and round in its dizzy car; or took my stand on a rising ground that overlooked the dance, an idle spectator in a busy throng. It was just where the village touched the outward border of the wood. There a little area had been levelled beneath the trees, surrounded by a painted rail, with a row of benches inside. The music was placed in a slight balcony, built around the trunk of a large tree in the centre; and the lamps, hanging from the branches above, gave a gay, fantastic, and fairy look to the scene. How often in such moments did I recall the lines of Goldsmith, describing those " kinder skies " beneath which " France displays her bright domain," and feel how true and masterly the sketch, —

" Alike all ages ; dames of ancient days
Have led their children through the mirthful maze,
And the gray grandsire, skilled in gestic lore,
Has frisked beneath the burden of threescore."

Nor must I forget to mention the *fête patro-nale*, — a kind of annual fair, which is held at midsummer, in honor of the patron saint of Auteuil. Then the principal street of the village is filled with booths of every description; strolling players, and rope-dancers, and jugglers, and giants, and dwarfs, and wild beasts, and all kinds of wonderful shows, excite the gaping curiosity of the throng; and in dust, crowds, and confusion, the village rivals the capital itself. Then the goodly dames of Passy descend into the village of Auteuil; then the brewers of Billancourt and the tanners of Sèvres dance lustily under the greenwood tree; and then, too, the sturdy fishmongers of Brétigny and Saint-Yon regale their wives with an airing in a swing, and their customers with eels and crawfish; or, as is more poetically set forth in an old Christmas carol, —

" Vous eussiez vu venir
    Tous ceux de Saint-Yon,
  Et ceux de Brétigny
    Apportant du poisson,
  Les barbeaux et gardons,
    Anguilles et carpettes

Etaient à bon marché
  Croyez,
A cette journée-là,
    Là, là,
Et aussi les perchettes."

I found another source of amusement in observing the various personages that daily passed and repassed beneath my window. The character which most of all arrested my attention was a poor blind fiddler, whom I first saw chanting a doleful ballad at the door of a small tavern near the gate of the village. He wore a brown coat, out at elbows, the fragment of a velvet waistcoat, and a pair of tight nankeen trousers, so short as hardly to reach below his calves. A little foraging-cap, that had long since seen its best days, set off an open, good-humored countenance, bronzed by sun and wind. He was led about by a brisk, middle-aged woman, in straw hat and wooden shoes; and a little barefooted boy, with clear, blue eyes and flaxen hair, held a tattered hat in his hand, in which he collected eleemosynary sous. The old fellow had a favorite song, which he used to sing with great glee to a merry, joyous air, the burden of which ran, *"Chantons l'amour et le plaisir!"* I often thought it would have been a good lesson for the crabbed and discontented rich man to have heard this remnant of humanity, — poor, blind, and in rags, and dependent upon casual charity for his daily bread, singing in so cheerful a voice the charms of existence, and, as it were, fiddling life away to a merry tune.

I was one morning called to my window by the sound of rustic music. I looked out and beheld a procession of villagers advancing along the road, attired in gay dresses, and marching merrily on in the direction of the church. I soon perceived that it was a marriage-festival. The procession was led by a long orang-outang of a man, in a straw hat and white dimity bob-coat, playing on an asthmatic clarionet, from which he contrived to blow unearthly sounds, ever and anon squeaking off at right angles from his tune, and winding up with a grand flourish on the guttural notes. Behind him, led by his little boy, came the blind fiddler, his honest features glowing with all the hilarity of a rustic bridal, and as he stumbled along, sawing away upon his fiddle till he made all crack again. Then came the happy bridegroom, dressed in his Sunday suit of blue, with a large nosegay in his button-hole; and close beside him his blushing bride, with downcast eyes, clad in a white robe and slippers, and wearing a wreath of white roses in her hair. The friends and relatives brought up the procession; and a troop of village urchins came shouting along in the rear, scrambling among themselves for the largess of sous and sugar-plums that now and then issued in large handfuls from the pockets of a lean man in black, who seemed to officiate as master of ceremonies on the occasion. I gazed on the procession till it was out of sight; and when the last wheeze of the clarionet died upon my ear, I could not help thinking how happy were they who were thus to dwell together in the peaceful bosom of their native village, far from the gilded misery and the pestilential vices of the town.

On the evening of the same day, I was sitting by the window, enjoying the freshness of the air and the beauty and stillness of the hour, when I heard the distant and solemn hymn of the Catholic burial-service, at first so faint and indistinct that it seemed an illusion. It rose mournfully on the hush of evening, — died gradually away, — then ceased. Then it rose again, nearer and more distinct, and soon after a funeral procession appeared, and passed directly beneath my window. It was led by a priest, bearing the banner of the church, and followed by two boys, holding long flambeaux in their hands. Next came a double file of priests in their surplices, with a missal in one hand and a lighted wax taper in the other, chanting the funeral dirge at intervals, — now pausing, and then again taking up the mournful burden of their lamentation, accompanied by others, who played upon a rude kind of bassoon, with a dismal and wailing sound. Then followed various symbols of the church, and the bier borne on the shoulders of four men. The coffin was covered with a velvet pall, and a chaplet of white flowers lay upon it, indicating that the deceased was unmarried. A few of the villagers came behind, clad in mourning robes, and bearing lighted tapers. The procession passed slowly along the same street that in the morning had been thronged by the gay bridal company. A melancholy train of thought forced itself home upon my mind. The joys and sorrows of this world are so strikingly mingled! Our mirth and grief are brought so mournfully in contact! We laugh while others weep, — and others rejoice when we are sad! The light heart and the heavy walk side by side and go about together! Beneath the same roof are spread the wedding-feast and the funeral-pall! The bridal-song mingles with the burial-hymn! One goes to the marriage-bed, another to the grave; and all is mutable, uncertain, and transitory.

It is with sensations of pure delight that I recur to the brief period of my existence which was passed in the peaceful shades of Auteuil. There is one kind of wisdom which we learn from the world, and another kind which can be acquired in solitude only. In cities we study those around us; but in the retirement of the country we learn to know ourselves. The voice within us is more distinctly audible in the stillness of the place; and the gentler affections of our nature spring up more freshly in its tranquillity and sunshine, — nurtured by the healthy principle which we inhale with the pure air, and invigorated by the genial influences which descend into the heart from the quiet of the sylvan solitude around, and the soft serenity of the sky above.

JACQUELINE.

Death lies on her, like an untimely frost
Upon the sweetest flower of all the field.
                                    SHAKESPEARE.

"DEAR mother, is it not the bell I hear?"

"Yes, my child; the bell for morning prayers. It is Sunday to-day."

"I had forgotten it. But now all days are alike to me. Hark! it sounds again, — louder, — louder. Open the window, for I love the sound. The sunshine and the fresh morning air revive me. And the church-bell, — O mother, — it reminds me of the holy Sunday mornings by the Loire, — so calm, so hushed, so beautiful! Now give me my prayer-book, and draw the curtain back, that I may see the green trees and the church-spire. I feel better to-day, dear mother."

It was a bright, cloudless morning in August. The dew still glistened on the trees; and a slight breeze wafted to the sick-chamber of Jacqueline the song of the birds, the rustle of the leaves, and the solemn chime of the church-bells. She had been raised up in bed, and, reclining upon the pillow, was gazing wistfully upon the quiet scene without. Her mother gave her the prayer-book, and then turned away to hide a tear that stole down her cheek.

At length the bells ceased. Jacqueline crossed herself, kissed a pearl crucifix that hung around her neck, and opened the silver clasps of her missal. For a time she seemed wholly absorbed in her devotions. Her lips moved, but no sound was audible. At intervals the solemn voice of the priest was heard at a distance, and then the confused responses of the congregation, dying away in inarticulate murmurs. Ere long the thrilling chant of the Catholic service broke upon the ear. At first it was low, solemn, and indistinct; then it became more earnest and entreating, as if interceding and imploring pardon for sin; and then arose louder and louder, full, harmonious, majestic, as it wafted the song of praise to heaven — and suddenly ceased. Then the sweet tones of the organ were heard, — trembling, thrill-

ing, and rising higher and higher, and filling the whole air with their rich, melodious music. What exquisite accords! — what noble harmonies! — what touching pathos! The soul of the sick girl seemed to kindle into more ardent devotion, and to be rapt away to heaven in the full, harmonious chorus, as it swelled onward, doubling and redoubling, and rolling upward in a full burst of rapturous devotion! Then all was hushed again. Once more the low sound of the bell smote the air, and announced the elevation of the host. The invalid seemed entranced in prayer. Her book had fallen beside her, — her hands were clasped, — her eyes closed, — her soul retired within its secret chambers. Then a more triumphant peal of bells arose. The tears gushed from her closed and swollen lids; her cheek was flushed; she opened her dark eyes, and fixed them with an expression of deep adoration and penitence upon an image of the Saviour on the cross, which hung at the foot of her bed, and her lips again moved in prayer. Her countenance expressed the deepest resignation. She seemed to ask only that she might die in peace, and go to the bosom of her Redeemer.

The mother was kneeling by the window, with her face concealed in the folds of the curtain. She arose, and going to the bedside of her child, threw her arms around her and burst into tears.

"My dear mother, I shall not live long; I feel it here. This piercing pain, — at times it seizes me, and I cannot — cannot breathe."

"My child, you will be better soon."

"Yes, mother, I shall be better soon. All tears, and pain, and sorrow will be over. The hymn of adoration and entreaty I have just heard, I shall never hear again on earth. Next Sunday, mother, kneel again by that window as to-day. I shall not be here, upon this bed of pain and sickness; but when you hear the solemn hymn of worship, and the beseeching tones that wing the spirit up to God, think, mother, that I am there, with my sweet sister who has gone before us, — kneeling at our Saviour's feet, and happy, — oh, how happy!"

The afflicted mother made no reply, — her heart was too full to speak.

"You remember, mother, how calmly Amie died. She was so young and beautiful! I always pray that I may die as she did. I do not fear death, as I did before she was taken from us. But, oh, — this pain, — this cruel pain! — it seems to draw my mind back from heaven. When it leaves me, I shall die in peace."

"My poor child! God's holy will be done!"

The invalid soon sank into a quiet slumber. The excitement was over, and exhausted nature sought relief in sleep.

The persons between whom this scene passed were a widow and her sick daughter, from the neighborhood of Tours. They had left the banks of the Loire to consult the more experienced physicians of the metropolis, and had been directed to the *maison de santé* at Auteuil for the benefit of the pure air. But all in vain. The health of the uncomplaining patient grew worse and worse, and it soon became evident that the closing scene was drawing near.

Of this Jacqueline herself seemed conscious; and towards evening she expressed a wish to receive the last sacraments of the church. A priest was sent for; and ere long the tinkling of a little bell in the street announced his approach. He bore in his hand a silver chalice containing the consecrated wafer, and a small vessel filled with the holy oil of the extreme unction hung from his neck. Before him walked a boy carrying a little bell, whose sound announced the passing of these symbols of the Catholic faith. In the rear, a few of the villagers, bearing lighted wax tapers, formed a short and melancholy procession. They soon entered the sick-chamber, and the glimmer of the tapers mingled with the red light of the setting sun that shot his farewell rays through the open window. The vessel of oil and the silver chalice were placed upon the table in front of a crucifix that hung upon the wall, and all present, excepting the priest, threw themselves upon their knees. The priest then approached the bed of the dying girl, and said, in a slow and solemn tone, —

"The King of kings and Lord of lords has passed thy threshold. Is thy spirit ready to receive him?"

"It is, father."

"Hast thou confessed thy sins?"

"Holy father, no."

"Confess thyself, then, that thy sins may be forgiven, and thy name recorded in the book of life."

And, turning to the kneeling crowd around, he waved his hand for them to retire, and was left alone with the sick girl. He seated himself beside her pillow, and the subdued whisper of the confession mingled with the murmur of the evening air, which lifted the heavy folds of the curtains, and stole in upon the holy scene. Poor Jacqueline had few sins to confess, — a secret thought or two towards the pleasures and delights of the world, — a wish to live, unuttered, but which, to the eye of her self-accusing spirit, seemed to resist the wise providence of God; — no more. The confession of a meek and lowly heart is soon made. The door was again opened; the attendants entered, and knelt around the bed, and the priest proceeded, —

"And now prepare thyself to receive with contrite heart the body of our blessed Lord and Redeemer. Dost thou believe that our Lord Jesus Christ was conceived by the Holy Spirit, and born of the Virgin Mary?"

"I believe."

And all present joined in the solemn response, —

"I believe."

"Dost thou believe that the Father is God, that the Son is God, and that the Holy Spirit is God, — three persons and one God?"

"I believe."

"Dost thou believe that the Son is seated on the right hand of the Majesty on high, whence he shall come to judge the quick and the dead?"

"I believe."

"Dost thou believe that by the holy sacraments of the church thy sins are forgiven thee, and that thus thou art made worthy of eternal life?"

"I believe."

"Dost thou pardon, with all thy heart, all who have offended thee in thought, word, or deed?"

"I pardon them."

"And dost thou ask pardon of God and thy neighbor for all offences thou hast committed against them, either in thought, word, or deed?"

"I do."

"Then repeat after me, — O Lord Jesus, I am not worthy, nor do I merit, that thy divine majesty should enter this poor tenement of clay; but, according to thy holy promises, be my sins forgiven, and my soul washed white from all transgression."

Then, taking a consecrated wafer from the vase, he placed it between the lips of the dying girl, and, while the assistant sounded the little silver bell, said, —

"*Corpus Domini nostri Jesu Christi custodiat animam tuam in vitam eternam.*"

And the kneeling crowd smote their breasts and responded in one solemn voice, —

"Amen!"

The priest then took a little golden rod, and, dipping it in holy oil, anointed the invalid upon the hands, feet, and breast, in the form of the cross. When these ceremonies were completed, the priest and his attendants retired, leaving the mother alone with her dying child, who, from the exhaustion caused by the preceding scene, sank into a deathlike sleep.

> "Between two worlds life hovered like a star,
> 'Twixt night and morn, upon the horizon's verge."

The long twilight of the summer evening stole on; the shadows deepened without, and the night-lamp glimmered feebly in the sick-chamber; but still she slept. She was lying with her hands clasped upon her breast, — her pallid cheek resting upon the pillow, and her bloodless lips apart, but motionless and silent as the sleep of death. Not a breath interrupted the silence of her slumber. Not a movement of the heavy and sunken eyelid, not a trembling of the lip, not a shadow on the marble brow, told when the spirit took its flight. It passed to a better world than this: —

> "There's a perpetual spring, — perpetual youth;
> No joint-benumbing cold, nor scorching heat,
> Famine, nor age, have any being there."

THE SEXAGENARIAN.

Do you set down your name in the scroll of youth, that are written down old, with all the characters of age? Have you not a moist eye, a dry hand, a yellow cheek, a white beard, a decreasing leg? SHAKESPEARE.

THERE he goes, in his long russet surtout, sweeping down yonder gravel-walk, beneath the trees, like a yellow leaf in autumn wafted along by a fitful gust of wind. Now he pauses, — now seems to be whirled round in an eddy, — and now rustles and brushes onward again. He is talking to himself in an undertone, as usual, and flourishes a pinch of snuff between his forefinger and his thumb, ever and anon drumming on the cover of his box, by way of emphasis, with a sound like the tap of a woodpecker. He always takes a morning walk in the garden, — in fact, I may say he passes the greater part of the day there, either strolling up and down the gravel-walks, or sitting on a rustic bench in one of the leafy arbors. He always wears that same dress, too; a bell-crowned hat, a frilled bosom, and white dimity waistcoat soiled with snuff, — light nankeen breeches, and, over all, that long and flowing surtout of russet-brown Circassian, hanging in wrinkles round his slender body, and toying with his thin, rakish legs. Such is his constant garb, morning and evening; and it gives him a cool and breezy look, even in the heat of a noonday in August.

The personage sketched in the preceding paragraph is Monsieur d'Argentville, a sexagenarian, with whom I became acquainted during my residence at the *maison de santé* of Auteuil. I found him there, and left him there. Nobody knew when he came, — he had been there from time immemorial; nor when he was going away, — for he himself did not

ARTIST: I. M. GAUGENGIGL.

THE SEXAGENARIAN.

know; nor what ailed him, — for though he was always complaining, yet he grew neither better nor worse, never consulted the physician, and ate voraciously three times a day. At table he was rather peevish, troubled his neighbors with his elbows, and uttered the monosyllable *pouah!* rather oftener than good-breeding and a due deference to the opinions of others seemed to justify. As soon as he seated himself at table, he breathed into his tumbler, and wiped it out with a napkin; then wiped his plate, his spoon, his knife and fork in succession, and each with great care. After this he placed the napkin under his chin; and, these preparations being completed, gave full swing to an appetite which was not inappropriately denominated, by one of our guests, "*une faim canine.*"

The old gentleman's weak side was an affectation of youth and gallantry. Though "written down old, with all the characters of age," yet at times he seemed to think himself in the heyday of life; and the assiduous court he paid to a fair countess, who was passing the summer at the *maison de santé*, was the source of no little merriment to all but himself. He loved, too, to recall the golden age of his amours; and would discourse with prolix eloquence, and a faint twinkle in his watery eye, of his *bonnes fortunes* in times of old, and the rigors that many a fair dame had suffered on his account. Indeed, his chief pride seemed to be to make his hearers believe that he had been a dangerous man in his youth, and was not yet quite safe.

As I also was a peripatetic of the garden, we encountered each other at every turn. At first our conversation was limited to the usual salutations of the day; but erelong our casual acquaintance ripened into a kind of intimacy. Step by step I won my way, — first into his society, — then into his snuff-box, — and then into his heart. He was a great talker, and he found in me what he found in no other inmate of the house, — a good listener, who never interrupted his long stories, nor contradicted his opinions. So he talked down one alley and up another, — from breakfast till dinner, — from dinner till midnight, — at all times and in all places, when he could catch me by the button,

till at last he had confided to my ear all the important and unimportant events of a life of sixty years.

Monsieur d'Argentville was a shoot from a wealthy family of Nantes. Just before the Revolution, he went up to Paris to study law at the University, and, like many other wealthy scholars of his age, was soon involved in the intrigues and dissipation of the metropolis. He first established himself in the Rue de l'Université; but a roguish pair of eyes at an opposite window soon drove from the field such heavy tacticians as Hugues Doneau and Gui Coquille. A flirtation was commenced in due form; and a flag of truce, offering to capitulate, was sent in the shape of a billet-doux. In the mean time he regularly amused his leisure hours by blowing kisses across the street with an old pair of bellows. One afternoon, as he was occupied in this way, a tall gentleman with whiskers stepped into the room, just as he had charged the bellows to the muzzle. He muttered something about an explanation, — his sister, — marriage, — and the satisfaction of a gentleman! Perhaps there is no situation in life so awkward to a man of real sensibility as that of being awed into matrimony or a duel by the whiskers of a tall brother. There was but one alternative; and the next morning a placard at the window of the Bachelor of Love, with the words "Furnished Apartment to let," showed that the former occupant had found it convenient to change lodgings.

He next appeared in the Chaussée-d'Antin, where he assiduously prepared himself for future exigencies by a course of daily lessons in the use of the small-sword. He soon after quarrelled with his best friend about a little actress on the Boulevard, and had the satisfaction of being jilted, and then run through the body at the Bois de Boulogne. This gave him new éclat in the fashionable world, and consequently he pursued pleasure with a keener relish than ever. He next had the *grande passion*, and narrowly escaped marrying an heiress of great expectations and a countless number of châteaux. Just before the catastrophe, however, he had the good fortune to discover that the lady's expectations were limited to his own pocket, and that, as for her châteaux, they were all Châteaux en Espagne.

About this time his father died; and the hopeful son was hardly well established in his inheritance when the Revolution broke out. Unfortunately he was a firm upholder of the divine right of kings, and had the honor of being among the first of the proscribed. He narrowly escaped the guillotine by jumping on board a vessel bound for America, and arrived at Boston with only a few francs in his pocket; but as he knew how to accommodate himself to circumstances, he contrived to live by teaching fencing and French, and keeping a dancing-school.

At the restoration of the Bourbons, he returned to France; and from that time to the day of our acquaintance had been engaged in a series of vexatious lawsuits, in the hope of recovering a portion of his property, which had been intrusted to a friend for safe-keeping at the commencement of the Revolution. His friend, however, denied all knowledge of the transaction, and the assignment was very diffi-

cult to prove. Twelve years of unsuccessful litigation had completely soured the old gentleman's temper, and made him peevish and misanthropic; and he had come to Auteuil merely to escape the noise of the city, and to brace his shattered nerves with pure air and quiet amusements. There he idled the time away, sauntering about the garden of the *maison de santé*, talking to himself when he could get no other listener, and occasionally reinforcing his misanthropy with a dose of the Maxims of La Rochefoucauld, or a visit to the scene of his duel in the Bois de Boulogne.

Poor Monsieur d'Argentville! What a miserable life he led, — or rather dragged on, from day to day! A petulant broken-down old man, who had outlived his fortune, and his friends, and his hopes, — yea, everything but the sting of bad passions and the recollection of a life ill-spent! Whether he still walks the the earth or slumbers in its bosom, I know not; but a lively recollection of him will always mingle with my reminiscences of Auteuil.

PÈRE LA CHAISE.

Our fathers find their graves in our short memories, and sadly tell us how we may be buried in our survivors.

Oblivion is not to be hired. The greater part must be content to be as though they had not been, — to be found in the register of God, not in the record of man.   Sir Thomas Browne's Urn Burial.

The cemetery of Père la Chaise is the Westminster Abbey of Paris. Both are the dwellings of the dead; but in one they repose in green alleys and beneath the open sky, — in the other their resting-place is in the shadowy aisle, and beneath the dim arches of an ancient abbey. One is a temple of nature; the other a temple of art. In one, the soft melancholy of the scene is rendered still more touching by the warble of birds and the shade of trees, and the grave receives the gentle visit of the sunshine and the shower: in the other, no sound but the passing footfall breaks the silence of the place; the twilight steals in through high and dusky windows; and the damps of the gloomy vault lie heavy on the heart, and leave their stain upon the mouldering tracery of the tomb.

Père la Chaise stands just beyond the Barrière d'Aulney, on a hill-side looking towards the city. Numerous gravel-walks, winding through shady avenues and between marble monuments, lead up from the principal entrance to a chapel on the summit. There is hardly a grave that has not its little enclosure planted with shrubbery; and a thick mass of foliage half conceals each funeral stone. The sighing of the wind, as the branches rise and fall upon it, — the occasional note of a bird among the trees, and the shifting of light and shade upon the tombs beneath, have a soothing effect upon the mind; and I doubt whether any one can enter that enclosure, where repose the dust and ashes of so many great and good men, without feeling the religion of the place steal over him, and seeing something of the dark and gloomy expression pass off from the stern countenance of death.

It was near the close of a bright summer afternoon that I visited this celebrated spot for the first time. The first object that arrested my attention, on entering, was a monument in the form of a small Gothic chapel, which stands near the entrance, in the avenue leading to the right hand. On the marble couch within are stretched two figures, carved in stone and dressed in the antique garb of the Middle Ages. It is the tomb of Abélard and Héloïse. The history of these unfortunate lovers is too well known to need recapitulation; but perhaps it is not so well known how often their ashes were disturbed in the slumber of the grave. Abélard died in the monastery of Saint Marcel, and was buried in the vaults of the church. His body afterwards was removed to the convent of the Paraclet, at the request of Héloïse, and at her death her own was deposited in the same tomb. Three centuries they reposed together; after which they were separated to different sides of the church, to calm the delicate scruples of the lady-abbess of the convent. More than a century afterward, they were again united in the same tomb; and when at length the Paraclet was destroyed, these mouldering remains were transported to the church of Nogent-sur-Seine. They were next deposited in an ancient cloister at Paris; and now repose near the gateway of the cemetery of Père la Chaise. What a singular destiny was theirs! that, after a life of such passionate and disastrous love, — such sorrows, and tears, and penitence, — their very dust should not be suffered to rest quietly in the grave! — that their death should so much resemble their life in its changes and vicissitudes, its partings and its meetings, its inquietudes and its persecutions! — that mistaken zeal should follow them down to the very tomb, — as if earthly passion could glimmer, like a funeral lamp, amid the damps of the charnel-house, and "even in their ashes burn their wonted fires!"

As I gazed on the sculptured forms before me, and the little chapel, whose Gothic roof seemed to protect their marble sleep, my busy memory swung back the dark portals of the past, and the picture of their sad and eventful lives came up before me in the gloomy distance. What a lesson for those who are endowed with the fatal gift of genius! It would seem, indeed, that He who "tempers the wind to the shorn lamb" tempers also his chastisements to the errors and infirmities of a weak and simple mind, — while the trangressions of him upon whose nature are more strongly marked the intellectual attributes of the Deity are followed, even upon earth, by severer tokens of the Divine displeasure. He who sins in the darkness of a benighted intellect sees not so clearly, through the shadows that surround him, the countenance of an offended God; but he who sins in the broad noonday of a clear and radiant mind, when at length the delirium of passion has subsided, and the cloud flits away from before the sun, trembles beneath the searching eye of that accusing power which is strong in the strength of a godlike intellect. Thus the mind and the heart are closely linked together, and the errors of genius bear with them their own chastisement, even upon earth. The history of Abélard and Héloïse is an illustration of this truth. But at length they sleep well. Their lives are like a tale that is told; their errors are "folded up like a book;" and what mortal hand shall break the seal that death has set upon them?

Leaving this interesting tomb behind me, I took a pathway to the left, which conducted me up the hill-side. I soon found myself in the deep shade of heavy foliage, where the branches of the yew and willow mingled, interwoven with the tendrils and blossoms of the honeysuckle. I now stood in the most populous part of this city of tombs. Every step awakened a new train of thrilling recollections; for at every step my eye caught the name of some one whose glory had exalted the character of his native land, and resounded across the waters of the Atlantic. Philosophers, historians, musicians, warriors, and poets slept side by side around me; some beneath the gorgeous monument, and some beneath the simple headstone. But the political intrigue, the dream of science, the historical research, the ravishing harmony of sound, the tried courage, the inspiration of the lyre, — where are they? With the living, and not with the dead! The right hand has lost its cunning in the grave; but the soul, whose high volitions it obeyed, still lives to reproduce itself in ages yet to come.

Among these graves of genius I observed here and there a splendid monument, which had been raised by the pride of family over the dust of men who could lay no claim either to the gratitude or remembrance of posterity. Their presence seemed like an intrusion into the sanctuary of genius. What had wealth to do there? Why should it crowd the dust of the great? That was no thoroughfare of business, — no mart of gain! There were no costly banquets there; no silken garments, nor gaudy liveries, nor obsequious attendants! "What servants," says Jeremy Taylor, "shall we have to wait upon us in the grave? what friends to visit us? what officious people to cleanse away the moist and unwholesome cloud reflected upon our faces from the sides of the weeping vaults, which are the longest weepers for our funerals?" Material wealth gives a factitious superiority to the living, but the treasures of intellect give a real superiority to the dead; and the rich man, who would not deign to walk the street with the starving and penniless man of genius, deems it an honor, when death has redeemed the fame of the neglected, to have his own ashes laid beside him, and to claim with him the silent companionship of the grave.

I continued my walk through the numerous winding paths, as chance or curiosity directed me. Now I was lost in a little green hollow, overhung with thick-leaved shrubbery, and then came out upon an elevation, from which, through an opening in the trees, the eye caught glimpses of the city, and the little esplanade, at the foot of the hill, where the poor lie buried. There poverty hires its grave, and takes but a short lease of the narrow house. At the end of a few months, or at most of a

few years, the tenant is dislodged to give place to another, and he in turn to a third. "Who," says Sir Thomas Browne, "knows the fate of his bones, or how often he is to be buried? Who hath the oracle of his ashes, or whither they are to be scattered?"

Yet, even in that neglected corner, the hand of affection had been busy in decorating the hired house. Most of the graves were surrounded with a slight wooden paling, to secure them from the passing footstep; there was hardly one so deserted as not to be marked with its little wooden cross, and decorated with a garland of flowers; and here and there I could perceive a solitary mourner, clothed in black, stooping to plant a shrub on the grave, or sitting in a motionless sorrow beside it.

As I passed on, amid the shadowy avenues of the cemetery, I could not help comparing my own impressions with those which others have felt when walking alone among the dwellings of the dead. Are, then, the sculptured urn and storied monument nothing more than symbols of family pride? Is all I see around me a memorial of the living more than of the dead, — an empty show of sorrow, which thus vaunts itself in mournful pageant and funeral parade? Is it indeed true, as some have said, that the simple wild-flower, which springs spontaneously upon the grave, and the rose, which the hand of affection plants there, are fitter objects wherewith to adorn the narrow house? No! I feel that it is not so! Let the good and the great be honored even in the grave. Let the sculptured marble direct our footsteps to the scene of their long sleep; let the chiselled epitaph repeat their names, and tell us where repose the nobly good and wise! It is not true that all are equal in the grave. There is no equality even there. The mere handful of dust and ashes, — the mere distinction of prince and beggar, — of a rich winding-sheet and a shroudless burial, — of a solitary grave and a family vault, — were this all, — then, indeed, it would be true that death is a common leveller. Such paltry distinctions as those of wealth and poverty are soon levelled by the spade and mattock; the damp breath of the grave blots them out forever. But there are other distinctions which even the mace of

death cannot level or obliterate. Can it break down the distinction of virtue and vice? Can it confound the good with the bad? the noble with the base? all that is truly great, and pure, and godlike, with all that is scorned, and sinful, and degraded? No! Then death is not a common leveller! Are all alike beloved in death and honored in their burial? Is that ground holy where the bloody hand of the murderer sleeps from crime? Does every grave awaken the same emotions in our hearts? and do the footsteps of the stranger pause as long beside each funeral-stone? No! Then all are not equal in the grave! And as long as the good and evil deeds of men live after them, so long will there be distinctions even in the grave. The superiority of one over another is in the nobler and better emotions which it excites; in its more fervent admonitions to virtue; in the livelier recollections which it awakens of the good and the great, whose bodies are crumbling to dust beneath our feet!

If, then, there are distinctions in the grave, surely it is not unwise to designate them by the external marks of honor. These outward appliances and memorials of respect, — the mournful urn, — the sculptured bust, the epitaph eloquent in praise, — cannot indeed create these distinctions, but they serve to mark them. It is only when pride or wealth builds them to honor the slave of mammon or the slave of appetite, when the voice from the grave rebukes the false and pompous epitaph, and the dust and ashes of the tomb seem struggling to maintain the superiority of mere worldly rank, and to carry into the grave the bawbles of earthly vanity, — it is then, and then only, that we feel how utterly worthless are all the devices of sculpture, and the empty pomp of monumental brass!

After rambling leisurely about for some time, reading the inscriptions on the various monuments which attracted my curiosity, and giving way to the different reflections they suggested, I sat down to rest myself on a sunken tombstone. A winding gravel-walk, overshaded by an avenue of trees, and lined on both sides with richly sculptured monuments, had gradually conducted me to the summit of the hill, upon whose slope the cemetery stands. Beneath me in the distance, and dim-discovered through the misty and smoky atmosphere of evening, rose the countless roofs and spires of the city. Beyond, throwing his level rays athwart the dusky landscape, sank the broad red sun. The distant murmur of the city rose upon my ear; and the toll of the evening bell came up, mingled with the rattle of the paved street and the confused sounds of labor. What an hour for meditation! What a contrast between the metropolis of the living and the metropolis of the dead! I could not help calling to my mind that allegory of mortality, written by a hand which has been many a long year cold : —

"Earth goeth upon earth as man upon mould,
  Like as earth upon earth never go should,

[1] I subjoin this relic of old English verse entire, and in its antiquated language, for those of my readers who may have antiquarian taste. It is copied from a book whose title I have forgotten, and of which I have but a single leaf, containing the poem. In describing the antiquities of the church of Stratford-upon-Avon, the writer gives the following account of a very old painting upon the wall, and of the poem which served as its motto. The painting is no longer visible, having been effaced in repairing the church.

"Against the west wall of the nave, on the south side of the arch, was painted the martyrdom of Thomas-à-Becket, while kneeling at the altar of St. Benedict in Canterbury cathedral; below this was the figure of an angel, probably St. Michael, supporting a long scroll, upon which were seven stanzas in old English, being an allegory of mortality : —

"Erthe oute of Erthe ys wondurly wroght
  Erth hath gotyn uppon erth a dygnyte of noght
  Erth ypon erth hath sett all hys thowht
  How erth apon erth may be hey browght

"Erth apon erth wold be a kyng
  But how that erth gott to erth he thyngkys nothyng
  When erth byddys erth hys rentys whom bryng
  Then schall erth apon erth have a hard ptyng

Earth goeth upon earth as glistening gold,
  And yet shall earth unto earth rather than he would.

"Lo, earth on earth, consider thou may,
  How earth cometh to earth naked alway,
  Why shall earth upon earth go stout or gay,
  Since earth out of earth shall pass in poor array." [1]

Before I left the graveyard the shades of evening had fallen, and the objects around me grown dim and indistinct. As I passed the gateway, I turned to take a parting look. I could distinguish only the chapel on the summit of the hill, and here and there a lofty obelisk of snow-white marble, rising from the black and heavy mass of foliage around, and pointing upward to the gleam of the departed sun, that still lingered in the sky, and mingled with the soft starlight of a summer evening.

"Erth apon erth wynnys castellys and towrys
  Then seth erth unto erth thys ys all owrys
  When erth apon erth hath bylde hys bowrys
  Then schall erth for erth suffur many hard schowrys

"Erth goth apon erth as man apon mowld
  Lyke as erth apon erth never goo schold
  Erth goth apon erth as gelsteryng gold
  And yet schall erth unto erth rather than he wold

"Why that erth loveth erth wondur me thynke
  Or why that erth wold for erth other swett or swynke
  When erth apon erth ys broght wt. yn the brynke
  Then schall erth apon erth have a fowll stynke

"Lo erth on erth consedur thow may
  How erth comyth to erth nakyd all way
  Why schall erth apon erth goo stowte or gay
  Seth erth owt of erth schall passe yn poor aray

"I counsill erth apon erth that ys wondurly wrogt
  The whyl yt. erth ys apon erth to torne hys thowht
  And pray to god upon erth yt. all erth wroght
  That all crystyn soullys to ye. blys may be broght

"Beneath were two men, holding a scroll over a body wrapped in a winding-sheet, and covered with some emblems of mortality," etc.

THE VALLEY OF THE LOIRE.

Je ne conçois qu'une manière de voyager plus agréable que d'aller à cheval ; c'est d'aller à pied. On part à son moment, on s'arrête à sa volonté, on fait tant et si peu d'exercise qu'on veut.

Quand on ne veut qu'arriver, on peut courir en chaise de poste ; mais quand on veut voyager, il faut aller à pied.

ROUSSEAU.

IN the beautiful month of October, I made a foot excursion along the banks of the Loire, from Orléans to Tours. This luxuriant region is justly called the garden of France. From Orléans to Blois, the whole valley of the Loire is one continued vineyard. The bright green foliage of the vine spreads, like the undulations of the sea, over all the landscape, with here and there a silver flash of the river, a sequestered hamlet, or the towers of an old château, to enliven and variegate the scene.

The vintage had already commenced. The peasantry were busy in the fields, — the song that cheered their labor was on the breeze, and the heavy wagon tottered by, laden with the clusters of the vine. Everything around me wore that happy look which makes the heart glad. In the morning I arose with the lark ; and at night I slept where sunset overtook me. The healthy exercise of foot-travelling, the pure, bracing air of autumn, and the cheerful aspect of the whole landscape about me, gave fresh elasticity to a mind not overburdened with care, and made me forget not only the fatigue of walking, but also the consciousness of being alone.

My first day's journey brought me at evening to a village, whose name I have forgotten, situated about eight leagues from Orléans. It is a small, obscure hamlet, not mentioned in the guide-book, and stands upon the precipitous banks of a deep ravine, through which a noisy brook leaps down to turn the ponderous wheel of a thatch-roofed mill. The village inn stands upon the highway ; but the village itself is not visible to the traveller as he passes. It is completely hidden in the lap of a wooded valley, and so embowered in trees that not a roof nor a chimney peeps out to betray its hiding-place. It is like the nest of a ground-swallow, which the passing footstep almost treads upon, and yet it is not seen. I passed by without suspecting that a village was near ; and the little inn had a look so uninviting that I did not even enter it.

After proceeding a mile or two farther, I perceived, upon my left, a village spire rising over the vineyards. Towards this I directed my footsteps ; but it seemed to recede as I advanced, and at last quite disappeared. It was evidently many miles distant; and as the path I followed descended from the highway, it had gradually sunk beneath a swell of the vine-clad landscape. I now found myself in the midst of an extensive vineyard. It was just sunset; and the last golden rays lingered on the rich and mellow scenery around me. The peasantry were still busy at their task; and the occasional bark of a dog, and the distant sound of an evening bell, gave fresh romance to the scene. The reality of many a day-dream of childhood, of many a poetic revery of youth, was before me. I stood at sunset amid the luxuriant vineyards of France !

The first person I met was a poor old woman, a little bowed down with age, gathering grapes into a large basket. She was dressed like the poorest class of peasantry, and pursued her solitary task alone, heedless of the cheerful gossip and the merry laugh which came from a band of more youthful vintagers at a short distance from her. She was so intently engaged in her work, that she did not perceive my approach until I bade her good evening. On hearing my voice, she looked up from her labor, and returned the salutation ; and, on my asking her if there were a tavern or a farm-house in the neighborhood where I could pass the night, she showed me the pathway through the vineyard that led to the village, and then added, with a look of curiosity, —

" You must be a stranger, sir, in these parts."

132

" Yes ; my home is very far from here."

" How far ? "

" More than a thousand leagues."

The old woman looked incredulous.

" I came from a distant land beyond the sea."

" More than a thousand leagues ! " at length repeated she ; " and why have you come so far from home ? "

" To travel ; — to see how you live in this country."

" Have you no relations in your own ? "

" Yes ; I have both brothers and sisters, a father and " —

" And a mother ? "

" Thank Heaven, I have."

" And did you leave *her ?* "

Here the old woman gave me a piercing look of reproof; shook her head mournfully, and, with a deep sigh, as if some painful recollections had been awakened in her bosom, turned again to her solitary task. I felt rebuked ; for there is something almost prophetic in the admonitions of the old. The eye of age looks meekly into my heart ! the voice of age echoes mournfully through it ! the hoary head and palsied hand of age plead irresistibly for its sympathies ! I venerate old age ; and I love not the man who can look without emotion upon the sunset of life, when the dusk of evening begins to gather over the watery eye, and the shadows of twilight grow broader and deeper upon the understanding !

I pursued the pathway which led towards the village, and the next person I encountered was an old man, stretched lazily beneath the vines upon a little strip of turf, at a point where four paths met, forming a crossway in the vineyard. He was clad in a coarse garb of gray, with a pair of long gaiters or spatterdashes. Beside him lay a blue cloth-cap, a staff, and an old weather-beaten knapsack. I saw at once that he was a foot-traveller like myself, and therefore, without more ado, entered into conversation with him. From his language, and the peculiar manner in which he now and then wiped his upper lip with the back of his hand, as if in search of the mustache which was no longer there, I judged that he had been a soldier. In this opinion

I was not mistaken. He had served under Napoleon, and had followed the imperial eagle across the Alps, and the Pyrenees, and the burning sands of Egypt. Like every *vieille moustache*, he spake with enthusiasm of the Little Corporal, and cursed the English, the Germans, the Spanish, and every other race on earth, except the Great Nation, — his own.

" I like," said he, " after a long day's march, to lie down in this way upon the grass, and enjoy the cool of the evening. It reminds me of the bivouacs of other days, and of old friends who are now up there."

Here he pointed with his finger to the sky.

" They have reached the last *étape* before me, in the long march. But I shall go soon. We shall all meet again at the last roll-call. *Sacré nom de* —— ! There 's a tear ! "

He wiped it away with his sleeve.

Here our colloquy was interrupted by the approach of a group of vintagers, who were returning homeward from their labor. To this party I joined myself, and invited the old soldier to do the same ; but he shook his head.

" I thank you ; my pathway lies in a different direction."

" But there is no other village near, and the sun has already set."

" No matter, I am used to sleeping on the ground. Good-night."

I left the old man to his meditations, and walked on in company with the vintagers. Following a well-trodden pathway through the vineyards, we soon descended the valley's slope, and I suddenly found myself in the bosom of one of those little hamlets from which the laborer rises to his toil as the skylark to his song. My companions wished me a goodnight, as each entered his own thatch-roofed cottage, and a little girl led me out to the very inn which an hour or two before I had disdained to enter.

When I awoke in the morning, a brilliant autumnal sun was shining in at my window. The merry song of birds mingled sweetly with the sound of rustling leaves and the gurgle of the brook. The vintagers were going forth to their toil ; the wine-press was busy in the shade, and the clatter of the mill kept time to the miller's song. I loitered about the village with a feeling of calm delight. I was unwilling to leave the seclusion of this sequestered hamlet; but at length, with reluctant step, I took the cross-road through the vineyard, and in a moment the little village had sunk again, as if by enchantment, into the bosom of the earth.

I breakfasted at the town of Mer; and, leaving the high-road to Blois on the right, passed down to the banks of the Loire, through a long, broad avenue of poplars and sycamores. I crossed the river in a boat, and in the after part of the day I found myself before the high and massive walls of the château of Chambord. This château is one of the finest specimens of the ancient Gothic castle to be found in Europe. The little river Cosson fills its deep and ample moat, and above it the huge towers and heavy battlements rise in stern and solemn grandeur, moss-grown with age, and blackened by the storms of three centuries. Within, all is mournful and deserted. The grass has overgrown the pavement of the courtyard, and the rude sculpture upon the walls is broken and defaced. From the courtyard I entered the central tower, and, ascending the principal staircase, went out upon the battlements. I seemed to have stepped back into the precincts of the feudal ages; and, as I passed along through echoing corridors, and vast, deserted halls, stripped of their furniture, and mouldering silently away, the distant past came back upon me; and the times when the clang of arms, and the tramp of mail-clad men, and the sounds of music and revelry and wassail, echoed along those high-vaulted and solitary chambers!

My third day's journey brought me to the ancient city of Blois, the chief town of the department of Loire-et-Cher. This city is celebrated for the purity with which even the lower classes of its inhabitants speak their native tongue. It rises precipitously from the northern bank of the Loire; and many of its streets are so steep as to be almost impassable for carriages. On the brow of the hill, overlooking the roofs of the city, and commanding a fine view of the Loire and its noble bridge, and the surrounding country, sprinkled with cottages and châteaux, runs an ample terrace,

planted with trees, and laid out as a public walk. The view from this terrace is one of the most beautiful in France. But what most strikes the eye of the traveller at Blois is an old, though still unfinished, castle. Its huge parapets of hewn stone stand upon either side of the street; but they have walled up the wide gateway, from which the colossal drawbridge was to have sprung high in air, connecting together the main towers of the building, and the two hills upon whose slope its foundations stand. The aspect of this vast pile is gloomy and desolate. It seems as if the strong hand of the builder had been arrested in the midst of his task by the stronger hand of death; and the unfinished fabric stands a lasting monument both of the power and weakness of man, — of his vast desires, his sanguine hopes, his ambitious purposes, — and of the unlooked-for conclusion, where all these desires, and hopes, and purposes are so often arrested. There is also at Blois another ancient château, to which some historic interest is attached, as being the scene of the massacre of the Duke of Guise.

On the following day, I left Blois for Amboise; and, after walking several leagues along the dusty highway, crossed the river in a boat to the little village of Moines, which lies amid luxuriant vineyards upon the southern bank of the Loire. From Moines to Amboise the road is truly delightful. The rich lowland scenery, by the margin of the river, is verdant even in October; and occasionally the landscape is diversified with the picturesque cottages of the vintagers, cut in the rock along the roadside, and overhung by the thick foliage of the vines above them.

At Amboise I took a cross-road, which led me to the romantic borders of the Cher and the château of Chenonceau. This beautiful château, as well as that of Chambord, was built by the gay and munificent Francis the First. One is a specimen of strong and massive architecture, — a dwelling for a warrior; but the other is of a lighter and more graceful construction, and was destined for those soft languishments of passion with which the fascinating Diane de Poitiers had filled the bosom of that voluptuous monarch.

The château of Chenonceau is built upon arches across the river Cher, whose waters are made to supply the deep moat at each extremity. There is a spacious courtyard in front, from which a drawbridge conducts to the outer hall of the castle. There the armor of Francis the First still hangs upon the wall, — his shield, and helm, and lance, — as if the chivalrous prince had just exchanged them for the silken robes of the drawing-room. From this hall a door opens into a long gallery, extending the whole length of the building across the Cher. The walls of the gallery are hung with the faded portraits of the long line of the descendants of Hugh Capet ; and the windows, looking up and down the stream, command a fine reach of pleasant river scenery. This is said to be the only château in France in which the ancient furniture of its original age is preserved. In one part of the building, you are shown the bed-chamber of Diane de Poitiers, with its antique chairs covered with faded damask and embroidery, her bed, and a portrait of the royal favorite hanging over the mantelpiece. In another you see the apartment of the infamous Catherine de' Medici ; a venerable arm-chair and an autograph letter of Henry the Fourth ; and in an old laboratory, among broken crucibles, and neckless retorts, and drums, and trumpets, and skins of wild beasts, and other ancient lumber, of various kinds, are to be seen the bed-posts of Francis the First ! Doubtless the naked walls and the vast solitary chambers of an old and desolate château inspire a feeling of greater solemnity and awe ; but when the antique furniture of the olden time remains, — the faded tapestry on the walls, and the arm-chair by the fireside, — the effect upon the mind is more magical and delightful. The old inhabitants of the place, long gathered to their fathers, though living still in history, seem to have left their halls for the chase or the tournament ; and as the heavy door swings upon its reluctant hinge one almost expects to see the gallant princes and courtly dames enter those halls again, and sweep in stately procession along the silent corridors.

Rapt in such fancies as these, and gazing on the beauties of this noble edifice, and the soft scenery around it, I lingered, unwilling to depart, till the rays of the setting sun, streaming through the dusty windows, admonished me that the day was drawing rapidly to a close. I sallied forth from the southern gate of the château, and crossing the broken drawbridge, pursued a pathway along the bank of the river, still gazing back upon those towering walls, now bathed in the rich glow of sunset, till a turn in the road and a clump of woodland at length shut them out from my sight.

A short time after candle-lighting, I reached the little tavern of the Boule d'Or, a few leagues from Tours, where I passed the night. The following morning was lowering and sad. A veil of mist hung over the landscape, and ever and anon a heavy shower burst from the overburdened clouds, that were driving by before a high and piercing wind. This unpropitious state of the weather detained me until noon, when a cabriolet for Tours drove up ; and taking a seat within it, I left the hostess of the Boule d'Or in the middle of a long story about a rich countess, who always alighted there when she passed that way. We drove leisurely along through a beautiful country, till at length we came to the brow of a steep hill, which commands a fine view of the city of Tours and its delightful environs. But the scene was shrouded by the heavy drifting mist, through which I could trace but indistinctly the graceful sweep of the Loire, and the spires and roofs of the city far below me.

The city of Tours and the delicious plain in which it lies have been too often described by other travellers to render a new description, from so listless a pen as mine, either necessary or desirable. After a sojourn of two cloudy and melancholy days, I set out on my return to Paris, by the way of Vendôme and Chartres. I stopped a few hours at the former place, to examine the ruins of a château built by Jeanne d'Albret, mother of Henry the Fourth. It stands upon the summit of a high and precipitous hill, and almost overhangs the town beneath. The French Revolution has completed the ruin that time had already begun ; and nothing now remains, but a broken and crumbling bastion, and here and there a solitary tower dropping slowly to decay. In one of these is the grave of Jeanne d'Albret. A marble entablature in the wall above contains the inscription, which is nearly effaced, though enough still remains to tell the curious traveller that there lies buried the mother of the "Bon Henri." To this is added a prayer that the repose of the dead may be respected.

Here ended my foot excursion. The object of my journey was accomplished; and, delighted with this short ramble through the valley of the Loire, I took my seat in the diligence for Paris, and on the following day was again swallowed up in the crowds of the metropolis, like a drop in the bosom of the sea.

THE TROUVÈRES.

> Quant recommence et revient biaux estez,
> Que foille et flor resplendit par boschage,
> Que li froiz tanz de l'hyver est passez,
> Et cil oisel chantent en lor langage,
> Lors chanterai
> Et envoisiez serai
> De cuer verai.
>
> JACQUES DE CHISON.

THE literature of France is peculiarly rich in poetry of the olden time. We can trace up the stream of song until it is lost in the deepening shadows of the Middle Ages. Even there it is not a shallow tinkling rill; but it comes like a mountain stream, rushing and sounding onward through the enchanted regions of romance, and mingles its voice with the tramp of steeds and the brazen sound of arms.

The glorious reign of Charlemagne,[1] at the close of the eighth and the commencement of the ninth century, seems to have breathed a spirit of learning as well as of chivalry throughout all France. The monarch established schools and academies in different parts of his realm, and took delight in the society and conversation of learned men. It is amusing to see with what evident self-satisfaction some of the magi whom he gathered around

him speak of their exertions in widening the sphere of human knowledge, and pouring in light upon the darkness of their age. "For some," says Alcuin, the director of the school of St. Martin de Tours, "I cause the honey of the Holy Scriptures to flow; I intoxicate others with the old wine of ancient history; these I nourish with the fruits of grammar, gathered by my own hands; and those I enlighten by pointing out to them the stars, like lamps attached by the vaulted ceiling of a great palace!"

Besides this classic erudition of the schools, the age had also its popular literature. Those who were untaught in scholastic wisdom were learned in traditional lore; for they had their ballads, in which were described the valor and achievements of the early kings of the Franks. These ballads, of which a collection was made by order of Charlemagne, animated the rude

---

[1] The following amusing description of this Restorer of Letters, as his biographers call him, is taken from the fabulous *Chronicle of John Turpin*, chap. xx.

"The Emperor was of a ruddy complexion, with brown hair; of a well-made, handsome form, but a stern visage. His height was about eight of his own feet, which were very long. He was of a strong, robust make; his legs and thighs very stout, and his sinews firm. His face was thirteen inches long; his beard a palm; his nose half a palm; his forehead a foot over. His lion-like eyes flashed fire like carbuncles; his eyebrows were half a palm over.

When he was angry, it was a terror to look upon him. He required eight spans for his girdle beside what hung loose. He ate sparingly of bread; but a whole quarter of lamb, two fowls, a goose, or a large portion of pork; a peacock, a crane, or a whole hare. He drank moderately of wine and water. He was so strong that he could at a single blow cleave asunder an armed soldier on horseback, from the head to the waist, and the horse likewise. He easily vaulted over four horses harnessed together; and could raise an armed man from the ground to his head, as he stood erect upon his hand."

soldier as he rushed to battle, and were sung in the midnight bivouacs of the camp. "Perhaps it is not too much to say," observes the literary historian Schlegel, "that we have still in our possession, if not the original language and form, at least the substance, of many of those ancient poems which were collected by the orders of that prince;—I refer to the Nibelungenlied, and the collection which goes by the name of the Heldenbuch."

When at length the old Tudesque language, which was the court language of Charlemagne, had given place to the Langue d'Oil, the northern dialect of the French Romance, these ancient ballads passed from the memories of the descendants of the Franks, and were succeeded by the romances of Charlemagne and his Twelve Peers,—of Rowland, and Olivir, and the other paladins who died at Roncesvalles. Robert Wace, a Norman Trouvère of the twelfth century, says in one of his poems, that a minstrel named Taillefer, mounted on a swift horse, went in front of the Norman army at the battle of Hastings, singing these ancient poems.

These *Chansons de Geste*, or old historic romances of France, are epic in their character, though, without doubt, they were written to be chanted to the sound of an instrument. To what period many of them belong, in their present form, has never yet been fully determined; and should it finally be proved by philological research that they can claim no higher antiquity than the twelfth or thirteenth century, still there can be little doubt that in their original form many of them reached far back into the ninth or tenth. The long prevalent theory, that the romances of the Twelve Peers of France all originated in the fabulous chronicle of Charlemagne and Rowland, written by the Archbishop Turpin in the twelfth century, if not as yet generally exploded, is nevertheless fast losing ground.

To the twelfth and thirteenth centuries also belong most of the Fabliaux, or metrical tales of the Trouvères. Many of these compositions are remarkable for the inventive talent they display, but as poems they have, generally speaking, little merit, and at times exhibit such a want of refinement, such open and gross obscenity, as to be highly offensive.

It is a remarkable circumstance in the literary history of France, that, while her antiquarians and scholars have devoted themselves to collecting and illustrating the poetry of the Troubadours, the early lyric poets of the South, that of the Trouvères, or the Troubadours of the North, has been almost entirely neglected. By a singular fatality, too, what little time and attention have hitherto been bestowed upon the fathers of French poetry have been so directed as to save from oblivion little of the most valuable portions of their writings; while the more tedious and worthless parts have been brought forth to the public eye, as if to deaden curiosity, and put an end to further research. The ancient historic romances of the land have, for the most part, been left to slumber unnoticed; while the lewd and tiresome Fabliaux have been ushered into the world as fair specimens of the ancient poetry of France. This has created unjust prejudices in the minds of many against the literature of the olden time, and has led them to regard it as nothing more than a confused mass of coarse and vulgar fictions, adapted to a rude and inelegant state of society.

Of late, however, a more discerning judgment has been brought to the difficult task of ancient research; and, in consequence of this, the long-established prejudices against the crumbling monuments of the national literature of France during the Middle Ages is fast disappearing. Several learned men are engaged in rescuing from oblivion the ancient poetic romances of Charlemagne and the Twelve Peers of France, and their labors seem destined to throw new light, not only upon the state of literature, but upon the state of society, during the twelfth and thirteenth centuries.

Among the voluminous remains of Troubadour literature, little else has yet been discovered than poems of a lyric character. The lyre of the Troubadour seems to have responded to the impulse of momentary feelings only,—to the touch of local and transitory circumstances. His song was a sudden burst of excited feeling;—it ceased when the passion was subdued, or rather when its first feverish excitement passed away; and as the liveliest feelings are the most transitory, the songs which embodied them are short, but full of spirit and energy. On the other hand, the great mass of the poetry of the Trouvères is of a narrative or epic character. The genius of the North seems always to have delighted in romantic fiction; and whether we attribute the origin of modern romance to the Arabians or to the Scandinavians, this at least is certain, that there existed marvellous tales in the Northern languages, and from these, in part at least, the Trouvères imbibed the spirit of narrative poetry. There are no traces of lyric compositions among their writings, till about the commencement of the thirteenth century; and it seems probable that the spirit of song-writing was imbibed from the Troubadours of the South.

Unfortunately, the neglect which has so long attended the old historic and heroic romances of the North of France has also befallen in some degree its early lyric poetry. Little has yet been done to discover and bring forth its riches; and doubtless many a sweet little ballad and melancholy complaint lies buried in the dust of the thirteenth century. It is not, however, my object, in this paper, to give an historical sketch of this ancient and almost forgotten poetry, but simply to bring forward a few specimens which shall exhibit its most striking and obvious characteristics.

In these examples it would be in vain to look for high-wrought expressions suited to the prevailing taste of the present day. Their most striking peculiarity, and perhaps their greatest merit, consists in the simple and direct expression of feeling which they contain. This feeling, too, is one which breathes the languor of that submissive homage which was paid to beauty in the days of chivalry; and I am aware, that, in this age of masculine and matter-of-fact thinking, the love-conceits of a more poetic state of society are generally looked upon as extremely trivial and puerile. Nevertheless I shall venture to present one or two of these simple poems, which, by recalling the distant age wherein they were composed, may peradventure please by the power of contrast.

I have just remarked that one of the greatest beauties of these ancient ditties is *naïveté*

of thought and simplicity of expression. These I shall endeavor to preserve as far as possible in the translation, though I am fully conscious how much the sparkling beauty of an original loses in being filtered through the idioms of a foreign language.

The favorite theme of the ancient lyric poets of the North of France is the wayward passion of love. They all delight to sing "*les douces dolors et li mal plaisant de fine amor.*" With such feelings the beauties of the opening spring are naturally associated. Almost every love-ditty of the old poets commences with some such exordium as this: — " When the snows of winter have passed away, when the soft and gentle spring returns, and the flower and leaf shoot in the groves, and the little birds warble to their mates in their own sweet lauguage, — then will I sing my lady-love ! "

Another favorite introduction to these little rhapsodies of romantic passion is the approach of morning and its sweet-voiced herald, the lark. The minstrel's song to his lady-love frequently commences with an allusion to the hour.

> " When the rose-bud opes its een,
> And the bluebells droop and die,
> And upon the leaves so green
> Sparkling dew-drops lie."

The following is at once the simplest and prettiest piece of this kind which I have met with among the early lyric poets of the North of France. It is taken from an anonymous poem, entitled " The Paradise of Love." A lover, having passed the " livelong night in tears, as he was wont," goes forth to beguile his sorrows with the fragrance and beauty of morning. The carol of the vaulting skylark salutes his ear, and to this merry musician he makes his complaint.

> " Hark ! hark !
> Pretty lark !
> Little heedest thou my pain !
> But if to these longing arms
> Pitying Love would yield the charms
> Of the fair
> With smiling air,
> Blithe would beat my heart again.

> " Hark ! hark !
> Pretty lark !

Little heedest thou my pain !
Love may force me still to bear,
While he lists, consuming care ;
    But in anguish
    Though I languish,
Faithful shall my heart remain.

    " Hark ! hark !
    Pretty lark !
Little heedest thou my pain !
Then cease, Love, to torment me so ;
But rather than all thoughts forego
    Of the fair
    With flaxen hair,
Give me back her frowns again.

    " Hark ! hark !
    Pretty lark !
Little heedest thou my pain ! "

Besides the " woful ballad made to his mistress's eyebrow," the early lyric poet frequently indulges in more calmly analyzing the philosophy of love, or in questioning the object and destination of a sigh. Occasionally these quaint conceits are prettily expressed, and the little song flutters through the page like a butterfly. The following is an example : —

" And whither goest thou, gentle sigh,
    Breathed so softly in my ear ?
    Say, dost thou bear his fate severe
To Love's poor martyr doomed to die ?
Come, tell me quickly, — do not lie ;
    What secret message bring'st thou here ?
And whither goest thou, gentle sigh,
    Breathed so softly in my ear ?

" May Heaven conduct thee to thy will,
    And safely speed thee on thy way ;
    This only I would humbly pray, —
Pierce deep, — but oh ! forbear to kill.
And whither goest thou, gentle sigh,
    Breathed so softly in my ear ? "

The ancient lyric poets of France are generally spoken of as a class, and their beauties and defects referred to them collectively, and not individually. In truth, there are few characteristic marks by which any individual author can be singled out and ranked above the rest. The lyric poets of the thirteenth and fourteenth centuries stand upon nearly the same level. But in the fifteenth century there were two who surpassed all their contemporaries in the beauty and delicacy of their senti-

ments ; and in the sweetness of their diction, and the structure of their verse, stand far in advance of the age in which they lived. These are Charles d'Orléans and Clotilde de Surville.

Charles, Duke of Orléans, the father of Louis the Twelfth, and uncle of Francis the First, was born in 1391. In the general tenor of his life, the peculiar character of his mind, and his talent for poetry, there is a striking resemblance between this noble poet and James the First of Scotland, his contemporary. Both were remarkable for learning and refinement ; both passed a great portion of their lives in sorrow and imprisonment ; and both cheered the solitude of their prison-walls with the charms of poetry. Charles d'Orléans was taken prisoner at the battle of Agincourt, in 1415, and carried into England, where he remained twenty-five years in captivity. It was there that he composed the greater part of his poetry.

The poems of this writer exhibit a singular delicacy of thought and sweetness of expression. The following little *Renouveaux*, or songs on the return of spring, are full of delicacy and beauty.

" Now Time throws off his cloak again
    Of ermined frost, and wind, and rain,
    And clothes him in the embroidery
    Of glittering sun and clear blue sky.
With beast and bird the forest rings,
Each in his jargon cries or sings ;
And Time throws off his cloak again
Of ermined frost, and wind, and rain.

" River, and fount, and tinkling brook
    Wear in their dainty livery
    Drops of silver jewelry ;
In new-made suit they merry look ;
And Time throw off his cloak again
Of ermined frost, and wind, and rain."

The second upon the same subject presents a still more agreeable picture of the departure of winter and the return of spring.

"Gentle spring ! — in sunshine clad,
    Well dost thou thy power display !
For winter maketh the light heart sad,
    And thou, — thou makest the sad heart gay.
He sees thee, and calls to his gloomy train,
The sleet, and the snow, and the wind, and the rain ;
And they shrink away, and they flee in fear,
    When thy merry step draws near.

"Winter giveth the fields and the trees so old
   Their beards of icicles and snow ;
And the rain, it raineth so fast and cold,
   We must cower over the embers low ;
And, snugly housed from the wind and weather,
Mope like birds that are changing feather.
But the storm retires, and the sky grows clear,
   When thy merry step draws near.

"Winter maketh the sun in the gloomy sky
   Wrap him round in a mantle of cloud ;
But, Heaven be praised, thy step is nigh ;
   Thou tearest away the mournful shroud,
And the earth looks bright, — and winter surly,
Who has toiled for naught both late and early,
Is banished afar by the new-born year,
   When thy merry step draws near."

The only person of that age who can dispute the laurel with Charles d'Orléans is Clotilde de Surville. This poetess was born in the Bas-Vivarais, in the year 1405. Her style is singularly elegant and correct ; and the reader who will take the trouble to decipher her rude provincial orthography will find her writings full of quiet beauty. The following lines, which breath the very soul of maternal tenderness, are part of a poem to her first-born.

"Sweet babe ! true portrait of thy father's face,
   Sleep on the bosom that thy lips have pressed !
Sleep, little one ; and closely, gently place
   Thy drowsy eyelid on thy mother's breast !

"Upon that tender eye, my little friend,
   Soft sleep shall come that cometh not to me !
I watch to see thee, nourish thee, defend ; —
   'T is sweet to watch for thee, — alone for thee !

"His arms fall down ; sleep sits upon his brow ;
   His eye is closed ; he sleeps, — how still and calm !

Wore not his cheek the apple's ruddy glow,
   Would you not say he slept on Death's cold arm ?

"Awake, my boy ! — I tremble with affright !
   Awake, and chase this fatal thought ! — unclose
Thine eye but for one moment on the light !
   Even at the price of thine, give me repose !

"Sweet error ! — he but slept ; — I breathe again ;
   Come, gentle dreams, the hour of sleep beguile !
Oh, when shall he for whom I sigh in vain
   Beside me watch to see thy waking smile ? "

———

But upon this theme I have written enough, perhaps too much.

"'This may be poetry, for aught I know,'
   Says an old, worthy friend of mine, while leaning
Over my shoulder as I write, — 'although
   I can't exactly comprehend its meaning.'"

I have touched upon the subject before me in a brief and desultory manner, and have purposely left my remarks unencumbered by learned reference and far-sought erudition ; for these are ornaments which would ill become so trivial a pen as this wherewith I write, though, perchance, the want of them will render my essay unsatisfactory to the scholar and the critic. But I am emboldened thus to skim with a light wing over this poetic lore of the past, by the reflection, that the greater part of my readers belong not to that grave and serious class who love the deep wisdom which lies in quoting from a quaint, forgotten tome, and who are ready on all occasions to say, " Commend me to the owl ! "

THE BAPTISM OF FIRE.

The more you mow us down, the thicker we rise; the Christian blood you spill is like the seed you sow, — it springs from the earth again and fructifies the more.
                                                                                TERTULLIAN.

As day was drawing to a close, and the rays of the setting sun climbed slowly up the dungeon wall, the prisoner sat and read in a tome with silver clasps. He was a man in the vigor of his days, with a pale and noble countenance, that wore less the marks of worldly care than of high and holy thought. His temples were already bald; but a thick and curling beard bespoke the strength of manhood; and his eye, dark, full, and eloquent, beamed with all the enthusiasm of a martyr.

The book before him was a volume of the early Christian Fathers. He was reading the Apologetic of the eloquent Tertullian, the oldest and ablest writer of the Latin Church. At times he paused, and raised his eyes to heaven as if in prayer, and then read on again in silence. At length a passage seemed to touch his inmost soul. He read aloud: —

"Give us, then, what names you please; from the instruments of cruelty you torture us by, call us Sarmenticians and Semaxians, because you fasten us to trunks of trees, and stick us about with fagots to set us on fire; yet let me tell you, when we are thus begirt and dressed about with fire, we are then in our most illustrious apparel. These are our victorious palms and robes of glory; and, mounted on our funeral pile, we look upon ourselves as in our triumphal chariot. No wonder, then, such passive heroes please not those they vanquish with such conquering sufferings. And therefore we pass for men of despair, and violently bent upon our own destruction. However, what you are pleased to call madness and despair in us are the very actions which, under virtue's standard, lift up your sons of fame and glory, and emblazon them to future ages."

He arose and paced the dungeon to and fro, with folded arms and a firm step. His thoughts held communion with eternity.

"Father which art in heaven!" he exclaimed, "give me strength to die like those holy men of old, who scorned to purchase life at the expense of truth. That truth has made me free; and though condemned on earth, I know that I am absolved in heaven!"

He again seated himself at his table, and read in that tome with silver clasps.

This solitary prisoner was Anne Du Bourg, a man who feared not man; once a merciful judge in that august tribunal upon whose voice hung the life and death of those who were persecuted for conscience' sake, he was now himself an accused, a convicted heretic, condemned to the Baptism of Fire, because he would not unrighteously condemn others. He had dared to plead the cause of suffering humanity before that dread tribunal, and, in the presence of the king himself, to declare that it was an offence to the majesty of God to shed man's blood in his name. Six weary months — from June to December — he had lain a prisoner in that dungeon, from which a death by fire was soon to set him free. Such was the clemency of Henry the Second!

As the prisoner read, his eyes were filled with tears. He still gazed upon the printed page, but it was a blank before his eyes. His thoughts were far away amid the scenes of his childhood, amid the green valleys of Riom and the Golden Mountains of Auvergne. Some simple word had called up the vision of the past. He was a child again. He was playing with the pebbles of the brook, — he was shouting to the echo of the hills, — he was praying at his mother's knee, with his little hands clasped in hers.

This dream of childhood was broken by the grating of bolts and bars, as the jailer opened his prison door. A moment afterward, his former colleague, De Harley, stood at his side.

"Thou here!" exclaimed the prisoner, surprised at the visit. "Thou in the dungeon of a heretic! On what errand hast thou come?"

"On an errand of mercy," replied De Harley. "I come to tell thee" —

"That the hour of my death draws near?"

"That thou mayst still be saved."

"Yes; if I will bear false witness against my God, — barter heaven for earth, — an eternity for a few brief days of worldly existence. Lost, thou shouldst say, — lost, not saved!"

"No! saved!" cried De Harley with warmth; "saved from a death of shame and an eternity of woe! Renounce this false doctrine, — this abominable heresy, — and return again to the bosom of the church which thou dost rend with strife and dissension."

"God judge between thee and me, which has embraced the truth."

"His hand already smites thee."

"It has fallen more heavily upon those who so unjustly persecute me. Where is the king? — he who said that with his own eyes he would behold me perish at the stake? — he to whom the undaunted Du Faur cried, like Elijah to Ahab, 'It is thou who troublest Israel!' — Where is the king? Called, through a sudden and violent death, to the judgment-seat of Heaven! — Where is Minard, the persecutor of the just? Slain by the hand of an assassin! It was not without reason that I said to him, when standing before my accusers, 'Tremble! believe the word of one who is about to appear before God; thou likewise shalt stand there soon, — thou that sheddest the blood of the children of peace.' He has gone to his account before me."

"And that menace has hastened thine own condemnation. Minard was slain by the Huguenots, and it is whispered that thou wast privy to his death."

"This, at least, might have been spared a dying man!" replied the prisoner, much agitated by so unjust and so unexpected an accusation. "As I hope for mercy hereafter, I am innocent of the blood of this man, and of all knowledge of so foul a crime. But, tell me, hast thou come here only to embitter my last hours with such an accusation as this? If so, I pray thee, leave me. My moments are precious. I would be alone."

"I came to offer thee life, freedom, and happiness."

"Life, — freedom, — happiness! At the price thou hast set upon them, I scorn them all! Had the apostles and martyrs of the early Christian Church listened to such paltry bribes as these, where were now the faith in which we trust? These holy men of old shall answer for me. Hear what Justin Martyr says, in his earnest appeal to Antonine the Pious, in behalf of the Christians who in his day were unjustly loaded with public odium and oppression."

He opened the volume before him and read:

"I could wish you would take this also into consideration, that what we say is really for your own good; for it is in our power at any time to escape your torments by denying the faith, when you question us about it: but we scorn to purchase life at the expense of a lie; for our souls are winged with a desire of a life of eternal duration and purity, of an immediate conversation with God, the Father and Maker of all things. We are in haste to be confessing and finishing our faith; being fully persuaded that we shall arrive at this blessed state, if we approve ourselves to God by our works, and by our obedience express our passion for that divine life which is never interrupted by any clashing evil."

The Catholic and the Huguenot reasoned long and earnestly together; but they reasoned in vain. Each was firm in his belief; and they parted to meet no more on earth.

On the following day, Du Bourg was summoned before his judges to receive his final sentence. He heard it unmoved, and with a prayer to God that he would pardon those who had condemned him according to their consciences. He then addressed his judges in an oration full of power and eloquence. It closed with these words: —

"And now, ye judges, if, indeed, you hold the sword of God as ministers of his wrath, to take vengeance upon those who do evil, beware, I charge you, beware how you condemn us. Consider well what evil we have done, and, before all things, decide whether it be just that we should listen unto you rather than unto God. Are you so drunken with the wine-cup of the great sorceress, that you drink poison for nourishment? Are you not those who make the people sin by turning them away from the service of God? And if you regard more the opinion of men than that of Heaven, in what esteem are you held by other nations, and principalities, and powers, for the martyrdoms you have caused in obedience to this blood-stained Phalaris? God grant, thou cruel tyrant, that by thy miserable death thou mayst put an end to our groans!

"Why weep ye? What means this delay? Your hearts are heavy within you, — your consciences are haunted by the judgment of God. And thus it is that the condemned rejoice in the fires you have kindled, and think they never live better than in the midst of consuming flames. Torments affright them not, — insults enfeeble them not; their honor is redeemed by death, — he that dies is the conqueror, and the conquered he that mourns.

"No! whatever snares are spread for us, whatever suffering we endure, you cannot separate us from the love of Christ. Strike, then, — slay, — grind us to powder! Those that die in the Lord shall live again; we shall all be raised together. Condemn me as you will, — I am a Christian; yes, I am a Christian, and am ready to die for the glory of our Lord, — for the truth of the Evangelists.

"Quench, then, your fires! Let the wicked abandon his way, and return unto the Lord, and he will have compassion on him. Live, — be happy, — and meditate on God, ye judges! As for me, I go rejoicing to my death. What wait ye for? Lead me to the scaffold!"

They bound the prisoner's hands, and, leading him forth from the council-chamber, placed him upon the cart that was to bear him to the Place de Grève. Before and behind marched a guard of five hundred soldiers; for Du Bourg was beloved by the people, and a popular tumult was apprehended. The day was overcast and sad; and ever and anon the sound of the tolling bell mingled its dismal clang with the solemn notes of the funeral march. They soon reached the place of execution, which was already filled with a dense and silent crowd. In the centre stood the gallows, with a pile of fagots beneath it, and the executioner with a

burning torch in his hand. But this funeral apparel inspired no terror in the heart of Du Bourg. A look of triumph beamed from his eye, and his countenance shone like that of an angel. With his own hands he divested himself of his outer garments, and, gazing round upon the breathless and sympathizing crowd, exclaimed, —

"My friends, I come not hither as a thief or a murderer; but it is for the Gospel's sake!"

A cord was then fastened round his waist, and he was drawn up into the air. At the same moment the burning torch of the executioner was applied to the fagots beneath, and the thick volumes of smoke concealed the martyr from the horror-stricken crowd. One stifled groan arose from all that vast multitude, like the moan of the sea, and all was hushed again; save the crackling of the fagots, and at intervals the funeral knell, that smote the very soul. The quivering flames darted upward and around; and an agonizing cry broke from the murky cloud, —

"My God! my God! forsake me not, that I forsake not thee!"

The wind lifted the reddening smoke like a veil, and the form of the martyr was seen to fall into the fire beneath. In a moment it rose again, its garments all in flame; and again the faint, half-smothered cry of agony was heard, —

"My God! my God! forsake me not, that I forsake not thee!"

Once more the quivering body descended into the flames; and once more it was lifted into the air, a blackened, burning cinder. Again and again this fiendish mockery of baptism was repeated; till the martyr, with a despairing, suffocating voice, exclaimed, —

"O God! I cannot die!"

The executioner came forward, and, either in mercy to the dying man or through fear of the populace, threw a noose over his neck, and strangled the almost lifeless victim. At the same moment the cord which held the body was loosened, and it fell into the fire to rise no more. And thus was consummated the martyrdom of the Baptism of Fire.

COQ-À-L'ÂNE.

My brain, methinks, is like an hour-glass,
Wherein my imaginations run like sands,
Filling up time ; but then are turned, and turned,
So that I know not what to stay upon
And less to put in art.

　　　　　　　　BEN JONSON.

A RAINY and gloomy winter was just drawing to its close, when I left Paris for the South of France. We started at sunrise ; and as we passed along the solitary streets of the vast and silent metropolis, drowsily one by one its clanging horologes chimed the hour of six. Beyond the city gates the wide landscape was covered with a silvery network of frost ; a wreath of vapor overhung the windings of the Seine ; and every twig and shrub, with its sheath of crystal, flashed in the level rays of the rising sun. The sharp, frosty air seemed to quicken the sluggish blood of the old postilion and his horses ; — a fresh team stood ready in harness at each stage ; and notwithstanding the slippery pavement of the causeway, the long and tedious climbing of the hillside, and the equally long and tedious descent with chained wheels and the drag, just after nightfall the lumbering vehicle of Vincent Caillard stopped at the gateway of the " Three Emperors," in the famous city of Orléans.

I cannot pride myself much upon being a good travelling-companion, for the rocking of a coach always lulls me into forgetfulness of the present ; and no sooner does the hollow, monotonous rumbling of the wheels reach my ear, than, like Nick Bottom, " I have an exposition of sleep come upon me." It is not, however, the deep, sonorous slumber of a laborer, " stuffed with distressful bread," but a kind of day-dream, wherein the creations of fancy seem realities, and the real world, which swims dizzily before the half-shut, drowsy eye, becomes mingled with the imaginary world within. This is doubtless a very great failing in a traveller ; and I confess, with all humility, that at times the line of demarcation between truth and fiction is rendered thereby so indefi-nite and indistinct, that I cannot always determine, with unerring certainty, whether an event really happened to me, or whether I only dreamed it.

On this account I shall not attempt a detailed description of my journey from Paris to Bordeaux. I was travelling like a bird of passage ; and five weary days and four weary nights I was on the way. The diligence stopped only to change horses, and for the travellers to take their meals ; and by night I slept with my head under my wing in a snug corner of the coach.

Strange as it may appear to some of my readers, this night-travelling is at times far from being disagreeable ; nay, if the country is flat and uninteresting, and you are favored with a moon, it may be very pleasant. As the night advances, the conversation around you gradually dies away, and is imperceptibly given up to some garrulous traveller who finds himself belated in the midst of a long story ; and when at length he puts out his feelers in the form of a question, discovers, by the silence around him, that the breathless attention of his audience is owing to their being asleep. All is now silent. You let down the window of the carriage, and the fresh night-air cools your flushed and burning cheek. The landscape, though in reality dull and uninteresting, seems beautiful as it floats by in the soft moonshine. Every ruined hovel is changed by the magic of night to a trim cottage, every straggling and dilapidated hamlet becomes as beautiful as those we read of in poetry and romance. Over the lowland hangs a silver mist ; over the hills peep the twinkling stars. The keen night-air is a spur to the postilion and his horses. In the words of the German ballad, —

> "Halloo ! halloo ! away they go,
> 　Unheeding wet or dry,
> And horse and rider snort and blow,
> 　And sparkling pebbles fly.
> And all on which the moon doth shine
> 　Behind them flees afar,
> And backward sped, scud overhead,
> 　The sky and every star."

Anon you stop at the relay. The drowsy hostler crawls out of the stable-yard ; a few gruff words and strange oaths pass between him and the postilion, — then there is a coarse joke in *patois*, of which you understand the ribaldry only, and which is followed by a husky laugh, a sound between a hiss and a growl ; — and then you are off again in a crack. Occasionally a way-traveller is un-caged, and a new-comer takes the vacant perch at your elbow. Meanwhile your busy fancy speculates upon all these things, and you fall asleep amid its thousand vagaries. Soon you wake again and snuff the morning air. It was but a moment, and yet the night is gone. The gray of twilight steals into the window, and gives a ghastly look to the countenances of the sleeping group around you. One sits bolt up-right in a corner, offending none, and stiff and motionless as an Egyptian mummy ; another sits equally straight and immovable, but snores like a priest ; the head of a third is dangling over his shoulder, and the tassel of his night-cap tickles his neighbor's ear ; a fourth has lost his hat, — his wig is awry, and his under-lip hangs lolling about like an idiot's. The whole scene is a living caricature of man, present-ing human nature in some of the grotesque at-titudes she assumes when that pragmatical schoolmaster, Propriety, has fallen asleep in his chair, and the unruly members of his charge are freed from the thraldom of the rod.

On leaving Orléans, instead of following the great western mail-route through Tours, Poi-tiers, and Angoulême, and thence on to Bor-deaux, I struck across the departments of the Indre, Haute-Vienne, and the Dordogne, pass-ing through the provincial capitals of Château-roux, Limoges, and Périgueux. South of the Loire the country assumes a more mountainous aspect, and the landscape is broken by long sweeping hills and fertile valleys. Many a fair scene invites the traveller's foot to pause ; and his eye roves with delight over the pictur-esque landscape of the valley of the Creuse, and the beautiful highland scenery near Péri-gueux. There are also many objects of art and antiquity which arrest his attention. Argen-ton boasts its Roman amphitheatre, and the ruins of an old castle built by King Pepin ; at Chalus the tower beneath which Richard Cœur-de-Lion was slain is still pointed out to the cu-rious traveller ; and Périgueux is full of crum-bling monuments of the Middle Ages.

Scenes like these, and the constant chatter of my fellow-travellers, served to enliven the te-dium of a long and fatiguing journey. The French are preëminently a talking people ; and every new object afforded a topic for light and animated discussion. The affairs of church and state were, however, the themes oftenest touched upon. The bill for the suppression of the liberty of the press was then under discus-sion in the Chamber of Peers, and excited the most lively interest through the whole king-dom. Of course it was a subject not likely to be forgotten in a stage-coach.

"Ah ! mon Dieu ! " said a brisk little man, with snow-white hair and a blazing red face, at the same time drawing up his shoulders to a level with his ears ; " the ministry are deter-mined to carry their point at all events. They mean to break down the liberty of the press, cost what it will."

"If they succeed," added the person who sat opposite, " we may thank the Jesuits for it. It is all their work. They rule the mind of our imbecile monarch, and it is their miserable policy to keep the people in darkness."

" No doubt of that," rejoined the first speaker. "Why, no longer ago than yesterday I read in the 'Figaro' that a printer had been prosecuted for publishing the moral lessons of the Evangelists without the miracles."

"Is it possible ? " said I. "And are the people so stupid as thus patiently to offer their shoulders to the pack-saddle ? "

" Most certainly not ! We shall have an-other revolution."

"If history speaks true, you have had revo-lutions enough, during the last century or two, to satisfy the most mercurial nation on earth.

You have hardly been quiet a moment since the day of the Barricades and the memorable war of the *pots-de-chambre* in the times of the Grand Condé."

"You are pleased to speak lightly of our revolutions, sir," rejoined the politician, growing warm. "You must, however, confess that each successive one has brought us nearer to our object. Old institutions, whose foundations lie deep in the prejudices of a great nation, are not to be toppled down by the springing of a single mine. You must confess, too, that our national character is much improved since the days you speak of. The youth of the present century are not so frivolous as those of the last. They have no longer that unbounded levity and light-heartedness so generally ascribed to them. From this circumstance we have everything to hope. Our revolutions, likewise, must necessarily change their character and secure to us more solid advantages than heretofore."

"Luck makes pluck, as the Germans say. You go on bravely; but it gives me pain to see religion and the church so disregarded."

"Superstition and the church, you mean," said the gray-headed man. "Why, sir, the church is nothing now-a-days but a tumbledown, dilapidated tower for rooks and daws, and such silly birds, to build their nests in!"

It was now very evident that I had unearthed a radical; and there is no knowing when his harangue would have ended, had not his voice been drowned by the noise of the wheels, as we entered the paved street of the city of Limoges.

A breakfast of boiled capon stuffed with truffles, and accompanied by a *Pâté de Périgueux*, a dish well-known to French gourmands, restored us all to good-humor. While we were at breakfast, a personage stalked into the room, whose strange appearance arrested my attention, and gave subject for future conversation to our party. He was a tall, thin figure, armed with a long whip, brass spurs, and black whiskers. He wore a bell-crowned, varnished hat, a blue frock-coat with standing collar, a red waistcoat, a pair of yellow leather breeches, and boots that reached to the knees. I at first took him for a postilion, or a private cour-

ier; but upon inquiry, I found that he was only the son of a notary-public, and that he dressed in this strange fashion to please his own fancy. As soon as we were comfortably seated in the diligence, I made some remark on the singular costume of the personage whom I had just seen at the tavern.

"These things are so common with us," said the politician, "that we hardly notice them."

"What you want in liberty of speech, then, you make up in liberty of dress?"

"Yes; in this, at least, we are a free people."

"I had not been long in France, before I discovered that a man may dress as he pleases, without being stared at. The most opposite styles of dress seem to be in vogue at the same moment. No strange garment nor desperate hat excites either ridicule or surprise. French fashions are known and imitated all the world over."

"Very true, indeed," said a little man in gosling-green. "We give fashions to all other nations."

"Fashions!" said the politician with a kind of growl, — "fashions! Yes, sir, and some of us are simple enough to boast of it, as if we were a nation of tailors."

Here the little man in gosling-green pulled up the horns of his cotton shirt-collar.

"I recollect," said I, "that your Madame de Pompadour in one of her letters says something to this effect: 'We furnish our enemies with hair-dressers, ribbons, and fashions; and they furnish us with laws.'"

"That is not the only silly thing she said in her lifetime. Ah! sir, these Pompadours and Maintenons, and Montespans were the authors of much woe to France. Their follies and extravagances exhausted the public treasury, and made the nation poor. They built palaces, and covered themselves with jewels, and ate from golden plate; while the people who toiled for them had hardly a crust to keep their own children from starvation! And yet they preach to us the divine right of kings!"

My radical had got upon his high horse again; and I know not whither it would have carried him, had not a thin man with a black, seedy coat, who sat at his elbow, at that moment crossed his path by one of those abrupt and sudden transitions which leave you aghast at the strange association of ideas in the speaker's mind.

"*Apropos de bottes!*" exclaimed he, "speaking of boots, and notaries public, and such matters, — excuse me for interrupting you, sir, — a little story has just popped into my head which may amuse the company; and as I am not very fond of political discussions, — no offence, sir, — I will tell it, for the sake of changing the conversation."

Whereupon, without further preamble or apology, he proceeded to tell his story in, as nearly as may be, the following words.

THE NOTARY OF PÉRIGUEUX.

Do not trust thy body with a physician. He 'll make thy foolish bones go without flesh in a fortnight, and thy soul walk without a body a sennight after.   SHIRLEY.

YOU must know, gentlemen, that there lived some years ago, in the city of Périgueux, an honest notary-public, the descendant of a very ancient and broken-down family, and the occupant of one of those old weather-beaten tenements which remind you of the times of your great-grandfather. He was a man of an unoffending, quiet disposition; the father of a family, though not the head of it, — for in that family "the hen overcrowed the cock," and the neighbors, when they spake of the notary, shrugged their shoulders, and exclaimed, "Poor fellow! his spurs want sharpening." In fine, — you understand me, gentlemen, — he was hen-pecked.

Well, finding no peace at home, he sought it elsewhere, as was very natural for him to do; and at length discovered a place of rest, far beyond the cares and clamors of domestic life. This was a little *Café Estaminet*, a short way out of the city, whither he repaired every evening to smoke his pipe, drink sugar-water, and play his favorite game of domino. There he met the boon companions he most loved; heard all the floating chitchat of the day; laughed when he was in merry mood; found consolation when he was sad; and at all times gave vent to his opinions, without fear of being snubbed short by a flat contradiction.

Now, the notary's bosom-friend was a dealer in claret and cognac, who lived about a league from the city, and always passed his evenings at the *Estaminet*. He was a gross, corpulent fellow, raised from a full-blooded Gascon breed, and sired by a comic actor of some reputation in his way. He was remarkable for nothing but his good-humor, his love of cards, and a strong propensity to test the quality of his own liquors by comparing them with those sold at other places.

As evil communications corrupt good manners, the bad practices of the wine-dealer won insensibly upon the worthy notary; and before he was aware of it, he found himself weaned from domino and sugar-water, and addicted to piquet and spiced wine. Indeed, it not unfrequently happened, that, after a long session at the *Estaminet*, the two friends grew so urbane, that they would waste a full half-hour at the door in friendly dispute which should conduct the other home. Though this course of life agreed well enough with the sluggish, phlegmatic temperament of the wine-dealer, it soon began to play the very deuse with the more sensitive organization of the notary, and finally put his nervous system completely out of tune. He lost his appetite, became gaunt and haggard, and could get no sleep. Legions of blue-devils haunted him by day, and by night strange faces peeped through his bed-curtains, and the nightmare snorted in his ear. The worse he grew, the more he smoked and tippled; and the more he smoked and tippled, — why, as a matter of course, the worse he grew. His wife alternately stormed, remonstrated, entreated; but all in vain. She made the house too hot for him, — he retreated to the tavern; she broke his long-stemmed pipes upon the andirons, — he substituted a short-stemmed one, which, for safe-keeping, he carried in his waistcoat-pocket.

Thus the unhappy notary ran gradually down at the heel. What with his bad habits and his domestic grievances, he became completely hipped. He imagined that he was going to die; and suffered in quick succession all the diseases that ever beset mortal man. Every shooting pain was an alarming symptom, — every uneasy feeling after dinner a sure prognostic of some mortal disease. In vain did his friends endeavor to reason, and then to laugh him out of his strange whims; for when did ever jest or reason cure a sick imagination? His only answer was, "Do let me alone; I know better than you what ails me."

Well, gentlemen, things were in this state, when, one afternoon in December, as he sat moping in his office, wrapped in an overcoat, with a cap on his head and his feet thrust into a pair of furred slippers, a cabriolet stopped at the door, and a loud knocking without aroused him from his gloomy revery. It was a message from his friend the wine-dealer, who had been suddenly attacked with a violent fever, and growing worse and worse, had now sent in the greatest haste for the notary to draw up his last will and testament. The case was urgent, and admitted neither excuse nor delay; and the notary, tying a handkerchief round his face, and buttoning up to the chin, jumped into the cabriolet, and suffered himself, though not without some dismal presentiments and misgivings of heart, to be driven to the wine-dealer's house.

When he arrived, he found everything in the greatest confusion. On entering the house, he ran against the apothecary, who was coming down-stairs, with a face as long as your arm; and a few steps farther he met the housekeeper — for the wine-dealer was an old bachelor — running up and down, and wringing her hands, for fear that the good man should die without making his will. He soon reached the chamber of his sick friend, and found him tossing about in a paroxysm of fever, and calling aloud for a draught of cold water. The notary shook his head; he thought this a fatal symptom; for ten years back the wine-dealer had been suffering under a species of hydrophobia, which seemed suddenly to have left him.

When the sick man saw who stood by his bedside, he stretched out his hand and exclaimed, —

135

"Ah! my dear friend! have you come at last? You see it is all over with me. You have arrived just in time to draw up that — that passport of mine. Ah, *grand diable!* how hot it is here! Water, — water, — water! Will nobody give me a drop of cold water?"

As the case was an urgent one, the notary made no delay in getting his papers in readiness; and in a short time the last will and testament of the wine-dealer was drawn up in due form, the notary guiding the sick man's hand as he scrawled his signature at the bottom.

As the evening wore away, the wine-dealer grew worse and worse, and at length became delirious, mingling in his incoherent ravings the phrases of the Credo and Paternoster with the shibboleth of the dram-shop and the card-table.

"Take care! take care! There, now — *Credo in* — Pop! ting-a-ling-ling! give me some of that. Cent-é-dize! Why, you old publican, this wine is poisoned, — I know your tricks! — *Sanctam ecclesiam catholicam* — Well, well, we shall see. Imbecile! to have a tierce-major and a seven of hearts, and discard the seven! By St. Anthony, capot! You are lurched, — ha! ha! I told you so. I knew very well, — there, — there, — don't interrupt me — *Carnis resurrectionem et vitam eternam!*"

With these words upon his lips, the poor wine-dealer expired. Meanwhile the notary sat cowering over the fire, aghast at the fearful scene that was passing before him, and now and then striving to keep up his courage by a glass of cognac. Already his fears were on the alert; and the idea of contagion flitted to and fro through his mind. In order to quiet these thoughts of evil import, he lighted his pipe and began to prepare for returning home. At that moment the apothecary turned round to him and said, — "Dreadful sickly time, this! The disorder seems to be spreading."

"What disorder?" exclaimed the notary, with a movement of surprise.

"Two died yesterday, and three to-day," continued the apothecary, without answering the question. "Very sickly time, sir, — very."

"But what disorder is it? What disease has carried off my friend here so suddenly?"

"What disease? Why, scarlet fever, to be sure."

"And is it contagious?"

"Certainly!"

"Then I am a dead man!" exclaimed the notary, putting his pipe into his waistcoat-pocket, and beginning to walk up and down the room in despair. "I am a dead man! Now don't deceive me, — don't, will you? What — what are the symptoms?"

"A sharp burning pain in the right side," said the apothecary.

"Oh, what a fool I was to come here!"

In vain did the housekeeper and the apothecary strive to pacify him; — he was not a man to be reasoned with; he answered that he knew his own constitution better than they did, and insisted upon going home without delay. Unfortunately, the vehicle he came in had returned to the city; and the whole neighborhood was abed and asleep. What was to be done? Nothing in the world but to take the apothecary's horse, which stood hitched at the door, patiently waiting his master's will.

Well, gentlemen, as there was no remedy, our notary mounted this raw-boned steed, and set forth upon his homeward journey. The night was cold and gusty, and the wind right in his teeth. Overhead the leaden clouds were beating to and fro, and through them the newly risen moon seemed to be tossing and drifting along like a cock-boat in the surf; now swallowed up in a huge billow of cloud, and now lifted upon its bosom and dashed with silvery spray. The trees by the road-side groaned with a sound of evil omen; and before him lay three mortal miles, beset with a thousand imaginary perils. Obedient to the whip and spur, the steed leaped forward by fits and starts, now dashing away in a tremendous gallop, and now relaxing into a long, hard trot; while the rider, filled with symptoms of disease and dire presentiments of death, urged him on, as if he were fleeing before the pestilence.

In this way, by dint of whistling and shouting, and beating right and left, one mile of the fatal three was safely passed. The apprehensions of the notary had so far subsided, that he even suffered the poor horse to walk up hill; but these apprehensions were suddenly revived again with tenfold violence by a sharp pain in the right side, which seemed to pierce him like a needle.

"It is upon me at last!" groaned the fear-stricken man. "Heaven be merciful to me, the greatest of sinners! And must I die in a ditch, after all? He! get up, — get up!"

And away went horse and rider at full speed, — hurry-scurry, — up hill and down, — panting and blowing like a whirlwind. At every leap the pain in the rider's side seemed to increase. At first it was a little point like the prick of a needle, — then it spread to the size of a half-franc piece, — then covered a place as large as the palm of your hand. It gained upon him fast. The poor man groaned aloud in agony; faster and faster sped the horse over the frozen ground, — farther and farther spread the pain over his side. To complete the dismal picture, the storm commenced, — snow mingled with rain. But snow, and rain, and cold were naught to him; for, though his arms and legs were frozen to icicles, he felt it not; the fatal symptom was upon him; he was doomed to die, — not of cold, but of scarlet fever!

At length, he knew not how, more dead than alive, he reached the gate of the city. A band of ill-bred dogs, that were serenading at a corner of the street, seeing the notary dash by, joined in the hue and cry, and ran barking and yelping at his heels. It was now late at night, and only here and there a solitary lamp twinkled from an upper story. But on went the notary, down this street and up that, till at last he reached his own door. There was a light in his wife's bedroom. The good woman came to the window, alarmed at such a knocking, and howling, and clattering at her door so late at night; and the notary was too deeply absorbed in his own sorrows to observe that the lamp cast the shadow of two heads on the window-curtain.

"Let me in! let me in! Quick! quick!" he exclaimed, almost breathless from terror and fatigue.

"Who are you that come to disturb a lone woman at this hour of the night?" cried a sharp voice from above. "Begone about your business, and let quiet people sleep."

"Come down and let me in! I am your

husband. Don't you know my voice? Quick, I beseech you; for I am dying here in the street!"

After a few moments of delay and a few more words of parley, the door was opened, and the notary stalked into his domicile, pale and haggard in aspect, and as stiff and straight as a ghost. Cased from head to heel in an armor of ice, as the glare of the lamp fell upon him, he looked like a knight-errant mailed in steel. But in one place his armor was broken. On his right side was a circular spot, as large as the crown of your hat, and about as black!

"My dear wife!" he exclaimed, with more tenderness than he had exhibited for many years, "Reach me a chair. My hours are numbered. I am a dead man!"

Alarmed at these exclamations, his wife stripped off his overcoat. Something fell from beneath it, and was dashed to pieces on the hearth. It was the notary's pipe! He placed his hand upon his side, and, lo! it was bare to the skin! Coat, waistcoat, and linen were burnt through and through, and there was a blister on his side as large as your hand!

The mystery was soon explained, symptom and all. The notary had put his pipe into his pocket without knocking out the ashes! And so my story ends.

———

"Is that all?" asked the radical, when the story-teller had finished.

"That is all."

"Well, what does your story prove?"

"That is more than I can tell. All I know is that the story is true."

"And did he die?" said the nice little man in gosling-green.

"Yes; he died afterwards," replied the story-teller, rather annoyed by the question.

"And what did he die of?" continued gosling-green, following him up.

"What did he die of? why, he died — of a sudden!"

THE JOURNEY INTO SPAIN.

A l'issue de l'yver que le joly temps de primavère commence, et qu'on voit arbres verdoyer, fleurs espanouir, et qu'on oit les oisillons chanter en toute joie et doulceur, tant que les verts bocages retentissent de leurs sons et que cœurs tristes pensifs y dolens s'en esjouissent, s'émeuvent à delaisser deuil et toute tristesse, et se parforcent à valoir mieux. — LA PLAISANTE HISTOIRE DE GUERIN DE MONGLAVE.

SOFT-BREATHING Spring! how many pleasant thoughts, how many delightful recollections, does thy name awaken in the mind of a traveller! Whether he has followed thee by the banks of the Loire or the Guadalquiver, or traced thy footsteps slowly climbing the sunny slope of Alp or Apennine, the thought of thee shall summon up sweet visions of the past, and thy golden sunshine and soft vapory atmosphere become a portion of his day-dreams and of him. Sweet images of thee, and scenes that have oft inspired the poet's song, shall mingle in his recollections of the past. The shooting of the tender leaf, — the sweetness and elasticity of the air, — the blue sky, — the fleet-drifting cloud, — and the flocks of wild fowl wheeling in long-drawn phalanx through the air, and screaming from their dizzy height, — all these shall pass like a dream before his imagination,

> "And gently o'er his memory come at times
> A glimpse of joys that had their birth in thee,
> Like a brief strain of some forgotten tune."

It was at the opening of this delightful season of the year that I passed through the South of France, and took the road of St. Jean de Luz for the Spanish frontier. I left Bordeaux amid all the noise and gayety of the last scene of Carnival. The streets and public walks of the city were full of merry groups in masks, — at every corner crowds were listening to the discordant music of the wandering ballad-singer; and grotesque figures, mounted on high stilts, and dressed in the garb of the peasants of the Landes of Gascony, were stalking up and down like so many long-legged cranes; others were amusing themselves with the tricks and grimaces of little monkeys, disguised like little men, bowing to the ladies, and figuring away in red coats and ruffles; and here and there a band of chimney-sweeps were staring in stupid wonder at the miracles of a showman's box. In a word, all was so full of mirth and merrimake, that even beggary seemed to have forgotten that it was wretched, and gloried in the ragged masquerade of one poor holiday.

To this scene of noise and gayety succeeded the silence and solitude of the Landes of Gascony. The road from Bordeaux to Bayonne winds along through immense pine-forests and sandy plains, spotted here and there with a dingy little hovel, and the silence is interrupted only by the dismal hollow roar of the wind among the melancholy and majestic pines. Occasionally, however, the way is enlivened by a market-town or a straggling village; and I still recollect the feelings of delight which I experienced, when, just after sunset, we passed through the romantic town of Roquefort, built upon the sides of the green valley of the Douze, which has scooped out a verdant hollow for it to nestle in, amid those barren tracts of sand.

On leaving Bayonne, the scene assumes a character of greater beauty and sublimity. To the vast forests of the Landes of Gascony succeeds a scene of picturesque beauty, delightful to the traveller's eye. Before him rise the snowy Pyrenees, — a long line of undulating hills, —

> "Bounded afar by peak aspiring bold,
> Like giant capped with helm of burnished gold."

To the left, as far as the eye can reach, stretch the delicious valleys of the Nive and Adour; and to the right the sea flashes along the pebbly margin of its silver beach, forming a thousand little bays and inlets, or comes tumbling in among the cliffs of a rock-bound coast, and beats against its massive barriers with a distant, hollow, continual roar.

Should these pages meet the eye of any solitary traveller who is journeying into Spain by the road I here speak of, I would advise him

ARTIST : MARCUS WATERMAN.

A SPANISH COURTYARD.

to travel from Bayonne to St. Jean de Luz on horseback. At the gate of Bayonne he will find a steed ready caparisoned for him, with a dark-eyed Basque girl for his companion and guide, who is to sit beside him upon the same horse. This style of travelling is, I believe, peculiar to the Basque provinces; at all events, I have seen it nowhere else. The saddle is constructed with a large frame-work extending on each side, and covered with cushions; and the traveller and his guide, being placed on the opposite extremities, serve as a balance to each other. We overtook many travellers mounted in this way, and I could not help thinking it a mode of travelling far preferable to being cooped up in a diligence. The Basque girls are generally beautiful; and there was one of these merry guides we met upon the road to Bidart whose image haunts me still. She had large and expressive black eyes, teeth like pearls, a rich and sunburnt complexion, and hair of a glossy blackness, parted on the forehead, and falling down behind in a large braid, so long as almost to touch the ground with the little ribbon that confined it at the end. She wore the common dress of the peasantry of the South of France, and a large gypsy straw hat was thrown back over her shoulder, and tied by a ribbon about her neck. There was hardly a dusty traveller in the coach who did not envy her companion the seat he occupied beside her.

Just at nightfall we entered the town of St. Jean de Luz, and dashed down its narrow streets at full gallop. The little madcap postilion cracked his knotted whip incessantly, and the sound echoed back from the high dingy walls like the report of a pistol. The coachwheels nearly touched the houses on each side of us; the idlers in the street jumped right and left to save themselves; window-shutters flew open in all directions; a thousand heads popped out from cellar and upper story; "*Sacrr-ré mâtin!*" shouted the postilion, — and we ratled on like an earthquake.

St. Jean de Luz is a smoky little fishing-town, situated on the low grounds at the mouth of the Nivelle, and a bridge connects it with the faubourg of Sibourne, which stands on the opposite bank of the river. I had no time,

however, to note the peculiarities of the place, for I was whirled out of it with the same speed and confusion with which I had been whirled in, and I can only recollect the sweep of the road across the Nivelle, — the church of Sibourne by the water's edge, — the narrow streets, the smoky-looking houses with red window-shutters, and "a very ancient and fish-like smell."

I passed by moonlight the little river Bidasoa, which forms the boundary between France and Spain; and when the morning broke, found myself far up among the mountains of San Salvador, the most westerly links of the great Pyrenean chain. The mountains around me were neither rugged nor precipitous, but they rose one above another in a long, majestic swell, and the trace of the ploughshare was occasionally visible to their summits. They seemed entirely destitute of trees; and as the season of vegetation had not yet commenced, their huge outlines lay black, and barren, and desolate against the sky. But it was a glorious morning, and the sun rose up into a cloudless heaven, and poured a flood of gorgeous splendor over the mountain landscape, as if proud of the realm he shone upon. The scene was enlivened by the dashing of a swollen mountain-brook, whose course we followed for miles down the valley, as it leaped onward to its journey's end, now breaking into a white cascade, and now foaming and chafing beneath a rustic bridge. Now and then we drove through a dilapidated town, with a group of idlers at every corner, wrapped in tattered brown cloaks, and smoking their little paper cigars in the sun; then would succeed a desolate tract of country, cheered only by the tinkle of a mule-bell, or the song of a muleteer; then we would meet a solitary traveller mounted on horseback, and wrapped in the ample folds of his cloak, with a gun hanging at the pommel of his saddle. Occasionally, too, among the bleak, inhospitable hills, we passed a rude little chapel, with a cluster of ruined cottages around it; and whenever our carriage stopped at the relay, or loitered slowly up the hillside, a crowd of children would gather around us, with little images and crucifixes for sale, curiously ornamented with ribbons and bits of tawdry finery.

A day's journey from the frontier brought us to Vitoria, where the diligence stopped for the night. I spent the scanty remnant of daylight in rambling about the streets of the city, with no other guide than the whim of the moment. Now I plunged down a dark and narrow alley, now emerged into a wide street or a spacious market-place, and now aroused the drowsy echoes of a church or cloister with the sound of my intruding footsteps. But descriptions of churches and public squares are dull and tedious matters for those readers who are in search of amusement and not of instruction; and if any one has accompanied me thus far on my fatiguing journey towards the Spanish capital, I will readily excuse him from the toil of an evening ramble through the streets of Vitoria.

On the following morning we left the town, long before daybreak, and during our forenoon's journey the postilion drew up at an inn, on the southern slope of the Sierra de San Lorenzo, in the province of Old Castile. The house was an old, dilapidated tenement, built of rough stone, and coarsely plastered upon the outside. The tiled roof had long been the sport of wind and rain, the motley coat of plaster was broken and time-worn, and the whole building sadly out of repair; though the fanciful mouldings under the eaves, and the curiously carved wood-work that supported the little balcony over the principal entrance, spoke of better days gone by. The whole building reminded me of a dilapidated Spanish Don, down at the heel and out at elbows, but with here and there a remnant of former magnificence peeping through the loopholes of his tattered cloak.

A wide gateway ushered the traveller into the interior of the building, and conducted him to a low-roofed apartment, paved with round stones, and serving both as a court-yard and a stable. It seemed to be a neutral ground for man and beast, — a little republic, where horse and rider had common privileges, and mule and muleteer lay cheek by jowl. In one corner a poor jackass was patiently devouring a bundle of musty straw, — in another, its master lay sound asleep with his saddle-cloth for a pillow; here a group of muleteers were quar-

relling over a pack of dirty cards, — and there the village barber, with a self-important air, stood laving the Alcalde's chin from the helmet of Mambrino. On the wall, a little taper glimmered feebly before an image of St. Anthony; directly opposite these a leathern wine-bottle hung by the neck from a pair of ox-horns; and the pavement below was covered with a curious medley of boxes, and bags, and cloaks, and pack-saddles, and sacks of grain, and skins of wine, and all kinds of lumber.

A small door upon the right led us into the inn-kitchen. It was a room about ten feet square, and literally all chimney; for the hearth was in the centre of the floor, and the walls sloped upward in the form of a long, narrow pyramid, with an opening at the top for the escape of the smoke. Quite round this little room ran a row of benches, upon which sat one or two grave personages smoking paper cigars. Upon the hearth blazed a handful of fagots, whose bright flame danced merrily among a motley congregation of pots and kettles, and a long wreath of smoke wound lazily up through the huge tunnel of the roof above. The walls were black with soot, and ornamented with sundry legs of bacon and festoons of sausages; and as there were no windows in this dingy abode, the only light which cheered the darkness within, came flickering from the fire upon the hearth, and the smoky sunbeams that peeped down the long-necked chimney.

I had not been long seated by the fire, when the tinkling of mule-bells, the clatter of hoofs, and the hoarse voice of a muleteer in the outer apartment, announced the arrival of new guests. A few moments afterward the kitchen-door opened, and a person entered, whose appearance strongly arrested my attention. It was a tall, athletic figure, with the majestic carriage of a grandee, and a dark, sunburnt countenance, that indicated an age of about fifty years. His dress was singular, and such as I had not before seen. He wore a round hat with wide, flapping brim, from beneath which his long, black hair hung in curls upon his shoulders; a leather jerkin, with cloth sleeves, descended to his hips; around his waist was closely buckled a leather belt, with a cartouch-box on one side; a pair of loose trousers of black serge hung in ample folds to the knees, around which they were closely gathered by embroidered garters of blue silk; and black broadcloth leggins, buttoned close to the calves, and strapped over a pair of brown leather shoes, completed the singular dress of the stranger. He doffed his hat as he entered, and, saluting the company with a "*Dios guarde á Ustedes, caballeros*" (God guard you, gentlemen), took a seat by the fire, and entered into conversation with those around him. As my curiosity was not a little excited by the peculiar dress of this person, I inquired of a travelling companion, who sat at my elbow, who and what this new-comer was. From him I learned that he was a muleteer of the Maragatería, — a name given to a cluster of small towns which lie in the mountainous country between Astorga and Villafranca, in the western corner of the kingdom of Leon.

"Nearly every province in Spain," said he, "has its peculiar costume, as you will see, when you have advanced farther into our country. For instance, the Catalonians wear crimson caps, hanging down upon the shoulder like a sack; wide pantaloons of green velvet, long enough in the waistband to cover the whole breast; and a little strip of a jacket, made of the same material, and so short as to bring the pocket directly under the armpit. The Valencians, on the contrary, go almost naked: a linen shirt, white linen trousers, reaching no lower than the knees, and a pair of coarse leather sandals complete their simple garb; it is only in mid-winter that they indulge in the luxury of a jacket. The most beautiful and expensive costume, however, is that of Andalusia; it consists of a velvet jacket,

faced with rich and various-colored embroidery, and covered with tassels and silken cord; a waistcoat of some gay color; a silken handkerchief round the neck, and a crimson sash round the waist; breeches that button down each side; gaiters and shoes of white leather; and a handkerchief of bright-colored silk wound about the head like a turban, and surmounted by a velvet cap or a little round hat, with a wide band, and an abundance of silken loops and tassels. The Old Castilians are more grave in their attire: they wear a leather breastplate instead of a jacket, breeches and leggins, and a montera cap. This fellow is a Maragato; and in the villages of the Maragatería the costume varies a little from the rest of Leon and Castile."

"If he is indeed a Maragato," said I jestingly, "who knows but he may be a descendant of the muleteer who behaved so naughtily at Cacabelos, as related in the second chapter of the veracious history of Gil Blas de Santillana?"

"*¿ Quien sabe?*" was the reply. "Notwithstanding the pride which even the meanest Castilian feels in counting over a long line of good-for-nothing ancestors, the science of genealogy has become of late a very intricate study in Spain."

Here our conversation was cut short by the *Mayoral* of the diligence, who came to tell us that the mules were waiting; and before many hours had elapsed we were scrambling through the square of the ancient city of Burgos. On the morrow we crossed the river Duero and the Guadarrama Mountains, and early in the afternoon entered the "Heróica Villa," of Madrid, by the Puerta de Fuencarral.

SPAIN.

Santiago y cierra España !
SPANISH WAR-CRY.

IT is a beautiful morning in June; — so beautiful, that I almost fancy myself in Spain. The tesselated shadows of the honeysuckle lies motionless upon the floor, as if it were a figure in the carpet; and through the open window comes the fragrance of the wild-brier and the mock-orange, reminding me of that soft, sunny clime where the very air is laden, like the bee, with sweetness, and the south wind

> "Comes over gardens, and the flowers
> That kissed it are betrayed."

The birds are carolling in the trees, and their shadows flit across the window as they dart to and fro in the sunshine; while the murmur of the bee, the cooing of doves from the eaves, and the whirring of a little humming-bird that has its nest in the honeysuckle, send up a sound of joy to meet the rising sun. How like the climate of the South! How like a summer morning in Spain!

My recollections of Spain are of the most lively and delightful kind. The character of the soil and of its inhabitants, — the stormy mountains and free spirits of the North, — the prodigal luxuriance and gay voluptuousness of the South, — the history and traditions of the past, resembling more the fables of romance than the solemn chronicle of events, — a soft and yet majestic language that falls like martial music on the ear, and a literature rich in the attractive lore of poetry and fiction, — these, but not these alone, are my reminiscences of Spain. With these I recall the thousand little circumstances and enjoyments which always give a coloring to our recollections of the past; the clear sky, — the pure, balmy air, — the delicious fruits and flowers, — the wild-fig and the aloe, and the olive by the wayside, — all, all that makes existence so joyous, and renders the sons and daughters of that clime the children of impulse and sensation.

As I write these words, a shade of sadness steals over me. When I think what that glorious land might be, and what it is, — what nature intended it should be, and what man has made it, — my very heart sinks within me. My mind instinctively reverts from the degradation of the present to the glory of the past; or, looking forward with strong misgivings, but with yet stronger hopes, interrogates the future.

The burnished armor of the Cid stands in the archives of the royal museum of Madrid, and there, too, is seen the armor of Ferdinand and of Isabel, of Guzman the Good and of Gonzalo de Córdova, and other early champions of Spain; but what hand shall now wield the sword of the Campeador, or lift up the banner of Leon and Castile? The ruins of Christian castle and Moorish alcazar still look forth from the hills of Spain; but where, oh where is the spirit of freedom that once fired the children of the Goth? Where is the spirit of Bernardo del Carpio, and Perez de Vargas, and Alonzo de Aguilar? Shall it forever sleep? Shall it never again beat high in the hearts of their sons? Shall the descendants of Pelayo bow forever beneath an iron yoke, " like cattle whose despair is dumb?"

The dust of the Cid lies mingling with the dust of Old Castile; but his spirit is not buried with his ashes. It sleeps, but is not dead. The day will come, when the foot of the tyrant shall be shaken from the neck of Spain; when a brave and generous people, though now ignorant, degraded, and much abused, shall " know their rights, and knowing dare maintain."

Of the national character of Spain I have brought away this impression; that its prominent traits are a generous pride of birth, a superstitious devotion to the dogmas of the Church, and an innate dignity, which exhibits itself even in the common and every-day employments of life. Castilian pride is proverbial. A beggar wraps his tattered cloak around him with all the dignity of a Roman senator;

and a muleteer bestrides his beast of burden with the air of a grandee.

I have thought, too, that there was a tinge of sadness in the Spanish character. The national music of the land is remarkable for its melancholy tone; and at times the voice of a peasant, singing amid the silence and solitude of the mountains, falls upon the ear like a funeral chant. Even a Spanish holiday wears a look of sadness, — a circumstance which some writers attribute to the cruel and overbearing spirit of the municipal laws. "On the greatest festivals," says Jovellanos, "instead of that boisterous merriment and noise which should bespeak the joy of the inhabitants, there reigns throughout the streets and market-places a

ful a phenomenon? This is not, indeed, the place to expose the errors which conspire to produce it; but, whatever those errors may be, one point is clear, — that they are all to be found in the laws!"[1]

Of the same serious, sombre character is the favorite national sport, — the bull-fight. It is a barbarous amusement, but of all others the most exciting, the most spirit-stirring; and in Spain, the most popular. "If Rome lived content with bread and arms," says the author I have just quoted, in a spirited little discourse entitled *Pan y Toros*, "Madrid lives content with bread and bulls."

Shall I describe a Spanish bull-fight? No. It has been so often and so well described by

slothful inactivity, a gloomy stillness, which cannot be remarked without mingled emotions of surprise and pity. The few persons who leave their houses seem to be driven from them by listlessness, and dragged as far as the threshold, the market, or the church-door; there, muffled in their cloaks, leaning against a corner, seated on a bench, or lounging to and fro, without object, aim, or purpose, they pass their hours, their whole evenings, without mirth, recreation, or amusement. When you add to this picture the dreariness and filth of the villages, the poor and slovenly dress of the inhabitants, the gloominess and silence of their air, the laziness, the want of concert and union so striking everywhere, who but would be astonished, who but would be afflicted by so mourn-

other pens that mine shall not undertake it, though it is a tempting theme. I cannot, however, refuse myself the pleasure of quoting here a few lines from one of the old Spanish ballads upon this subject. It is entitled "The Bull-fight of Ganzul." The description of the bull, which is contained in the passage I here extract, is drawn with a master's hand. It is rather a paraphrase than a translation, by Mr. Lockhart.

135

"From Guadiana comes he not, he comes not from Xenil,
From Guadalarif of the plain, nor Barves of the hill;
But where from out the forest burst Xarama's waters clear,
Beneath the oak-trees was he nursed, this proud and stately steer.

[1] *Informe dado á la Real Academia de Historia sobre Juegos, Espectáculos, y Diversiones Públicas.*

" Dark is his hide on either side, but the blood within doth
　　boil,
And the dun hide glows, as if on fire, as he paws to the
　　turmoil.
His eyes are jet, and they are set in crystal rings of
　　snow ;
But now they stare with one red glare of brass upon
　　the foe.

" Upon the forehead of the bull the horns stand close and
　　near,
From out the broad and wrinkled skull like daggers
　　they appear ;
His neck is massy, like the trunk of some old, knotted
　　tree,
Whereon the monster's shaggy mane, like billows
　　curled, ye see.

" His legs are short, his hams are thick, his hoofs are
　　black as night ;
Like a strong flail he holds his tail, in fierceness of his
　　might ;

Like something molten out of iron, or hewn from forth
　　the rock.
Harpado of Xarama stands, to bide the Alcayde's shock.

" Now stops the drum, — close, close they come ; thrice
　　meet and thrice give back ;
The white foam of Harpado lies on the charger's
　　breast of black ;
The white foam of the charger on Harpado's front of
　　dun ; —
Once more advance upon his lance, — once more, thou
　　fearless one ! "

There are various circumstances closely
connected with the train of thought I have
here touched upon ; but I forbear to mention
them, for fear of drawing out this chapter to
too great a length. Some of them will naturally find a place hereafter. Meanwhile let us
turn the leaf to a new chapter, and to subjects
of a livelier nature.

A TAILOR'S DRAWER.

Nedyls, threde, thymbell, shers, and all suche knackes.
THE FOUR Ps.

I.

A TAILOR'S drawer, did you say ?

Yes ; a tailor's drawer. It is, indeed, rather
a quaint rubric for a chapter in the pilgrim's
breviary ; albeit it well befits the motley character of the following pages. It is a title
which the Spaniards give to a desultory discourse, wherein various and discordant themes
are touched upon, and which is crammed full of
little shreds and patches of erudition ; and certainly it is not inappropriate to a chapter
whose contents are of every shape and hue, and
" do no more adhere and keep pace together
than the hundreth psalm to the tune of Green
Sleeves."

II.

It is recorded in the Adventures of Gil Blas
de Santillana, that, when this renowned personage first visited the city of Madrid, he took
lodgings at the house of Mateo Melandez, in
the Puerta del Sol. In chosing a place of
abode in the Spanish court, I followed, as far
as practicable, this illustrious example ; but, as
the kind-hearted Mateo had been long gathered to his fathers, I was content to take up
my residence in the hired house of Valentin
Gonzalez, at the foot of the Calle de la Montera. My apartments were in the third story,
above the dust, though not beyond the rattle,
of the street ; and my balconies looked down
into the Puerta del Sol, the heart of Madrid,
through which circulates the living current of
its population at least once every twenty-four
hours.

The Puerta del Sol is a public square, from
which diverge the five principal streets of the
metropolis. It is the great rendezvous of
grave and gay, — of priest and layman, — of
gentle and simple, — the mart of business and
of gossip, — the place where the creditor seeks
his debtor, where the lawyer seeks his client,
where the stranger seeks amusement, where
the friend seeks his friend, and the foe his foe ;
where the idler seeks the sun in winter, and
the shade in summer, and the busybody seeks
the daily news, and picks up the crumbs of
gossip to fly away with them in his beak to
the *tertulia* of Doña Paquita !

Tell me, ye who have sojourned in foreign
lands, and know in what bubbles a traveller's

happiness consists, — is it not a blessing to have your window overlook a scene like this ?

III.

There, — take that chair upon the balcony, and let us look down upon the busy scene beneath us. What a continued roar the crowded throughfare sends up ! Though three stories high, we can hardly hear the sound of our own voices ! The London cries are whispers, when compared with the cries of Madrid.

See, — yonder stalks a gigantic peasant of New Castile, with a montera cap, brown jacket and breeches, and coarse blue stockings, forcing his way through the crowd, and leading a donkey laden with charcoal, whose sonorous bray is in unison with the harsh voice of his master. Close at his elbow goes a rosy-cheeked damsel, selling calico. She is an Asturian from the mountains of Santander. How do you know ? By her short yellow petticoats, — her blue bodice, — her coral necklace and earrings. Through the middle of the square struts a peasant of Old Castile, with his yellow leather jerkin strapped about his waist, — his brown leggings and his blue garters, — driving before him a flock of gabbling turkeys, and crying, at the top of his voice, " *Pao, pao, pavitos, paos !* " Next comes a Valencian, with his loose linen trousers and sandal shoon, holding a huge sack of watermelons upon his shoulder with his left hand, and with his right balancing high in air a specimen of the luscious fruit, upon which is perched a little pyramid of the crimson pulp, while he tempts the passers-by with " *A cala, y calando ; una sandía vendo-o-o. Si esto es sangre !* " (By the slice, — come and try it, — watermelon for sale. This is blood !) His companion near him has a pair of scales thrown over his shoulder, and holds both arms full of muskmelons. He chimes into the harmonious ditty with " *Melo — melo-o-o — meloncitos ; aquí está el azúcar !* " (Melons, melons ; here is the sugar !) Behind them creeps a slow-moving Asturian, in heavy wooden shoes, crying watercresses ; and a peasant woman from the Guadarrama Mountains, with a montera cocked up in front, and a blue kerchief tied under her chin, swings in each hand a bunch of live chickens, — that hang by the claws, head downwards, fluttering, scratching, crowing with all their might, while the good woman tries to drown their voices in the discordant cry of " ¿ *Quien me compra un gallo, — un par de gallinas ?* " (Who buys a cock, — a pair of fowls ?) That tall fellow in blue, with a pot of flowers upon his shoulder, is a wag beyond all dispute. See how cunningly he cocks his eye up at us, and cries, " *Si yo tuviera balcon !* " (If I only had a balcony !)

What next ? A Manchego with a sack of oil under his arm ; a Gallego with a huge water-jar upon his shoulders ; an Italian pedler with images of saints and madonnas ; a razor-grinder with his wheel ; a mender of pots and kettles, making music, as he goes, with a shovel and a frying-pan ; and, in fine, a noisy, patchwork, ever-changing crowd, whose discordant cries mingle with the rumbling of wheels, the clatter of hoofs, and the clang of church-bells ; and make the Puerta del Sol, at certain hours of the day, like a street in Babylon the Great.

IV.

Chiton ! A beautiful girl, with flaxen hair, blue eyes, and the form of a fairy in a midsummer night's dream, has just stepped out on the balcony beneath us ! See how coquettishly she crosses her arms upon the balcony, thrusts her dainty little foot through the bars, and plays with her slipper ! She is an Andalusian, from Malaga. Her brother is a bold dragoon, and wears a long sword ; so beware ! and " let not the creaking of shoes and the rustling of silks betray thy poor heart to woman." Her mother is a vulgar woman, " fat and forty " ; eats garlic in her salad, and smokes cigars. But mind ! that is a secret ; I tell it to you in confidence.

V.

The following little ditty I translate from the Spanish. It is as delicate as a dew-drop.

> She is a maid of artless grace,
> Gentle in form, and fair of face.
>
> Tell me, thou ancient mariner,
>   That sailest on the sea,
> If ship, or sail, or evening star
>   Be half so fair as she !

Tell me, thou gallant cavalier,
　　Whose shining arms I see,
If steed, or sword, or battle-field
　　Be half so fair as she !

Tell me, thou swain, that guard'st thy flock
　　Beneath the shadowy tree,
If flock, or vale, or mountain-ridge
　　Be half so fair as she !

VI.

A miller has just passed by, covered with flour from head to foot, and perched upon the tip end of a little donkey, crying *"Arre bor-rico !"* and at every cry swinging a cudgel in his hand, and giving the ribs of the poor beast what in the vulgar dialect is called a *cachipor-razo.* I could not help laughing, though I felt provoked at the fellow for his cruelty. The truth is, I have great regard for a jackass. His meekness, and patience, and long-suffer-ing are very amiable qualities, and, consider-ing his situation, worthy of all praise. In Spain, a donkey plays as conspicuous a part as a priest or a village alcalde. There would be no getting along without him. And yet, who so beaten and abused as he ?

VII.

Here comes a gay gallant, with white kid gloves, an eye-glass, a black cane, with a white ivory pommel, and a little hat, cocked pertly on one side of his head. He is an exquisite fop, and a great lady's man. You will always find him on the Prado at sunset, when the crowd and dust are thickest, ogling through his glass, flourishing his cane, and humming between his teeth some favorite air of the "Semiramis," or the "Barber of Seville." He is a great amateur, and patron of the Italian Opera, — beats time with his cane, — nods his head, and cries *Bravo!* — and fancies himself in love with the Prima Donna. The height of his ambition is to be thought the gay Lothario, — the gallant Don Cortejo of his little sphere. He is a poet withal, and daily besieges the heart of the cruel Doña Inez with sonnets and madrigals. She turns a deaf ear to his song, and is inexorable : —

> "Mas que no sea mas piadosa
> 　A dos escudos en prosa,
> 　　No puede ser."

VIII.

What a contrast between this personage and the sallow, emaciated being who is now crossing the street ! It is a barefooted Carmel-ite, — a monk of an austere order, — wasted by midnight vigils and long penance. Absti-nence is written on that pale cheek, and the bowed head and downcast eye are in accord-ance with the meek profession of a mendicant brotherhood.

What is this world to thee, thou man of pen-itence and prayer? What hast thou to do with all this busy, turbulent scene about thee, — with all the noise, and gayety, and splendor of this thronged city ? Nothing. The wide world gives thee nothing, save thy daily crust, thy crucifix, thy convent-cell, thy pallet of straw ! Pilgrim of heaven ! thou hast no home on earth. Thou art journeying onward to "a house not made with hands ; " and, like the first apostles of thy faith, thou takest neither gold, nor silver, nor brass, nor scrip for thy journey. Thou hast shut thy heart to the en-dearments of earthly love, — thy shoulder bear-eth not the burden with thy fellow-man, — in all this vast crowd thou hast no friends, no hopes, no sympathies. Thou standest aloof from man, — and art thou nearer God? I know not. Thy motives, thy intentions, thy desires are registered in heaven. I am thy fel-low-man, — and not thy judge.

"Who is the greater ? " says the German moralist ; " the wise man who lifts himself above the storms of time, and from aloof looks down upon them, and yet takes no part there-in, — or he who, from the height of quiet and repose, throws himself boldly into the battle-tumult of the world? Glorious is it, when the eagle through the beating tempest flies into the bright blue heaven upward ; but far more glo-rious, when, poising in the blue sky over the black storm-abyss, he plunges downward to his aerie on the cliff, where cower his unfledged brood and tremble."

IX.

Sultry grows the day, and breathless ! The lately crowded street is silent and deserted, — hardly a footfall, — hardly here and there a solitary figure stealing along in the narrow strip of shade beneath the eaves! Silent, too, and deserted is the Puerta del Sol; so silent, that even at this distance the splashing of its fountain is distinctly audible, — so deserted, that not a living thing is visible there, save the outstretched and athletic form of a Galician water-carrier, who lies asleep upon the pavement in the cool shadow of the fountain! There is not air enough to stir the leaves of the jasmine upon the balcony, or break the thin column of smoke that issues from the cigar of Don Diego, master of the noble Spanish tongue, *y hombre de muchos dingolondangos.* He sits bolt upright between the window and the door, with the collar of his snuff-colored frock thrown back upon his shoulders, and his toes turned out like a dancing-master, poring over the "Diario de Madrid," to learn how high the thermometer rose yesterday, — what patron saint has a festival to-day, — and at what hour to-morrow the "King of Spain, Jerusalem, and the Canary Islands" will take his departure for the gardens of Aranjuez.

You have a proverb in your language, Don Diego, which says, —

"Despues de comer
    Ni un sobrescrito leer;" —

after dinner read not even the superscription of a letter. I shall obey, and indulge in the exquisite luxury of a *siesta.* I confess that I love this after-dinner nap. If I have a gift, a vocation for anything, it is for sleeping; and from my heart I can say with honest Sancho, "Blessed be the man that first invented sleep!" In a sultry clime, too, where the noontide heat unmans you, and the cool starry night seems made for anything but slumber, I am willing to barter an hour or two of intense daylight for an hour or two of tranquil, lovely, dewy night!

Therefore, Don Diego, *hasta la vista!*

X.

It is evening; the day is gone; fast gather and deepen the shades of twilight! In the words of a German allegory, "The babbling day has touched the hem of night's garment, and, weary and still, drops asleep in her bosom."

The city awakens from its slumber. The convent-bells ring solemnly and slow. The

streets are thronged again. Once more I hear the shrill cry, the rattling wheel, the murmur of the crowd. The blast of a trumpet sounds from the Puerta del Sol, — then the tap of a drum; a mounted guard opens the way, — the crowd doff their hats, and the king sweeps by in a gilded coach drawn by six horses, and followed by a long train of uncouth, antiquated vehicles drawn by mules.

The living tide now sets towards the Prado, and the beautiful gardens of the Retiro. Beautiful are they at this magic hour! Beautiful, with the almond-tree in blossom, with the broad green leaves of the sycamore and the chestnut, with the fragrance of the orange and the lemon, with the beauty of a thousand flowers, with the soothing calm and the dewy freshness of evening!

XI.

I love to linger on the Prado till the crowd is gone and the night far advanced. There musing and alone I sit, and listen to the lulling fall of waters in their marble fountains, and watch the moon as it rises over the gardens of the Retiro, brighter than a northern sun. The beautiful scene lies half in shadow, half in light, — almost a fairy-land. Occasionally the sound of a guitar, or a distant voice, breaks in upon my revery. Then the form of a monk, from the neighboring convent, sweeps by me like a shadow, and disappears in the gloom of the leafy avenues; and far away from the streets of the city comes the voice of the watchman telling the midnight hour.

Lovely art thou, O Night, beneath the skies of Spain! Day, panting with heat, and laden with a thousand cares, toils onward like a beast of burden; but Night, calm, silent, holy Night, is a ministering angel that cools with its dewy breath the toil-heated brow; and, like the Roman sisterhood, stoops down to bathe the pilgrim's feet. How grateful is the starry twilight! How grateful the gentle radiance of the moon! How grateful the delicious coolness of "the omnipresent and deep-breathing air!" Lovely art thou, O Night, beneath the skies of Spain!

ANCIENT SPANISH BALLADS.

I love a ballad but even too well, if it be doleful matter merrily set down, or a very pleasant thing indeed, and sung lamentably.   WINTER'S TALE.

How universal is the love of poetry! Every nation has its popular songs, the offspring of a credulous simplicity and an unschooled fancy. The peasant of the North, as he sits by the evening fire, sings the traditionary ballad to his children,

> "Nor wants he gleeful tales, while round
> The nut-brown bowl doth trot."

The peasant of the South, as he lies at noon in the shade of the sycamore, or sits by his door in the evening twilight, sings his amorous lay, and listlessly,

> "On hollow quills of oaten straw,
> He pipeth melody."

The muleteer of Spain carols with the early lark, amid the stormy mountains of his native land. The vintager of Sicily has his evening hymn; the fisherman of Naples his boat-song; the gondolier of Venice his midnight serenade. The goatherd of Switzerland and the Tyrol, — the Carpathian boor, — the Scotch Highlander, — the English ploughboy, singing as he drives his team afield, — peasant, — serf, — slave, — all, all have their ballads and traditionary songs. Music is the universal language of mankind, — poetry their universal pastime and delight.

The ancient ballads of Spain hold a prominent rank in her literary history. Their number is truly astonishing, and may well startle the most enthusiastic lover of popular song. The Romancero General[1] contains upwards of a thousand; and though upon many of these may justly be bestowed the encomium which

[1] Romancero General, en que se contiene todos los Romances que andan impresos. 4to. Madrid, 1604.

ARTIST: ROBERT BLUM.

STREET SCENE IN MADRID.

honest Izaak Walton pronounces upon the old English ballad of the Passionate Shepherd, — "old-fashioned poetry, but choicely good," — yet, as a whole, they are, perhaps, more remarkable for their number than for their beauty. Every great historic event, every marvellous tradition, has its popular ballad. Don Roderick, Bernardo del Carpio, and the Cid Campeador are not more the heroes of ancient chronicle than of ancient song; and the imaginary champions of Christendom, the twelve peers of Charlemagne, have found an historian in the wandering ballad-singer no less authentic than the good Archbishop Turpin.

Most of these ancient ballads had their origin during the dominion of the Moors in Spain. Many of them, doubtless, are nearly as old as the events they celebrate; though in their present form the greater part belong to the fourteenth century. The language in which they are now preserved indicates no higher antiquity; but who shall say how long they had been handed down by tradition, ere they were taken from the lips of the wandering minstrel, and recorded in a more permanent form?

The seven centuries of the Moorish sovereignty in Spain are the heroic ages of her history and her poetry. What the warrior achieved with his sword the minstrel published in his song. The character of those ages is seen in the character of their literature. History casts its shadow far into the land of song. Indeed, the most prominent characteristic of the ancient Spanish ballads is their warlike spirit. They shadow forth the majestic lineaments of the warlike ages; and through every line breathes a high and peculiar tone of chivalrous feeling. It is not the piping sound of peace, but a blast, — a loud, long blast from the war-horn, —

> "A trump with a stern breath,
> Which is cleped the trump of death."

And with this mingles the voice of lamentation, — the requiem for the slain, with a melancholy sweetness: —

> "Rio Verde, Rio Verde !
> Many a corpse is bathed in thee,

> Both of Moors and eke of Christians,
> Slain with swords most cruelly.

> "And thy pure and crystal waters
> Dappled are with crimson gore ;
> For between the Moors and Christians
> Long has been the fight and sore.

> "Dukes and counts fell bleeding near thee,
> Lords of high renown were slain,
> Perished many a brave hidalgo
> Of the noblemen of Spain."

Another prominent characteristic of these ancient ballads is their energetic and beautiful simplicity. A great historic event is described in the fewest possible words; there is no ornament, no artifice. The poet's intention was to narrate, not to embellish. It is truly wonderful to observe what force, and beauty, and dramatic power are given to the old romances by this single circumstance. When Bernardo del Carpio leads forth his valiant Leonese against the host of Charlemagne, he animates their courage by alluding to their battles with the Moors, and exclaims, "Shall the lions that have bathed their paws in Libyan gore now crouch before the Frank?" When he enters the palace of the treacherous Alfonso, to upbraid him for a broken promise, and the king orders him to be arrested for contumely, he lays his hand upon his sword and cries, "Let no one stir! I am Bernardo; and my sword is not subject even to kings!" When the Count Alarcos prepares to put to death his own wife at the king's command, she submits patiently to her fate, asks time to say a prayer, and then exclaims, "Now bring me my infant boy, that I may give him suck, as my last farewell!" Is there in Homer an incident more touching, or more true to nature?

The ancient Spanish ballads naturally divide themselves into three classes: the Historic, the Romantic, and the Moorish. It must be confessed, however, that the line of demarcation between these three classes is not well defined; for many of the Moorish ballads are historic, and many others occupy a kind of debatable ground between the historic and the romantic. I have adopted this classification for the sake of its convenience, and shall now make a few hasty observations upon each class, and illustrate my remarks by specimens of the ballads.

The historic ballads are those which recount the noble deeds of the early heroes of Spain: of Bernardo del Carpio, the Cid, Martin Pelaez, Garcia Perez de Vargas, Alonso de Aguilar, and many others whose names stand conspicuous in Spanish history. Indeed, these ballads may themselves be regarded in the light of historic documents; they are portraits of long-departed ages, and if at times their features are exaggerated and colored with too bold a contrast of light and shade, yet the free and spirited touches of a master's hand are recognized in all. They are instinct, too, with the spirit of Castilian pride, with the high and dauntless spirit of liberty that burned so fiercely of old in the heart of the brave hidalgo. Take, for example, the ballad of the Five Farthings. King Alfonso the Eighth, having exhausted his treasury in war, wishes to lay a tax of five farthings upon each of the Castilian hidalgos, in order to defray the expenses of a journey from Burgos to Cuenca. This proposition of the king was met with disdain by the noblemen who had been assembled on the occasion.

> "Don Nuño, Count of Lara,
>   In anger and in pride,
> Forgot all reverence for the king,
>   And thus in wrath replied : —
>
> "'Our noble ancestors,' quoth he,
>   'Ne'er such a tribute paid;
> Nor shall the king receive of us
>   What they have once gainsaid.
>
> "'The base-born soul who deems it just
>   May here with thee remain;
> But follow me, ye cavaliers,
>   Ye noblemen of Spain.'
>
> "Forth followed they the noble Count,
>   They marched to Glera's plain ;
> Out of three thousand gallant knights
>   Did only three remain.
>
> "They tied the tribute to their spears,
>   They raised it in the air,
> And they sent to tell their lord the king
>   That his tax was ready there.
>
> "'He may send and take by force,' said they,
>   'This paltry sum of gold ;

> But the goodly gift of liberty
>   Cannot be bought and sold.'"

The same gallant spirit breathes through all the historic ballads; but, perhaps, most fervently in those which relate to Bernardo del Carpio. How spirit-stirring are all the speeches which the ballad-writers have put into the mouth of this valiant hero! "Ours is the blood of the Goth," says he to King Alfonso; "sweet to us is liberty, and bondage odious!" "The king may give his castles to the Frank, but not his vassals; for kings themselves hold no dominion over the free will!" He and his followers would rather die freemen than live slaves! If these are the common watchwords of liberty at the present day, they were no less so among the high-souled Spaniards of the eighth century.

One of the finest of the historic ballads is that which describes Bernardo's march to Roncesvalles. He sallies forth "with three thousand Leonese and more," to protect the glory and freedom of his native land. From all sides, the peasantry of the land flock to the hero's standard.

> "The peasant leaves his plough afield,
>   The reaper leaves his hook,
> And from his hand the shepherd-boy
>   Lets fall the pastoral crook.
>
> "The young set up a shout of joy,
>   The old forget their years,
> The feeble man grows stout of heart,
>   No more the craven fears.
>
> "All rush to Bernard's standard,
>   And on liberty they call ;
> They cannot brook to wear the yoke,
>   When threatened by the Gaul.
>
> "'Free were we born,' 'tis thus they cry,
>   'And willingly pay we
> The duty that we owe our king,
>   By the divine decree.
>
> "'But God forbid that we obey
>   The laws of foreign knaves,
> Tarnish the glory of our sires,
>   And make our children slaves.
>
> "'Our hearts have not so craven grown,
>   So bloodless all our veins,
> So vigorless our brawny arms,
>   As to submit to chains.

"'Has the audacious Frank, forsooth,
   Subdued these seas and lands?
Shall he a bloodless victory have?
   No, not while we have hands.

"'He shall learn that the gallant Leonese
   Can bravely fight and fall;
But that they know not how to yield;
   They are Castilians all.

"'Was it for this the Roman power
   Of old was made to yield
Unto Numantia's valiant hosts,
   On many a bloody field?

"'Shall the bold lions that have bathed
   Their paws in Libyan gore,
Crouch basely to a feebler foe,
   And dare the strife no more?

"'Let the false king sell town and tower,
   But not his vassals free;
For to subdue the free-born soul
   No royal power hath he!'"

These short specimens will suffice to show the spirit of the old heroic ballads of Spain; the Romances del Cid, and those that rehearse the gallant achievements of many other champions, brave and stalwart knights of old, I must leave unnoticed, and pass to another field of chivalry and song.

The next class of the ancient Spanish ballads is the Romantic, including those which relate to the Twelve Peers of Charlemagne and other imaginary heroes of the days of chivalry. There is an exaggeration in the prowess of these heroes of romance which is in accordance with the warmth of a Spanish imagination; and the ballads which celebrate their achievements still go from mouth to mouth among the peasantry of Spain, and are hawked about the streets by the blind ballad-monger.

Among the romantic ballads, those of the Twelve Peers stand preëminent; not so much for their poetic merit as for the fame of their heroes. In them are sung the valiant knights whose history is written more at large in the prose romances of chivalry, — Orlando, and Oliver, and Montesinos, and Durandarte, and the Marques de Mantua, and the other paladins, "*que en una mesa comian pan.*" These ballads are of different length and various degrees of merit. Of some a few lines only remain; they are evidently fragments of larger

136

works; while others, on the contrary, aspire to the length and dignity of epic poems; — witness the ballads of the Conde de Irlos and the Marques de Mantua, each of which consists of nearly a thousand long and sonorous lines.

Among these ballads of the Twelve Peers there are many of great beauty; others possess little merit, and are wanting in vigor and conciseness. From the structure of the versification, I should rank them among the oldest of the Spanish ballads. They are all monorhythmic, with full consonant rhymes.

To the romantic ballads belong also a great number which recount the deeds of less celebrated heroes; but among them all none is so curious as that of Virgil. Like the old French romance writers of the Middle Ages, the early Spanish poets introduce the Mantuan bard as a knight of chivalry. The ballad informs us that a certain king kept him imprisoned seven years, for what old Brantôme would call *outrecuydance* with a certain Doña Isabel. But being at mass on Sunday, the recollection of Virgil comes suddenly into his mind, when he ought to be attending to the priest; and, turning to his knights, he asks them what has become of Virgil. One of them replies, " Your Highness has him imprisoned in your dungeons;" to which the king makes answer with the greatest coolness, by telling them that the dinner is waiting, and that after they have dined they will pay Virgil a visit in his prison. Then up and spake the queen like a true heroine; quoth she, " I will not dine without him"; and straightway they all repaired to the prison, where they find the incarcerated knight engaged in the pleasant pastime of combing his hair and arranging his beard. He tells the king very coolly that on that very day he has been a prisoner seven years; to this the king replies, " Hush, hush, Virgil; it takes three more to make ten." " Sire," says Virgil, with the same philosophical composure, " if your Highness so ordains, I will pass my whole life here." " As a reward for your patience, you shall dine with me to-day," says the king. " My coat is torn," says Virgil; " I am not in trim to make a leg." But this difficulty is removed by the promise of a new suit from the king; and they go to dinner. Virgil delights both knights and damsels, but most of all Doña Isabel. The archbishop is called in; they are married forthwith, and the ballad closes like a scene in some old play: "He takes her by the hand, and leads her to the garden."

Such is this curious ballad.

I now turn to one of the most beautiful of these ancient Spanish poems; — it is the Romance del Conde Alarcos; a ballad full of interest and of touching pathos. The story is briefly this. The Count Alarcos, after being secretly betrothed to the Infanta Solisa, forsakes her and weds another lady. Many years afterward, the princess, sitting alone, as she was wont, and bemoaning her forsaken lot, resolves to tell the cause of her secret sorrow to the king her father; and, after confessing her clandestine love for Count Alarcos, demands the death of the Countess, to heal her wounded honor. Her story awakens the wrath of the king; he acknowledges the justness of her demand, seeks an interview with the Count, and sets the case before him in so strong a light, that finally he wrings from him a promise to put his wife to death with his own hand. The Count returns homeward a grief-stricken man, weeping the sad destiny of his wife, and saying within himself, "How shall I look upon her smile of joy, when she comes forth to meet me?" The Countess welcomes his return with affectionate tenderness; but he is heavy at heart and disconsolate. He sits down to supper with his children around him, but the food is untasted; he hides his face in his hands, and weeps. At length they retire to their chamber. In the language of Mr. Lockhart's translation, —

"They came together to the bower, where they were used to rest, —
   None with them but the little babe that was upon the breast:
   The Count had barred the chamber-doors, — they ne'er were barred till then :
   'Unhappy lady,' he began, ' and I most lost of men !

" 'Now speak not so, my noble lord, my husband, and my life!
   Unhappy never can she be that is Alarcos' wife !'
   'Alas ! unhappy lady, 't is but little that you know;
   For in that very word you 've said is gathered all your woe.

" 'Long since I loved a lady, — long since I oaths did plight
   To be that lady's husband, to love her day and night ;
   Her father is our lord the king, — to him the thing is known;
   And now — that I the news should bring ! — she claims me for her own.

" 'Alas ! my love, alas ! my life, the right is on their side;
   Ere I had seen your face, sweet wife, she was betrothed my bride;
   But — oh, that I should speak the word ! — since in her place you lie,
   It is the bidding of our lord that you this night must die.'

" 'Are these the wages of my love, so lowly and so leal ?
   Oh, kill me not, thou noble Count, when at thy foot I kneel!
   But send me to my father's house, where once I dwelt in glee;
   There will I live a lone, chaste life, and rear my children three.'

" 'It may not be, — mine oath is strong, — ere dawn of day you die.'
   'Oh, well 't is seen how all alone upon the earth am I! —
   My father is an old, frail man; my mother 's in her grave ;
   And dead is stout Don Garci, — alas! my brother brave!

" ' 'T was at this coward king's command they slew my brother dear,
   And now I 'm helpless in the land ! — It is not death I fear,
   But loth, loth am I to depart, and leave my children so; —
   Now let me lay them to my heart, and kiss them, ere I go.'

" 'Kiss him that lies upon thy breast, — the rest thou mayst not see.'
   'I fain would say an Ave.' 'Then say it speedily.'
   She knelt her down upon her knee, — 'O Lord, behold my case !
   Judge not my deeds, but look on me in pity and great grace!'

" When she had made her orison, up from her knees she rose: —
   'Be kind, Alarcos, to our babes, and pray for my repose;
   And now give me my boy once more, upon my breast to hold,
   That he may drink one farewell drink before my breast be cold.'

" 'Why would you waken the poor child ? you see he is asleep;
   Prepare, dear wife, there is no time, the dawn begins to peep.'

'Now, hear me, Count Alarcos! I give thee pardon
    free :
I pardon thee for the love's sake wherewith I 've loved
    thee ; —

"'But they have not my pardon, — the king and his proud
    daughter ;
The curse of God be on them, for this unchristian
    slaughter.
I charge them with my dying breath, ere thirty days be
    gone,
To meet me in the realm of death, and at God's awful
    throne !'"

The Count then strangles her with a scarf, and the ballad concludes with the fulfilment of the dying lady's prayer, in the death of the king and the Infanta within twenty days of her own.

Few, I think, will be disposed to question the beauty of this ancient ballad, though a refined and cultivated taste may revolt from the seemingly unnatural incident upon which it is founded. It must be recollected that this is a scene taken from a barbarous age, when the life of even the most cherished and beloved was held of little value in comparison with a chivalrous but false and exaggerated point of honor. It must be borne in mind also, that, notwithstanding the boasted liberty of the Castilian hidalgos, and their frequent rebellions against the crown, a deep reverence for the divine right of kings, and a consequent disposition to obey the mandates of the throne, at almost any sacrifice, has always been one of the prominent traits of the Spanish character. When taken in connection with these circumstances, the story of this old ballad ceases to be so grossly improbable as it seems at first sight ; and, indeed, becomes an illustration of national character. In all probability, the story of the Conde Alarcos had some foundation in fact.[1]

The third class of the ancient Spanish ballads is the Moorish. Here we enter a new world, more gorgeous and more dazzling than that of Gothic chronicle and tradition. The stern spirits of Bernardo, the Cid, and Mudarra have passed away ; the mail-clad forms of Guarinos, Orlando, and Durandarte are not here :

the scene is changed ; it is the bridal of Andalla ; the bull-fight of Ganzul. The sunshine of Andalusia glances upon the marble halls of Granada, and green are the banks of the Xenil and the Darro. A band of Moorish knights gayly arrayed in gambesons of crimson silk, with scarfs of blue and jewelled tahalíes, sweep like the wind through the square of Vivarambla. They ride to the Tournament of Reeds ; the Moorish maiden leans from the balcony ; bright eyes glisten from many a lattice ; and the victorious knight receives the prize of valor from the hand of her whose beauty is like the star-lit night. These are the Xarifas, the Celindas, and Lindaraxas, — the Andallas, Ganzules, and Abenzaydes of Moorish song.

Then comes the sound of the silver clarion, and the roll of the Moorish atabal, down from the snowy pass of the Sierra Nevada and across the gardens of the Vega. Alhama has fallen ! woe is me, Alhama ! The Christian is at the gates of Granada ; the banner of the cross floats from the towers of the Alhambra ! And these, too, are themes for the minstrel, — themes sung alike by Moor and Spaniard.

Among the Moorish ballads are included not only those which were originally composed in Arabic, but all that relate to the manners, customs, and history of the Moors in Spain. In most of them the influence of an Oriental taste is clearly visible ; their spirit is more refined and effeminate than that of the historic and romantic ballads, in which no trace of such an influence is perceptible. The spirit of the Cid is stern, unbending, steel-clad ; his hand grasps his sword Tizona ; his heel wounds the flank of his steed Babieca ; —

    " La mano aprieta á Tizona,
      Y el talon fiere á Babieca."

But the spirit of Arbolan the Moor, though resolute in camps, is effeminate in courts ; he is a diamond among scymitars, yet graceful in the dance ; —

    " Diamante entre los alfanges.
      Gracioso en baylar las zambras."

Estrella de Sevilla, by Lope de Vega, and *Del Rey abajo Ninguno*, by Francisco de Rojas.

---

[1] This exaggerated reverence for the person and prerogatives of the king has furnished the groundwork of two of the best dramas in the Spanish language : *La*

The ancient ballads are stamped with the character of their heroes. Abundant illustrations of this could be given, but it is not necessary.

Among the most spirited of the Moorish ballads are those which are interwoven in the History of the Civil Wars of Granada. The following, entitled " A very mournful Ballad on the Siege and Conquest of Alhama," is very beautiful; and such was the effect it produced upon the Moors that it was forbidden, on pain of death, to sing it within the walls of Granada. The translation, which is executed with great skill and fidelity, is from the pen of Lord Byron.

> " The Moorish king rides up and down,
> 　　Through Granada's royal town;
> 　　From Elvira's gates to those
> 　　Of Bivarambla on he goes.
> 　　　　Woe is me, Alahama!
>
> " Letters to the monarch tell
> 　　How Alhama's city fell;
> 　　In the fire the scroll he threw,
> 　　And the messenger he slew.
> 　　　　Woe is me, Alhama!
>
> " He quits his mule, and mounts his horse,
> 　　And through the street directs his course;
> 　　Through the street of Zacatin
> 　　To the Alhambra spurring in.
> 　　　　Woe is me, Alhama!
>
> " When the Alhambra's walls he gained
> 　　On the moment he ordained
> 　　That the trumpet straight should sound
> 　　With the silver clarion round.
> 　　　　Woe is me, Alhama!
>
> " And when the hollow drums of war
> 　　Beat the loud alarm afar,
> 　　That the Moors of town and plain
> 　　Might answer to the martial strain, —
> 　　　　Woe is me, Alhama!
>
> " Then the Moors, by this aware
> 　　That bloody Mars recalled them there,
> 　　One by one, and two by two,
> 　　To a mighty squadron grew.
> 　　　　Woe is me, Alhama!
>
> " Out then spake an aged Moor
> 　　In these words the king before:
> 　　'Wherefore call on us, O king?
> 　　What may mean this gathering?'
> 　　　　Woe is me Alhama!

> " 'Friends! ye have, alas! to know
> 　　Of a most disastrous blow, —
> 　　That the Christians, stern and bold,
> 　　Have obtained Alhama's hold.'
> 　　　　Woe is me, Alhama!
>
> " Out then spake old Alfaqui,
> 　　With his beard so white to see :
> 　　'Good king, thou art justly served;
> 　　Good king, this thou hast deserved.
> 　　　　Woe is me, Alhama!
>
> " 'By thee were slain, in evil hour,
> 　　The Abencerrage, Granada's flower;
> 　　And strangers were received by thee
> 　　Of Córdova the chivalry.
> 　　　　Woe is me, Alhama!
>
> " 'And for this, O king! is sent
> 　　On thee a double chastisement;
> 　　Thee and thine, thy crown and realm,
> 　　One last wreck shall overwhelm.
> 　　　　Woe is me, Alhama!
>
> " He who holds no laws in awe,
> 　　He must perish by the law;
> 　　And Granada must be won,
> 　　And thyself with her undone.'
> 　　　　Woe is me, Alhama!
>
> " Fire flashed from out the old Moor's eyes,
> 　　The monarch's wrath began to rise,
> 　　Because he answered, and because
> 　　He spake exceeding well of laws.
> 　　　　Woe is me, Alhama!
>
> " 'There is no law to say such things
> 　　As may disgust the ear of kings!'
> 　　Thus, snorting with his choler, said
> 　　The Moorish king, and doomed him dead.
> 　　　　Woe is me, Alhama!"

Such are the ancient ballads of Spain; poems which, like the Gothic cathedrals of the Middle Ages, have outlived the names of their builders. They are the handiwork of wandering, homeless minstrels, who for their daily bread thus " built the lofty rhyme; " and whose names, like their dust and ashes, have long, long been wrapped in a shroud. " These poets," says an anonymous writer, " have left behind them no trace to which the imagination can attach itself; they have ' died and made no sign.' We pass from the infancy of Spanish poetry to the age of Charles, through a long vista of monuments without inscriptions, as the traveller approaches the noise and bustle of modern Rome through the lines of silent and unknown tombs that border the Appian Way."

Before closing this essay, I must allude to the unfavorable opinion which the learned Dr. Southey has expressed concerning the merit of these old Spanish ballads. In his preface to the Chronicle of the Cid, he says: "The heroic ballads of the Spaniards have been overrated in this country; they are infinitely and every way inferior to our own. There are some spirited ones in the Guerras Civiles de Granada, from which the rest have been estimated; but, excepting these, I know none of any value among the many hundred which I have perused." On this field I am willing to do battle, though it be with a veteran knight who bears enchanted arms, and whose sword, like that of Martin Antolinez, "illumines all the field." That the old Spanish ballads may have been overrated, and that as a whole they are inferior to the English, I concede; that many of the hundred ballads of the Cid are wanting in interest, and that many of those of the Twelve Peers of France are languid, and drawn out beyond the patience of the most patient reader, I concede; I willingly confess, also, that among them all I have found none that can rival in graphic power the short but wonderful ballad of Sir Patrick Spence, wherein the mariner sees "the new moon with the old moon in her arm," or the more modern one of the Battle of Agincourt, by Michael Drayton, beginning, —

> "Fair stood the wind for France,
> As we our sails advance,
> Nor now to prove our chance
>   Longer will tarry;
> But putting to the main,
> At Caux, the mouth of Seine,
> With all his martial train,
>   Landed King Harry."

All this I readily concede: but that the old Spanish ballads are infinitely and every way inferior to the English, and that among them all there are none of any value, save a few which celebrate the civil wars of Granada, — this I deny. The March of Bernardo del Carpio is hardly inferior to Chevy Chase; and the ballad of the Conde Alarcos, in simplicity and pathos, has hardly a peer in all English balladry, — it is superior to Edem o' Gordon.

But a truce to criticism. Already, methinks, I hear the voice of a drowsy and prosaic herald proclaiming, in the language of Don Quixote to the puppet-player, "Make an end, Master Peter, for it grows toward supper-time, and I have some symptoms of hunger upon me."

THE VILLAGE OF EL PARDILLO.

When the lawyer is swallowed up with business, and the statesman is preventing or contriving plots, then we sit on cowslip banks, hear the birds sing, and possess ourselves in as much quietness as these silent silver streams we now see glide so quietly by us.

                                                                    IZAAK WALTON.

IN that delicious season when the coy and capricious maidenhood of spring is swelling into the warmer, riper, and more voluptuous womanhood of summer, I left Madrid for the village of El Pardillo. I had already seen enough of the villages of the North of Spain to know that for the most part they have few charms to entice one from the city ; but I was curious to see the peasantry of the land in their native homes, — to see how far the shepherds of Castile resemble those who sigh and sing in the pastoral romances of Montemayor and Gaspar Gil Polo.

I love the city and its busy hum ; I love that glad excitement of the crowd which makes the pulse beat quick, the freedom from restraint, the absence of those curious eyes and idle tongues which persecute one in villages and provincial towns. I love the country, too, in its season ; and there is no scene over which my eye roves with more delight than the face of a summer landscape dimpled with soft sunny hollows, and smiling in all the freshness and luxuriance of June. There is no book in which I read sweeter lessons of virtue, or find the beauty of a quiet life more legibly recorded. My heart drinks in the tranquillity of the scene ; and I never hear the sweet warble of a bird from its native wood, without a silent wish that such a cheerful voice and peaceful shade were mine. There is a beautiful moral feeling connected with everything in rural life, which is not dreamed of in the philosophy of the city. The voice of the brook and the language of the winds and woods are no poetic fiction. What an impressive lesson is there in the opening bud of spring ! what an eloquent homily in the fall of the autumnal leaf ! How well does the song of a passing bird represent the glad but transitory days of youth ! and in the hollow tree and hooting owl what a melancholy image of the decay and imbecility of old age ! In the beautiful language of an English poet,

"Your voiceless lips, O flowers, are living preachers,
    Each cup a pulpit, every leaf a book,
Supplying to my fancy numerous teachers,
    From loneliest nook.

"'Neath cloistered boughs each floral bell that swingeth,
    And tolls its perfume on the passing air,
Makes Sabbath in the fields, and ever ringeth
    A call to prayer;

"Not to the domes where crumbling arch and column
    Attest the feebleness of mortal hand,
But to that fane most catholic and solemn
    Which God hath planned;

"To that cathedral, boundless as our wonder,
    Whose quenchless lamps the sun and moon supply, —
Its choir the winds and waves, its organ thunder,
    Its dome the sky.

"There, amid solitude and shade, I wander
    Through the green aisles, and, stretched upon the sod,
Awed by the silence, reverently ponder
    The ways of God."

But the traveller who journeys through the northern provinces of Spain will look in vain for the charms of rural scenery in the villages he passes. Instead of trim cottages, and gardens, and the grateful shade of trees, he will see a cluster of stone hovels roofed with red tiles, and basking in the hot sun, without a single tree to lend him shade or shelter ; and instead of green meadows and woodlands vocal with the song of birds, he will find bleak and rugged mountains, and vast extended plains, that stretch away beyond his ken.

It was my good fortune, however, to find, not many leagues from the metropolis, a village which could boast the shadow of a few trees. El Pardillo is situated on the southern slope of the Guadarrama Mountains, just where the last broken spurs of the sierra stretch forward into the vast table-land of New Castile. The village itself, like most other Castilian villages, is only a cluster of weather-stained and dilapidated houses, huddled together without beauty or regularity; but the scenery around it is picturesque, — a mingling of hill and dale, sprinkled with patches of cultivated land and clumps of forest-trees; and in the background the blue, vapory outline of the Guadarrama Mountains melting into the sky.

In this quiet place I sojourned for a season, accompanied by the publican Don Valentin and his fair daughter Florencia. We took up our abode in the cottage of a peasant named Lucas, an honest tiller of the soil, simple and good-natured; or, in the more emphatic language of Don Valentin, "*un hombre muy infeliz, y sin malicia ninguna.*" Not so his wife Matina; she was a Tartar, and so meddlesome withal, that poor Lucas skulked doggedly about his own premises, with his head down and his tail between his legs.

In this little village my occupations were few and simple. My morning's walk was to the Cross of Espalmado, a large wooden crucifix in the fields; the day was passed with books, or with any idle companion I was lucky enough to catch by the button, and bribe with a cigar into a long story, or a little village gossip; and I whiled away the evening in peeping round among the cottagers, studying the beautiful landscape that spread before me, and watching the occasional gathering of a storm about the blue peaks of the Guadarrama Mountains. My favorite haunt was a secluded spot in a little woodland valley, through which a crystal brook ran brawling along its pebbly channel. There, stretched in the shadow of a tree, I often passed the hours of noontide heat, now reading the magic numbers of Garcilaso, and anon listening to the song of the nightingale overhead; or watching the toil of a patient ant, as he rolled his stone, like Sisyphus, up hill, or the flight of a bee darting from flower to flower, and "hiding his murmurs in the rose."

Blame me not, thou studious moralist, — blame me not unheard for this idle dreaming; such moments are not wholly thrown away. In the language of Goethe, "I lie down in the grass near a falling brook, and close to the earth a thousand varieties of grasses become perceptible. When I listen to the hum of the little world between the stubble, and see the countless indescribable forms of insects, I feel the presence of the Almighty who has created us, — the breath of the All-benevolent who supports us in perpetual enjoyment."

The village church, too, was a spot around which I occasionally lingered of an evening, when in pensive or melancholy mood. And here, gentle reader, thy imagination will straightway conjure up a scene of ideal beauty, — a village church with decent white-washed walls, and modest spire just peeping forth from a clump of trees! No; I will not deceive thee; — the church of El Pardillo resembles not this picture of thy well-tutored fancy. It is a gloomy little edifice, standing upon the outskirts of the village, and built of dark and unhewn stone, with a spire like a sugar-loaf. There is no grass-plot in front, but a little esplanade beaten hard by the footsteps of the church-going peasantry. The tombstone of one of the patriarchs of the village serves as a doorstep, and a single solitary tree throws its friendly shade upon the portals of the little sanctuary.

One evening, as I loitered around this spot, the sound of an organ and the chant of youthful voices from within struck my ear; the church door was ajar, and I entered. There stood the priest, surrounded by a group of children, who were singing a hymn to the Virgin: —

> "Ave, Regina cœlorum,
> Ave, Domina angelorum."

There is something exceedingly thrilling in the voices of children singing. Though their music be unskilful, yet it finds its way to the heart with wonderful celerity. Voices of cherubs are they, for they breathe of paradise; clear, liquid tones, that flow from pure lips and innocent hearts, like the sweetest notes of a flute, or the falling of water from a fountain! When the chant was finished, the priest opened a little book which he held in his hand and began, with a voice as solemn as a funeral bell, to question this class of roguish catechumens, whom he was initiating into the mysterious doctrines of the mother church. Some of the questions and answers were so curious that I cannot refrain from repeating them here; and should any one doubt their authenticity, he will find them in the Spanish catechisms.

"In what consists the mystery of the Holy Trinity?"

"In one God, who is three persons; and three persons, who are but one God."

"But tell me, — three human persons, are they not three men?"

"Yes, father."

"Then why are not three divine persons three Gods?"

"Because three human persons have three human natures; but the three divine persons have only one divine nature."

"Can you explain this by an example?"

"Yes, father; so a tree which has three branches is still but one tree, since all the three branches spring from one trunk, so the three divine persons are but one God, because they all have the same divine nature."

"Where were these three divine persons before the heavens and the earth were created?"

"In themselves."

"Which of them was made man?"

"The Son."

"And after the Son was made man, was he still God?"

"Yes, father; for in becoming man he did not cease to be God, any more than a man when he becomes a monk ceases to be a man."

"How was the Son of God made flesh?"

"He was born of the most holy Virgin Mary."

"And can we still call her a virgin?"

"Yes, father; for as a ray of the sun may pass through a pane of glass, and the glass remain unbroken, so the Virgin Mary, after the birth of her son, was a pure and holy virgin as before." [1]

"Who died to save and redeem us?"

"The Son of God: as man, and not as God."

"How could he suffer and die as man only, being both God and man, and yet but one person?"

"As in a heated bar of iron upon which water is thrown, the heat only is affected and not the iron, so the Son of God suffered in his human nature and not in his divine."

"And when the spirit was separated from his most precious body, whither did the spirit go?"

"To limbo, to glorify the souls of the holy fathers."

"And the body?"

"It was carried to the grave."

"Did the divinity remain united with the spirit or with the body?"

"With both. As a soldier, when he unsheathes his sword, remains united both with the sword and the sheath, though these are separated from each other, so did the divinity remain united both with the spirit and the body of Christ, though the spirit was separated and removed from the body."

I did not quarrel with the priest for having been born and educated in a different faith from mine; but as I left the church and sauntered slowly homeward, I could not help asking myself, in a whisper, "Why perplex the spirit of a child with these metaphysical subtilties, these dark, mysterious speculations, which man in all his pride of intellect cannot fathom or explain?"

I must not forget, in this place, to make honorable mention of the little great men of El Pardillo. And first in order comes the priest. He was a short, portly man, serious in manner, and of grave and reverend presence; though at the same time there was a dash of the jolly-fat-friar about him; and on hearing a good joke or a sly innuendo, a smile would gleam in his eye, and play over his round face, like the light of a glowworm. His housekeeper was a brisk, smiling little woman, on the shady side of thirty, and a cousin of his to boot. Whenever she was mentioned, Don Valentin looked wise, as if this cousinship were apocryphal; but he said nothing, — not he;

---

[1] This illustration was also made use of during the dark ages. Pierre de Corbiac, a Troubadour of the thirteenth century, thus introduces it in a poem entitled "Prayer to the Virgin":—

" Domna, verges pur' e fina
Ans que fos l' enfantamens,

Et apres tot eissamens,
De vos trais sa carn humana
Jhesu-Christ nostre salvaire;
Si com ses trencamens faire
Intra'l bel rais quan solelha
Per la fenestra veirina."

what right had he to be peeping into other people's business, when he had only one eye to look after his own withal? Next in rank to the dominie was the alcalde, justice of the peace and quorum; a most potent, grave, and reverend personage, with a long beak of a nose, and a pouch under his chin, like a pelican. He was a man of few words, but great in authority; and his importance was vastly increased in the village by a pair of double-barrelled spectacles, so contrived, that, when bent over his desk and deeply buried in his musty papers, he could look up and see what was going on around him without moving his head, whereby he got the reputation of seeing twice as much as other people. There was the village surgeon, too, a tall man with a varnished hat and a starved dog; he had studied at the University of Salamanca, and was pompous and pedantic, ever and anon quoting some threadbare maxim from the Greek philosophers, and embellishing it with a commentary of his own. Then there was the gray-headed sacristan, who rang the church-bell, played on the organ, and was learned in tombstone lore; a politician, who talked me to death about taxes, liberty, and the days of the constitution; and a notary public, a poor man with a large family, who would make a paper cigar last half an hour, and who kept up his respectability in the village by keeping a horse.

Beneath the protecting shade of these great men full many an inhabitant of El Pardillo was born and buried. The village continued to flourish, a quiet, happy place, though all unknown to fame. The inhabitants were orderly and industrious, went regularly to mass and confession, kept every saint's day in the calendar, and devoutly hung **Judas** once a year in effigy. On Sundays and all other holidays, when mass was over, the time was devoted to sports and recreation; and the day passed off in social visiting, and athletic exercises, such as running, leaping, wrestling, pitching quoits, and heaving the bar. When evening came, the merry sound of the guitar summoned to the dance; then every nook and alley poured forth its youthful company, — light of heart and heel, and decked out in all the holiday finery of flowers, and ribbons, and crimson sashes.

137

A group gathered before the cottage door; the signal was given, and away whirled the merry dancers to the wild music of voice and guitar, and the measured beat of castanet and tambourine.

I love these rural dances, — from my heart I love them. This world, at best, is so full of care and sorrow, — the life of a poor man is so stained with the sweat of his brow, — there is so much toil, and struggling, and anguish, and disappointment here below, that I gaze with delight on a scene where all these are laid aside and forgotten, and the heart of the toil-worn peasant seems to throw off its load, and to leap to the sound of music, when merrily,

> " Beneath soft eve's consenting star,
> Fandango twirls his jocund castanet."

Not many miles from the village of El Pardillo stands the ruined castle of Villafranca, an ancient stronghold of the Moors of the fifteenth century. It is built upon the summit of a hill, of easy ascent upon one side, but precipitous and inaccessible on the other. The front presents a large square tower, constituting the main part of the castle; on one side of which an arched gateway leads to a spacious court-yard within, surrounded by battlements. The corner towers are circular, with beetling turrets; and here and there, apart from the main body of the castle, stand several circular basements, whose towers have fallen and mouldered into dust. From the balcony in the square tower, the eye embraces the level landscape for leagues and leagues around; and beneath, in the depth of the valley, lies a beautiful grove, alive with the song of the nightingale. The whole castle is in ruin, and occupied only as a hunting-lodge, being inhabited by a solitary tenant, who has charge of the adjacent domain.

One holiday, when mass was said and the whole village was let loose to play, we made a pilgrimage to the ruins of this old Moorish alcazar. Our cavalcade was as motley as that of old, — the pilgrims " that toward Canterbury wolden ride;" for we had the priest, and the doctor of physic, and the man of laws, and a wife of Bath, and many more whom I must leave unsung. Merrily flew the hours and fast;

and sitting after dinner in the gloomy hall of that old castle, many a tale was told, and many a legend and tradition of the past conjured up to satisfy the curiosity of the present.

Most of these tales were about the Moors who built the castle, and the treasures they had buried beneath it. Then the priest told the story of a lawyer who sold himself to the devil for a pot of money, and was burnt by the Holy Inquisition therefor. In his confession, he told how he had learned from a Jew the secret of raising the devil; how he went to the castle at midnight with a book which the Jew gave him, and, to make the charm sure, carried with him a loadstone, six nails from the coffin of a child of three years, six tapers of rosewax, made by a child of four years, the skin and blood of a young kid, an iron fork, with which the kid had been killed, a few hazel-rods, a flask of high-proof brandy, and some lignum-vitæ charcoal to make a fire. When he read in the book, the devil appeared in the shape of a man dressed in flesh-colored clothes, with long nails, and large fiery eyes, and he signed an agreement with him written in blood, promising never to go to mass, and to give him his soul at the end of eight years; in return for this, he was to have a million of dollars in good money, which the devil was to bring to him the next night; but when the next night came, and the lawyer had conjured from his book, instead of the devil, there appeared — who do you think? — the alcalde with half the village at his heels, and the poor lawyer was handed over to the Inquisition, and burnt for dealing in the black art.

I intended to repeat here some of the many tales that were told; but, upon reflection, they seem too frivolous, and must therefore give place to a more serious theme.

THE DEVOTIONAL POETRY OF SPAIN.

Heaven's dove, when highest he flies,
Flies with thy heavenly wings.
                              CRASHAW.

THERE is hardly a chapter in literary history more strongly marked with the peculiarities of national character than that which contains the moral and devotional poetry of Spain. It would naturally be expected that in this department of literature all the fervency and depth of national feeling would be exhibited. But still, as the spirit of morality and devotion is the same, wherever it exists, — as the enthusiasm of virtue and religion is everywhere essentially the same feeling, though modified in its degree and in its action by a variety of physical causes and local circumstances, — and as the subject of the didactic verse and the spiritual canticle cannot be materially changed by the change of nation and climate, it might at the first glance seem quite as natural to expect that the moral and devotional poetry of Christian countries would never be very strongly marked with national peculiarities. In other words, we should expect it to correspond to the warmth or coldness of national feeling, for it is the external and visible expression of this feeling; but not to the distinction of national character, because, its nature and object being everywhere the same, these distinctions become swallowed up in one universal Christian character.

In moral poetry this is doubtless true. The great principles of Christian morality being eternal and invariable, the verse which embodies and represents them must, from this very circumstance, be the same in its spirit through all Christian lands. The same, however, is not necessarily true of devotional or religious poetry. There, the language of poetry is something more than the visible image of a devotional spirit. It is also an expression of religious faith; shadowing forth, with greater or less distinctness, its various creeds and doctrines. As these are different in different nations, the spirit that breathes in religious song, and the letter that gives utterance to the doctrine of faith, will not be universally the same. Thus, Catholic nations sing the praises of the Virgin Mary in language in which nations of the Protestant faith do not unite ; and among Protestants themselves, the difference of interpretations, and the consequent belief or disbelief of certain doctrines, give a various spirit and expression to religious poetry. And yet, in all, the devotional feeling, the heavenward volition, is the same.

As far, then, as peculiarities of religious faith exercise an influence upon intellectual habits, and thus become a part of national character, so far will the devotional or religious poetry of a country exhibit the characteristic peculiarities resulting from this influence of faith, and its assimilation with the national mind. Now Spain is by preëminence the Catholic land of Christendom. Most of her historic recollections are more or less intimately associated with the triumphs of the Christian faith ; and many of her warriors — of her best and bravest — were martyrs in the holy cause, perishing in that war of centuries which was carried on within her own territories between the crescent of Mahomet and the cross of Christ. Indeed, the whole tissue of her history is interwoven with miraculous traditions. The intervention of her patron saint has saved her honor in more than one dangerous pass ; and the war-shout of " *Santiago, y cierra España !* " has worked like a charm upon the wavering spirit of the soldier. A reliance on the guardian ministry of the saints pervades the whole people, and devotional offerings for signal preservation in times of danger and distress cover the consecrated walls of churches. An enthusiasm of religious feeling, and of external ritual observances, prevails throughout the land. But more particularly is the name of the Virgin honored and adored. *Ave Maria* is the salutation of peace at the friendly threshold, and the God-speed to the wayfarer. It is the evening orison, when the toils of day are done ; and at midnight it echoes along the solitary streets in the voice of the watchman's cry.

These and similar peculiarities of religious faith are breathing and moving through a large portion of the devotional poetry of Spain. It is not only instinct with religious feeling, but incorporated with " the substance of things not seen." Not only are the poet's lips touched with a coal from the altar, but his spirit is folded in the cloud of incense that rises before the shrines of the Virgin Mother, and the glorious company of the saints and martyrs. His soul is not wholly swallowed up in the contemplation of the sublime attributes of the Eternal Mind ; but, with its lamp trimmed and burning, it goeth out to meet the bridegroom, as if he were coming in a bodily presence.

The history of the devotional poetry of Spain commences with the legendary lore of Maestro Gonzalo de Berceo, a secular priest, whose life was passed in the cloisters of a Benedictine convent, and amid the shadows of the thirteenth century. The name of Berceo stands foremost on the catalogue of Spanish poets, for the author of the poem of the Cid is unknown. The old patriarch of Spanish poetry has left a monument of his existence in upwards of thirteen thousand alexandrines celebrating the lives and miracles of saints and the Virgin, as he found them written in the Latin chronicles and dusty legends of his monastery. In embodying these in rude verse in *roman paladino*, or the old Spanish romance tongue, intelligible to the common people, Fray Gonzalo seems to have passed his life. His writings are just such as we should expect from the pen of a monk of the thirteenth century. They are more ghostly than poetical ; and throughout, unction holds the place of inspiration. Accordingly, they illustrate very fully the preceding remarks ; and the more so, inasmuch as they are written with the most ample and childish credulity, and the utmost singleness of faith touching the events and miracles described.

The following extract is taken from one of Berceo's poems, entitled " Vida de San Milan." It is a description of the miraculous appearance of Santiago and San Millan, mounted on snow-white steeds, and fighting for the cause of Christendom, at the battle of Simancas in the *Campo de Toro.*

" And when the kings were in the field, — their squadrons
     in array, —
   With lance in rest they onward pressed to mingle in the
      fray;
   But soon upon the Christians fell a terror of their
      foes, —
   These were a numerous army, — a little handful those.

" And while the Christian people stood in this uncertainty,
    Upward to heaven they turned their eyes, and fixed their
        thoughts on high;
    And there two figures they beheld, all beautiful and
        bright,
    Even than the pure new-fallen snow their garments were
        more white.

" They rode upon two horses more white than crystal
        sheen,
    And arms they bore such as before no mortal man had
        seen;
    The one, he held a crosier, — a pontiff's mitre wore;
    The other held a crucifix, — such man ne'er saw before.

" Their faces were angelical, celestial forms had they, —
    And downward through the fields of air they urged
        their rapid way;
    They looked upon the Moorish host with fierce and an-
        gry look,
    And in their hands, with dire portent, their naked sa-
        bres shook.

" The Christian host, beholding this, straightway take
        heart again;
    They fall upon their bended knees, all resting on the
        plain,
    And each one with his clenched fist to smite his breast
        begins,
    And promises to God on high he will forsake his sins.

" And when the heavenly knights drew near unto the bat-
        tle-ground,
    They dashed among the Moors and dealt unerring blows
        around;
    Such deadly havoc there they made the foremost ranks
        along,
    A panic terror spread unto the hindmost of the throng.

" Together with these two good knights, the champions of
        the sky,
    The Christians rallied and began to smite full sore and
        high;
    The Moors raised up their voices and by the Koran
        swore
    That in their lives such deadly fray they ne'er had seen
        before.

" Down went the misbelievers, — fast sped the bloody
        fight, —
    Some ghastly and dismembered lay, and some half dead
        with fright:
    Full sorely they repented that to the field they came,
    For they saw that from the battle they should retreat
        with shame.

" Another thing befell them, — they dreamed not of such
        woes, —
    The very arrows that the Moors shot from their twang-
        ing bows

Turned back against them in their flight and wounded
        them full sore,
And every blow they dealt the foe was paid in drops of
        gore.

.   .   .   .

" Now he that bore the crosier, and the papal crown had
        on,
    Was the glorified Apostle, the brother of Saint John ;
    And he that held the crucifix, and wore the monkish
        hood,
    Was the holy San Millan of Cogolla's neighborhood."

Berceo's longest poem is entitled *Miraclos de Nuestra Señora*, " Miracles of Our Lady." It consists of nearly four thousand lines, and contains the description of twenty-five miracles. It is a complete homily on the homage and devotion due to the glorious Virgin, *Madre de Jhu Xto*, Mother of Jesus Christ ; but it is written in a low and vulgar style, strikingly at variance with the elevated character of the subject. Thus, in the twentieth miracle, we have the account of a monk who became intoxicated in a wine-cellar. Having lain on the floor till the vesper-bell aroused him, he staggered off towards the church in most melancholy plight. The Evil One besets him on the way, assuming the various shapes of a bull, a dog, and a lion ; but from all these perils he is miraculously saved by the timely intervention of the Virgin, who finding him still too much intoxicated to make his way to bed, kindly takes him by the hand, leads him to his pallet, covers him with a blanket and a counterpane, smooths his pillow, and, after making the sign of the cross over him, tells him to rest quietly, for sleep will do him good.

To a certain class of minds there may be something interesting and even affecting in descriptions which represent the spirit of a departed saint as thus assuming a corporeal shape, in order to assist and console human nature even in its baser infirmities ; but it ought also to be considered how much such descriptions tend to strip religion of its peculiar sanctity, to bring it down from its heavenly abode, not merely to dwell among men, but, like an imprisoned culprit, to be chained to the derelict of principle, manacled with the base desire and earthly passion, and forced to do the menial offices of a slave. In descriptions of this kind, as in the representations of our Saviour and of sainted spirits in human shape, execution must of necessity fall far short of the conception. The handiwork cannot equal the glorious archetype, which is visible only to the mental eye. Painting and sculpture are not adequate to the task of embodying in a permanent shape the glorious visions, the radiant forms, the glimpses of heaven, which fill the imagination when purified and exalted by devotion. The hand of man unconsciously inscribes upon all his works the sentence of imperfection, which the finger of the invisible hand wrote upon the wall of the Assyrian monarch. From this it would seem to be not only a natural but a necessary conclusion, that all the descriptions of poetry which borrow anything, either directly or indirectly, from these bodily and imperfect representations, must partake of their imperfection, and assume a more earthly and material character than these which come glowing and burning from the more spiritualized perceptions of the internal sense.

It is very far from my intention to utter any sweeping denunciation against the divine arts of painting and sculpture, as employed in the exhibition of Scriptural scenes and personages. These I esteem meet ornaments for the house of God; though, as I have already said, their execution cannot equal the high conceptions of an ardent imagination, yet, whenever the hand of a master is visible, — when the marble almost moves before you, and the painting starts into life from the canvas, — the effect upon an enlightened mind will generally, if not universally, be to quicken its sensibilities and excite to more ardent devotion, by carrying the thoughts beyond the representations of bodily suffering, to the contemplation of the intenser mental agony, — the moral sublimity exhibited by the martyr. The impressions produced, however, will not be the same in all minds; they will necessarily vary according to the prevailing temper and complexion of the mind which receives them. As there is no sound where there is no ear to receive the impulses and vibrations of the air, so is there no moral impression, — no voice of instruction from all the works of nature, and all the imitations of art, — unless there be within the soul

itself a capacity for hearing the voice and receiving the moral impulse. The cause exists eternally and universally; but the effect is produced only when and where the cause has room to act, and just in proportion as it has room to act. Hence the various moral impressions, and the several degrees of the same moral impression, which an object may produce in different minds. These impressions will vary in kind and in degree according to the acuteness and the cultivation of the internal moral sense. And thus the representations spoken of above might exercise a very favorable influence upon an enlightened and well-regulated mind, and at the same time a very unfavorable influence upon an unenlightened and superstitious one. And the reason is obvious. An enlightened mind beholds all things in their just proportions, and receives from them the true impressions they are calculated to convey. It is not hoodwinked, — it is not shut up in a gloomy prison, till it thinks the walls of its own dungeon the limits of the universe, and the reach of its own chain the outer verge of all intelligence; but it walks abroad; the sunshine and the air pour in to enlighten and expand it; the various works of nature are its ministering angels; the glad recipient of light and wisdom, it develops new powers and acquires increased capacities, and thus, rendering itself less subject to error, assumes a nearer similitude to the Eternal Mind. But not so the dark and superstitious mind. It is filled with its own antique and mouldy furniture, — the moth-eaten tome, the gloomy tapestry, the dusty curtain. The straggling sunbeam from without streams through the stained window, and as it enters assumes the colors of the painted glass; while the half-extinguished fire within now smouldering in its ashes, and now shooting forth a quivering flame, casts fantastic shadows through the chambers of the soul. Within the spirit sits, lost in its own abstractions. The voice of nature from without is hardly audible; her beauties are unseen, or seen only in shadowy forms, through a colored medium, and with a strained and distorted vision. The invigorating air does not enter that mysterious chamber; it visits not that lonely inmate, who, breathing only a close, exhausted atmosphere, exhibits in the languid frame and feverish pulse the marks of lingering, incurable disease. The picture is not too strongly sketched; such is the contrast between the free and the superstitious mind. Upon the latter, which has little power over its ideas, — to generalize them, to place them in their proper light and position, to reason upon, to discriminate, to judge them in detail, and thus to arrive at just conclusions; but, on the contrary, receives every crude and inadequate impression as it first presents itself, and treasures it up as an ultimate fact, — upon such a mind, representations of Scripture-scenes, like those mentioned above, exercise an unfavorable influence. Such a mind cannot rightly estimate, it cannot feel, the work of a master; and a miserable painting, or a still more miserable caricature carved in wood, will serve

only the more to drag the spirit down to earth. Thus, in the unenlightened mind, these representations have a tendency to sensualize and desecrate the character of holy things. Being brought constantly before the eye, and represented in a real and palpable form to the external senses, they lose, by being made too familiar, that peculiar sanctity with which the mind naturally invests the unearthly and invisible.

It is curious to observe the influence of the circumstances just referred to upon the devotional poetry of Spain.[1] Sometimes it exhibits itself directly and fully, sometimes indirectly and incidentally, but always with sufficient clearness to indicate its origin. Sometimes it destroys the beauty of a poem by a miserable conceit; at other times it gives it the character of a beautiful allegory.[2]

---

[1] The following beautiful Latin hymn, written by Francisco Xavier, the friend and companion of Loyola, and from his zeal in the Eastern missions surnamed the Apostle of the Indies, would hardly have originated in any mind but that of one familiar with the representations of which I have spoken above.

> " O Deus! ego amo te:
> Nec amo te, ut salves me,
> Aut quia non amantes te
> Æterno punis igne.

> " Tu, tu, mi Jesu, totum me
> Amplexus es in cruce.
> Tulisti clavos, lanceam,
> Multamque ignominiam:
> Innumeros dolores,
> Sudores et angores,
> Ac mortem: et hæc propter me
> Ac pro me peccatore.

> " Cur igitur non amem te,
> O Jesu amantissime?
> Non ut in cœlo salves me,
> Aut ne æternum damnes me,
> Nec præmii ullius spe:
> Sed sicut tu amasti me,
> Sic amo et amabo te:
> Solum quia rex meus es,
> Et solum quia Deus es.
>   Amen."

" O God! my spirit loves but thee:
Not that in heaven its home may be,
Nor that the souls which love not thee
Shall groan in fire eternally.

> " But thou on the accursed tree
> In mercy hast embraced me.
> For me the cruel nails, the spear,
> The ignominious scoff, didst bear,
> Countless, unutterable woes, —
> The bloody sweat, — death's pangs and throes, —
> These thou didst bear, all these for me,
> A sinner and estranged from thee.

> " And wherefore no affection show,
> Jesus, to thee that lov'st me so?
> Not that in heaven my home may be,
> Not lest I die eternally, —
> Nor from the hopes of joys above me:
> But even as thou thyself didst love me,
> So love I, and will ever love thee:
> Solely because my King art thou,
> My God forevermore as now.
>   Amen."

[2] I recollect but few instances of this kind of figurative poetry in our language. There is, however, one of most exquisite beauty and pathos, far surpassing anything I have seen of the kind in Spanish. It is a passage from Cowper.

> " I was a stricken deer, that left the herd
> Long since: with many an arrow deep infixt
> My panting side was charged, when I withdrew
> To seek a tranquil death in distant shades.
> There was I found by one who had himself
> Been hurt by archers; in his side he bore,
> And in his hands and feet, the cruel scars.
> With gentle force soliciting the darts,
> He drew them forth, and healed, and bade me live."

The following sonnets will serve as illustrations. They are from the hand of the wonderful Lope de Vega: —

"Shepherd ! that with thine amorous sylvan song
Hast broken the slumber that encompassed me,
That madest thy crook from the accursed tree
On which thy powerful arms were stretched so long, —
Lead me to mercy's ever-flowing fountains,
For thou my shepherd, guard, and guide shalt be,
I will obey thy voice, and wait to see
Thy feet all beautiful upon the mountains.
Hear, Shepherd ! — thou that for thy flock art dying,
Oh, wash away these scarlet sins, for thou
Rejoicest at the contrite sinner's vow.
Oh, wait ! — to thee my weary soul is crying, —
Wait for me ! — yet why ask it when I see,
With feet nailed to the cross, thou art waiting still for
    me ?"

"Lord, what am I, that with unceasing care
Thou didst seek after me, — that thou didst wait,
Wet with unhealthy dews before my gate,
And pass the gloomy nights of winter there ?
O strange delusion ! — that I did not greet
Thy blessed approach ! and oh, to Heaven how lost,
If my ingratitude's unkindly frost
Hast chilled the bleeding wounds upon thy feet !
How oft my guardian angel gently cried,
'Soul, from thy casement look without and see
How he persists to knock and wait for thee !'
And oh, how often to that voice of sorrow,
'To-morrow we will open !' I replied;
And when the morrow came, I answered still, 'To-
    morrow !'"

The most remarkable portion of the devotional poetry of the Spaniards is to be found in their sacred dramas, their *Vidas de Santos* and *Autos Sacramentales*. These had their origin in the Mysteries and Moralities of the dark ages, and are indeed monstrous creations of the imagination. The *Vidas de Santos*, or Lives of Saints, are representations of their miracles, and of the wonderful traditions concerning them. The *Autos Sacramentales* have particular reference to the Eucharist and the ceremonies of the *Corpus Christi*. In these theatrical pieces are introduced upon the stage, not only angels and saints, but God, the Saviour, and the Virgin Mary ; and, in strange juxtaposition with these, devils, peasants, and kings ; in fine, they contain the strangest medley of characters, real and allegorical, which the imagination can conceive. As if this were

not enough, in the midst of what was intended as a solemn, religious celebration, scenes of low buffoonery are often introduced.

The most remarkable of the sacred dramas which I have read is *La Devocion de la Cruz,* " The Devotion of the Cross," by Calderon ; and it will serve as a specimen of that class of writing. The piece commences with a dialogue between Lisardo, the son of Curcio, a decayed nobleman, and Eusebio, the hero of the play and lover of Julia, Lisardo's sister. Though the father's extravagance has wasted his estates, Lisardo is deeply offended that Eusebio should aspire to an alliance with the family, and draws him into a secluded place in order to settle their dispute with the sword. Here the scene opens, and, in the course of the dialogue which precedes the combat, Eusebio relates that he was born at the foot of a cross, which stood in a rugged and desert part of those mountains ; that the virtue of this cross preserved him from the wild beasts ; that, being found by a peasant three days after his birth, he was carried to a neighboring village, and there received the name of Eusebio of the Cross ; that, being thrown by his nurse into a well, he was heard to laugh, and was found floating upon the top of the water, with his hands placed upon his mouth in the form of a cross ; that the house in which he dwelt being consumed by fire, he escaped unharmed amid the flames, and it was found to be Corpus Christi day ; and, in fine, after relating many other similar miracles, worked by the power of the cross, at whose foot he was born, he says that he bears its image miraculously stamped upon his breast. After this they fight, and Lisardo falls mortally wounded. In the next scene, Eusebio has an interview with Julia, at her father's house ; they are interrupted, and Eusebio conceals himself ; Curcio enters, and informs Julia that he has determined to send her that day to a convent, that she may take the veil, "*para ser de Cristo esposa.*" While they are conversing, the dead body of Lisardo is brought in by peasants, and Eusebio is declared to be the murderer. The scene closes by the escape of Eusebio. The second act, or *jornada*, discovers Eusebio as the leader of a band of robbers. They fire upon a traveller, who proves to be a priest, named Alberto, and who is seeking a spot in those solitudes wherein to establish a hermitage. The shot is prevented from taking effect by a book which the pious old man carries in his bosom, and which he says is a "treatise on the true origin of the divine and heavenly tree, on which, dying with courage and fortitude, Christ triumphed over death; in fine, the book is called the 'Miracles of the Cross.'" They suffer the priest to depart unharmed, who in consequence promises Eusebio that he shall not die without confession, but that wherever he may be, if he but call upon his name, he will hasten to absolve him. In the mean time Julia retires to a convent, and Curcio goes with an armed force in pursuit of Eusebio, who has resolved to gain admittance to Julia's convent. He scales the walls of the convent by night, and silently gropes his way along the corridor. Julia is discovered sleeping in her cell, with a taper beside her. He is, however, deterred from executing his malicious designs, by discovering upon her breast the form of a cross, similar to that which he bears upon his own, and "Heaven would not suffer him, though so great an offender, to lose his respect for the cross." To be brief, he leaps from the convent-walls and escapes to the mountains. Julia, counting her honor lost, having offended God, "*como á Dios, y como á esposa,*" pursues him, — descends the ladder from the convent-wall, and, when she seeks to return to her cell, finds the ladder has been removed. In her despair, she accuses Heaven of having withdrawn its clemency, and vows to perform such deeds of wickedness as shall terrify both heaven and hell.

The third *jornada* transports the scene back to the mountains. Julia, disguised in man's apparel, with her face concealed, is brought to Eusebio by a party of the banditti. She challenges him to single combat; and he accepts the challenge, on condition that his antagonist shall declare who he is. Julia discovers herself; and relates several horrid murders she has committed since leaving the convent. Their interview is here interrupted by the entrance of banditti, who inform Eusebio that Curcio, with an armed force, from all the

neighboring villages, is approaching. The attack commences. Eusebio and Curcio meet, but a secret and mysterious sympathy prevents them from fighting; and a great number of peasants, coming in at this moment, rush upon Eusebio in a body, and he is thrown down a precipice. There Curcio discovers him, expiring with his numerous wounds. The *dénouement* of the piece commences. Curcio, moved by compassion, examines a wound in Eusebio's breast, discovers the mark of the cross, and thereby recognizes him to be his son. Eusebio expires, calling on the name of Alberto, who shortly after enters, as if lost in those mountains. A voice from the dead body of Eusebio calls his name. I shall here transcribe a part of the scene.

ALBERTO.

Homeward now from Rome returning,
In the deep and silent pauses
Of the night, upon this mountain
I again have lost my way!
This must be the very region
Where my life Eusebio gave me,
And I fear from his marauders
Danger threatens me to-day!

EUSEBIO.

Ho! Alberto!

ALBERTO.

　　　　What breath is it
Of a voice so full of terror,
That aloud my name repeating
Sounded then upon mine ear?

EUSEBIO.

Ho! Alberto!

ALBERTO.

　　　　It pronounces
Yet again my name; methought it
Came in this direction. Let me
Go still nearer.

GIL.

　　　　Santo Dios!
'T is Eusebio, and my terror
Of all terrors is the greatest!

EUSEBIO.

Ho! Alberto!

ALBERTO.

　　　　Nearer sounds it!
O thou voice that ridest swift

On the wind my name repeating,
Who art thou?

EUSEBIO.

Eusebio am I.
Come, Alberto, hither hasten,
Hither, where I buried lie;
Come, and lift aside these branches;
Do not fear.

ALBERTO.

No fear have I.

GIL.

I have!

ALBERTO (*uncovering Eusebio*).
Now thou art uncovered,
Tell me, in the name of God,
What thou wishest.

EUSEBIO.

In his name
'T was my Faith, Alberto, called thee,
So that ere my life be ended
Thou shouldst hear me in confession.
Long ago I should have died,
For remained untenanted
By the spirit this dead body;
But the mighty blow of death
Only robbed it of its motion,
Did not sever it asunder.
He rises.
Come where I may make confession
Of my sins, Alberto, for they
More are than the sands of ocean,
Or the atoms of the sun!
So much doth avail with Heaven
The Devotion of the Cross!

Eusebio then retires to confess himself to Alberto; and Curcio afterward relates, that, when the venerable saint had given him absolution, his body again fell dead at his feet. Julia discovers herself, overwhelmed with the thoughts of her passion for Eusebio and her other crimes, and as Curcio, in a transport of indignation, endeavors to kill her, she seizes a cross which stands over Eusebio's grave, and with it ascends to heaven, while Alberto shouts, "*Gran milagro!*" and the curtain falls.

Thus far I have spoken of the devotional poetry of Spain as modified by the peculiarities of religious faith and practice. Considered apart from the dogmas of a creed, and as the expression of those pure and elevated feelings

of religion which are not the prerogative of any one sect or denomination, but the common privilege of all, it possesses strong claims to our admiration and praise. I know of nothing in any modern tongue so beautiful as some of its finest passages. The thought springs heavenward from the soul, — the language comes burning from the lip. The imagination of the poet seems spiritualized; with nothing of earth, and all of heaven, — a heaven like that of his own native clime, without a cloud, or a vapor of earth, to obscure its brightness. His voice, speaking the harmonious accents of that noble tongue, seems to flow from the lips of an angel, — melodious to the ear and to the internal sense, — breathing those

"Effectual whispers, whose still voice
The soul itself more feels than hears."

The following sonnets of Francisco de Aldana, a writer remarkable for the beauty of his conceptions and the harmony of his verse, are illustrations of this remark. In what glowing language he describes the aspirations of the soul for its paternal heaven, its celestial home! how beautifully he portrays in a few lines the strong desire, the ardent longing, of the exiled and imprisoned spirit to wing its flight away and be at rest! The strain bears our thoughts upward with it; it transports us to the heavenly country; it whispers to the soul, — Higher, immortal spirit! higher!

"Clear fount of light! my native land on high,
Bright with a glory that shall never fade!
Mansion of truth! without a veil or shade,
Thy holy quiet meets the spirit's eye.
There dwells the soul in its ethereal essence,
Gasping no longer for life's feeble breath;
But, sentinelled in heaven, its glorious presence
With pitying eye beholds, yet fears not death.
Beloved country! banished from thy shore,
A stranger in this prison-house of clay,
The exiled spirit weeps and sighs for thee!
Heavenward the bright perfections I adore
Direct, and the sure promise cheers the way,
That whither love aspires, there shall my dwelling be."

"O Lord! that seest from yon starry height
Centred in one the future and the past,
Fashioned in thine own image, see how fast
The world obscures in me what once was bright!
Eternal Sun! the warmth which thou hast given
To cheer life's flowery April fast decays;

> Yet in the hoary winter of my days,
> Forever green shall be my trust in Heaven.
> Celestial King! Oh, let thy presence pass
> Before my spirit, and an image fair
> Shall meet that look of mercy from on high,
> As the reflected image in a glass
> Doth meet the look of him who seeks it there,
> And owes its being to the gazer's eye."

The prevailing characteristics of Spanish devotional poetry are warmth of imagination, and depth and sincerity of feeling. The conception is always striking and original, and, when not degraded by dogmas, and the poor, puerile conceits arising from them, beautiful and sublime. This results from the frame and temperament of the mind, and is a general characteristic of the Spanish poets, not only in this department of song, but in all others. The very ardor of imagination which, exercised upon minor themes, leads them into extravagance and hyperbole, when left to act in a higher and wider sphere conducts them nearer and nearer to perfection. When imagination spreads its wings in the bright regions of devotional song, — in the pure empyrean, — judgment should direct its course, but there is no danger of its soaring too high. The heavenly land still lies beyond its utmost flight. There are heights it cannot reach; there are fields of air which tire its wing; there is a splendor which dazzles its vision; — for there is a glory " which eye hath not seen, nor ear heard, nor hath it entered into the heart of man to conceive."

But perhaps the greatest charm of the devotional poets of Spain is their sincerity. Most of them were ecclesiastics, — men who had in sober truth renounced the realities of this life for the hopes and promises of another. We are not to suppose that all who take holy orders are saints; but we should be still farther from believing that all are hypocrites. It would be even more absurd to suppose that none are sincere in their professions than that all are. Besides, with whatever feelings a man may enter the monastic life, there is something in its discipline and privations which has a tendency to wean the mind from earth, and to fix it upon heaven. Doubtless many have seemingly renounced the world from motives of worldly aggrandizement; and others have re-

nounced it because it has renounced them. The former have carried with them to the cloister their earthly ambition, and the latter their dark misanthropy; and though many have daily kissed the cross and yet grown hoary in iniquity, and shrived their souls that they might sin more gayly on, — yet solitude works miracles in the heart, and many who enter the cloister from worldly motives find it a school wherein the soul may be trained to more holy purposes and desires. There is not half the corruption and hypocrisy within the convent's walls that the church bears the shame of hiding there. Hermits may be holy men, though knaves have sometimes been hermits. Were they all hypocrites, who of old for their souls' sake exposed their naked bodies to the burning sun of Syria? Were they, who wandered houseless in the solitudes of Engaddi? Were they, who dwelt beneath the palm-trees by the Red Sea? Oh, no! They were ignorant, they were deluded, they were fanatic, but they were not hypocrites; if there be any sincerity in human professions and human actions, they were not hypocrites. During the Middle Ages, there was corruption in the church, — foul, shameful corruption; and now also hypocrisy may scourge itself in feigned repentance, and ambition hide its face beneath a hood; yet all is not therefore rottenness that wears a cowl. Many a pure spirit, through heavenly-mindedness, and an ardent though mistaken zeal, has fled from the temptations of the world to seek in solitude and self-communion a closer walk with God. And not in vain. They have found the peace they sought. They have felt, indeed, what many profess to feel, but do not feel, — that they are strangers and sojourners here, travellers who are bound for their home in a far country. It is this feeling which I speak of as giving a peculiar charm to the devotional poetry of Spain. Compare its spirit with the spirit which its authors have exhibited in their lives. They speak of having given up the world, and it is no poetical hyperbole; they speak of longing to be free from the weakness of the flesh, that they may commence their conversation in heaven, — and we feel that they had already begun it in lives of penitence, meditation, and prayer.

THE PILGRIM'S BREVIARY.

If thou vouchsafe to read this treatise, it shall seem no otherwise to thee than the way to an ordinary traveller, — sometimes fair, sometimes foul; here champaign, there enclosed; barren in one place, better soyle in another; by woods, groves, hills, dales, plains, I shall lead thee.　　　BURTON'S ANATOMIE OF MELANCHOLY.

THE glittering spires and cupolas of Madrid have sunk behind me. Again and again I have turned to take a parting look, till at length the last trace of the city has disappeared, and I gaze only upon the sky above it.

And now the sultry day is passed; the freshening twilight falls, and the moon and the evening star are in the sky. This river is the Xarama. This noble avenue of trees leads to Aranjuez. Already its lamps begin to twinkle in the distance. The hoofs of our weary mules clatter upon the wooden bridge; the public square opens before us; yonder, in the moonlight, gleam the walls of the royal palace, and near it, with a rushing sound, fall the waters of the Tagus.

We have now entered the vast and melancholy plains of La Mancha, — a land to which the genius of Cervantes has given a vulgo-classic fame. Here are the windmills, as of old; every village has its Master Nicholas, — every venta its Maritornes. Wondrous strong are the spells of fiction! A few years pass away, and history becomes romance, and romance, history. To the peasantry of Spain, Don Quixote and his squire are historic personages; and woe betide the luckless wight who unwarily takes the name of Dulcinea upon his lips within a league of El Toboso! The traveller, too, yields himself to the delusion; and as he traverses the arid plains of La Mancha, pauses with willing credulity to trace the footsteps of the mad Hidalgo, with his " velvet breeches on a holiday, and slippers of the same." The high-road from Aranjuez to Córdova crosses and recrosses the knight-errant's path. Between Manzanares and Valdepeñas stands the inn where he was dubbed a knight; to the northward, the spot where he encountered the windmills; to the westward, the inn where he made the balsam of Fierabras, the scenes of his adventures with the fulling-mills, and his tournament with the barber; and to the southward, the Sierra Morena, where he did penance, like the knights of olden time.

For my own part, I confess that there are seasons when I am willing to be the dupe of my imagination; and if this harmless folly but lends its wings to a dull-paced hour, I am even ready to believe a fairy tale.

On the fourth day of our journey we dined at Manzanares, in an old and sombre-looking inn, which, I think, some centuries back, must have been the dwelling of a grandee. A wide gateway admitted us into the inn-yard, which was a paved court, in the centre of the edifice, surrounded by a colonnade, and open to the sky above. Beneath this colonnade we were shaved by the village barber, a supple, smooth-faced Figaro, with a brazen lava and a gray montera cap. There, too, we dined in the open air, with bread as white as snow, and the rich red wine of Valdepeñas; and there in the listlessness of after-dinner, smoked the sleep-inviting cigar, while in the court-yard before us the muleteers danced a fandango with the maids of the inn, to such music as three blind musicians could draw from a violin, a guitar, and a clarinet. When this scene was over, and the blind men had groped their way out of the yard, I fell into a delicious slumber, from which I was soon awakened by music of another kind. It was a clear youthful voice, singing a national song to the sound of a guitar. I opened my eyes, and near me stood a tall, graceful figure, leaning against one of the pillars of the colonnade, in the attitude of a serenader. His dress was that of a Spanish student. He wore a black gown and cassock, a pair of shoes made of an ex-pair of boots, and a hat in the shape of a half-moon, with the handle of a wooden spoon sticking out on one side like a cockade. When he had finished his song, we invited him to the remnant of a Vich sausage, a bottle of Valdepeñas, bread at his own discretion, and a pure Havana cigar. The stranger made a leg, and accepted these signs of good company with the easy air of a man who is accustomed to earn his livelihood by hook or by crook; and as the wine was of that stark and generous kind which readily "ascends one into the brain," our gentleman with the half-moon hat grew garrulous and full of anecdote, and soon told us his own story, beginning with his birth and parentage, like the people in Gil Blas.

"I am the son of a barber," quoth he; "and first saw the light some twenty years ago, in the great city of Madrid. At a very early age, I was taught to do something for myself, and began my career of gain by carrying a slow-match in the Prado, for the gentlemen to light their cigars with, and catching the wax that dropped from the friars' tapers at funerals and other religious processions.

"At school I was noisy and unruly; and was finally expelled for hooking the master's son with a pair of ox-horns, which I had tied to my head, in order to personate the bull in a mock bull-fight. Soon after this my father died, and I went to live with my maternal uncle, a curate in Fuencarral. He was a man of learning, and resolved that I should be like him. He set his heart upon making a physician of me; and to this end taught me Latin and Greek.

"In due time I was sent to the University of Alcalá. Here a new world opened before me. What novelty, — what variety, — what excitement! But, alas! three months were hardly gone, when news came that my worthy uncle had passed to a better world. I was now left to shift for myself. I was penniless, and lived as I could, not as I would. I became a *sopista*, a soup-eater, — a knight of the wooden spoon. I see you do not understand me. In other words, then, I became one of that respectable body of charity scholars who go armed with their wooden spoons to eat the allowance of eleemosynary soup which is daily served out to them at the gate of the convents. I had no longer house nor home. But necessity is the mother of inven-

tion. I became a hanger-on of those who were more fortunate than myself; studied in other people's books, slept in other people's beds, and breakfasted at other people's expense. This course of life has been demoralizing, but it has quickened my wits to a wonderful degree.

"Did you ever read the life of the Gran Tacaño, by Quevedo? In the first book you have a faithful picture of life in a Spanish University. What was true in his day is true in ours. O Alcalá! Alcalá! if your walls had tongues as well as ears, what tales could they repeat! what midnight frolics! what madcap revelries! what scenes of merriment and mischief! How merry is a student's life, and yet how changeable! Alternate feasting and fasting, — alternate Lent and Carnival, — alternate want and extravagance! Care given to the winds, — no thought beyond the passing hour; yesterday, forgotten, — to-morrow, a word in an unknown tongue!

"Did you ever hear of raising the dead? not literally, — but such as the student raised, when he dug for the soul of the licentiate Pedro Garcias, at the fountain between Peñafiel and Salamanca, — money? No? Well, it is done after this wise. Gambling, you know, is our great national vice; and then gamblers are so dishonest! Now, our game is to cheat the cheater. We go at night to some noted gaming-house, — five or six of us in a body. We stand around the table, watch those that are at play, and occasionally put in a trifle ourselves to avoid suspicion. At length the favorable moment arrives. Some eager player ventures a large stake. I stand behind his chair. He wins. As quick as thought, I stretch my arm over his shoulder and seize the glittering prize, saying very coolly, 'I have won at last.' My gentleman turns round in a passion, and I meet his indignant glance with a look of surprise. He storms, and I expostulate; he menaces, — I heed his menaces no more than the buzzing of a fly that has burnt his wings in my lamp. He calls the whole table to witness; but the whole table is busy, each with his own gain or loss, and there stand my comrades, all loudly asserting that the stake was mine. What can he do? there was a mistake; he swallows the affront as best he may, and we bear away the booty. This we call raising the dead. You say it is disgraceful, — dishonest. Our maxim is, that all is fair among sharpers; *Baylar al son que se toca*, — Dance to any tune that is fiddled. Besides, as I said before, poverty is demoralizing. One loses the nice distinctions of right and wrong, of *meum* and *tuum*.

"Thus merrily pass the hours of term-time. When the summer vacations come round, I sling my guitar over my shoulder, and with a light heart, and a lighter pocket, scour the country, like a strolling piper or a mendicant friar. Like the industrious ant, in summer I provide for winter; for in vacation we have time for reflection, and make the great discovery, that there is a portion of time called the future. I pick up a trifle here and a trifle there, in all the towns and villages through which I pass, and before the end of my tour I find myself quite rich — for the son of a barber. This we call the *vida tunantesca*, — a rag-tag-and-bobtail sort of life. And yet the vocation is as honest as that of a begging Franciscan. Why not?

"And now, gentlemen, having dined at your expense, with your leave I will put this loaf of bread and the remains of this excellent Vich sausage into my pocket, and, thanking you for your kind hospitality, bid you a good afternoon. God be with you, gentlemen!"

In general, the aspect of La Mancha is desolate and sad. Around you lies a parched and sunburnt plain, which, like the ocean, has no limits but the sky; and straight before you, for many a weary league, runs the dusty and level road, without the shade of a single tree. The villages you pass through are poverty-stricken and half-depopulated; and the squalid inhabitants wear a look of misery that makes the heart ache. Every league or two, the ruins of a post-house, or a roofless cottage with shattered windows and blackened walls, tells a sad tale of the last war. It was there that a little band of peasantry made a desperate stand against the French, and perished by the bullet, the sword, or the bayonet. The lapse of many years has not changed the scene, nor repaired the battered wall; and at almost every step the traveller may pause and exclaim: —

"Here was the camp, the watch-flame, and the host;
Here the bold peasant stormed the dragon's nest."

From Valdepeñas southward the country wears a more lively and picturesque aspect. The landscape breaks into hill and valley, covered with vineyards and olive-fields; and before you rise the dark ridges of the Sierra Morena, lifting their sullen fronts into a heaven all gladness and sunshine. Ere long you enter the wild mountain-pass of Despeña-Perros. A sudden turn in the road brings you to a stone column, surmounted by an iron cross, marking the boundary line between La Mancha and Andalusia. Upon one side of this column is carved a sorry-looking face, not unlike the death's-heads on the tombstones of a country church-yard. Over it is written this inscription: "EL VERDADERO RETRATO DE LA SANTA CARA DEL DIOS DE XAEN," — The true portrait of the holy countenance of the God of Xaen! I was so much struck with this strange superscription that I stopped to copy it.

"Do you really believe that this is what it pretends to be?" said I to a muleteer, who was watching my movements.

"I don't know," replied he, shrugging his brawny shoulders; "they say it is."

"Who says it is?"

"The priest, — the Padre Cura."

"I supposed so. And how was this portrait taken?"

He could not tell. The Padre Cura knew all about it.

When I joined my companions, who were a little in advance of me with the carriage, I got the mystery explained. The Catholic Church boasts of three portraits of our Saviour, miraculously preserved upon the folds of a handkerchief, with which St. Veronica wiped the sweat from his brow, on the day of the crucifixion. One of these is at Toledo, another in the kingdom of Xaen, and the third at Rome.

The impression which this monument of superstition made upon my mind was soon effaced by the magnificent scene which now burst upon me. The road winds up the mountain-side with gradual ascent; wild, shapeless, gigantic crags overhang it upon the right, and upon the left the wary foot starts back from the brink of a fearful chasm hundreds of feet in depth. Its sides are black with ragged pines, and rocks that have toppled down from above; and at the bottom, scarcely visible, wind the silvery waters of a little stream, a tributary of the Gaudalquiver. The road skirts the ravine for miles, — now climbing the barren rock, and now sliding gently downward into shadowy hollows, and crossing some rustic bridge thrown over a wild mountain-brook.

At length the scene changed. We stood upon the southern slope of the Sierra, and looked down upon the broad, luxuriant valleys of Andalusia, bathed in the gorgeous splendor of a southern sunset. The landscape had already assumed the "burnished livery" of autumn; but the air I breathed was the soft and balmy breath of spring, — the eternal spring of Andalusia.

If ever you should be fortunate enough to visit this part of Spain stop for the night at the village of La Carolina. It is indeed a model for all villages, — with its broad streets, its neat, white houses, its spacious market-place surrounded with a colonnade, and its public walk ornamented with fountains and set out with luxuriant trees. I doubt whether all Spain can show a village more beautiful than this.

The approach to Córdova from the east is enchanting. The sun was just rising as we crossed the Gaudalquiver and drew near to the city; and, alighting from the carriage, I pursued my way on foot, the better to enjoy the scene and the pure morning air. The dew still glistened on every leaf and spray; for the burning sun had not yet climbed the tall hedge-row of wild figs and aloes which skirts the roadside. The highway wound along through gardens, orchards, and vineyards, and here and there above me towered the glorious palm in all its leafy magnificence. On my right, a swelling mountain-ridge, covered with verdure and

sprinkled with little white hermitages, looked forth towards the rising sun; and on the left, in a long, graceful curve, swept the bright waters of the Guadalquiver, pursuing their silent journey through a verdant reach of soft lowland landscape. There, amid all the luxuriance of this sunny clime, arises the ancient city of Córdova, though stripped, alas! of its former magnificence. All that reminds you of the past is the crumbling wall of the city, and a Saracen mosque, now changed to a Christian cathedral. The stranger, who is familiar with the history of the Moorish dominion in Spain, pauses with a sigh, and asks himself, Is this the imperial city of Alhakam the Just, and Abdoulrahman the Magnificent?

This, then, is Seville, that "pleasant city, famous for oranges and women." After all I have heard of its beauty, I am disappointed in finding it less beautiful than my imagination had painted it. The wise saw, —

> "Quien no ha visto Sevilla,
> No ha visto maravilla," —

He who has not seen Seville has seen no marvel, — is an Andalusian gasconade. This, however, is the judgment of a traveller weary and wayworn with a journey of twelve successive days in a carriage drawn by mules; and I am well aware how much our opinions of men and things are colored by these trivial ills. A sad spirit is like a rainy day; its mists and shadows darken the brightest sky, and clothe the fairest landscape in gloom.

I am, likewise, a disappointed man in another respect. I have come all the way from Madrid to Seville without being robbed! And this, too, when I journeyed at a snail's pace, and had bought a watch large enough for the clock of a village church, for the express purpose of having it violently torn from me by a fierce-whiskered highwayman, with his blunderbuss and his "*Boca abajo, ladrones!*" If I print this in a book, I am undone. What! travel in Spain and not be robbed! To be sure, I came very near it more than once. Almost every village we passed through had its tale to tell of atrocities committed in the neighborhood. In one place, the stage-coach had been stopped and plundered; in another, a man had been murdered and thrown into the river; here and there a rude wooden cross and a shapeless pile of stones marked the spot where some unwary traveller had met his fate; and at night, seated around the blazing hearth of the inn-kitchen, my fellow-travellers would converse in a mysterious undertone of the dangers we were to pass through on the morrow But the morrow came and went, and, alas! neither *salteador*, nor *ratero* moved a finger. At one place, we were a day too late; at another, a day too early.

I am now at the *Fonda de los Americanos*. My chamber-door opens upon a gallery, beneath which is a little court paved with marble, having a fountain in the centre. As I write, I can just distinguish the tinkling of its tiny jet, falling into the circular basin with a murmur so gentle that it scarcely breaks the silence of the night. At day-dawn I start for Cadiz, promising myself a pleasant sail down the Guadalquivir. All I shall be able to say of Seville is what I have written above, — that it is "a pleasant city, famous for oranges and women."

———

I am at length in Cadiz. I came across the bay yesterday morning in an open boat from Santa Maria, and have established myself in very pleasant rooms, which look out upon the *Plaza de San Antonio*, the public square of the city. The morning sun awakes me, and at evening the sea-breeze comes in at my window. At night the square is lighted by lamps suspended from the trees, and thronged with a brilliant crowd of the young and gay.

Cadiz is beautiful almost beyond imagination. The cities of our dreams are not more enchanting. It lies like a delicate sea-shell upon the brink of the ocean, so wondrous fair that it seems not formed for man. In sooth, the Paphian queen, born of the feathery sea-foam, dwells here. It is the city of beauty and of love.

The women of Cadiz are world-renowned for their loveliness. Surely earth has none more dazzling than a daughter of that bright, burning clime. What a faultless figure! what a

dainty foot! what dignity! what matchless grace!

"What eyes, — what lips, — what everything about her!
  How like a swan she swims her pace, and bears
  Her silver breasts!"

The Gaditana is not ignorant of her charms. She knows full well the necromancy of a smile. You see it in the flourish of her fan, — a magic wand, whose spell is powerful; you see it in her steady gaze, the elastic step,

"The veil,
  Thrown back a moment with the glancing hand,
  While the o'erpowering eye, that turns you pale,
  Flashes into the heart."

When I am grown old and gray, and sit by the fireside wrapped in flannels, if, in a listless moment, recalling what is now the present, but will then be the distant and almost forgotten past, I turn over the leaves of this journal till my watery eye falls upon the page I have just written, I shall smile at the enthusiasm with which I have sketched this portrait. And where will then be the bright forms that now glance before me, like the heavenly creations of a dream? All gone, — all gone! Or, if perchance a few still linger upon earth, they will be bowed with age and sorrow, saying their paternosters with a tremulous voice.

Old age is a Pharisee; for he makes broad his phylacteries, and wears them upon his brow, inscribed with prayer, but in the "crooked autograph" of a palsied hand. "I see with pain," says Madame de Pompadour, "that there is nothing durable upon the earth. We bring into the world a fair face, and lo! in less than thirty years it is covered with wrinkles; after which a woman is no longer good for anything."

Were I to translate these sombre reflections into choice Castilian, and read them to the bright-eyed maiden who is now leaning over the balcony opposite, she would laugh, and laughing say, "*Cuando el demonio es viejo, se mete frayle.*"

———

THE devotion paid at the shrine of the Virgin is one of the most prominent and characteristic features of the Catholic religion. In

Spain it is one of the most attractive features. In the southern provinces, in Granada and in Andalusia, which the inhabitants call "*La tierra de María Santísima*,"—the land of the most holy Mary, — this admiration is ardent and enthusiastic. There is one of its outward observances which struck me as peculiarly beautiful and impressive. I refer to the Ave Maria, an evening service of the Virgin. Just as the evening twilight commences, the bell tolls to prayer. In a moment, throughout the crowded city, the hum of business is hushed, the thronged streets are still; the gay multitudes that crowd the public walks stand motionless; the angry dispute ceases; the laugh of merriment dies away; life seems for a moment to be arrested in its career, and to stand still. The multitude uncover their heads, and, with the sign of the cross, whisper their evening prayer to the Virgin. Then the bells ring a merrier peal; the crowds move again in the streets, and the rush and turmoil of business recommence. I have always listened with feelings of solemn pleasure to the bell that sounded forth the Ave Maria. As it announced the close of day, it seemed also to call the soul from its worldly occupations to repose and devotion. There is something beautiful in thus measuring the march of time. The hour, too, naturally brings the heart into unison with the feelings and sentiments of devotion. The close of the day, the shadows of evening, the calm of twilight, inspire a feeling of tranquillity; and though I may differ from the Catholic in regard to the object of his supplication, yet it seems to me a beautiful and appropriate solemnity, that, at the close of each daily epoch of life, — which, if it have not been fruitful in incidents to ourselves, has, nevertheless, been so to many of the great human family, — the voice of a whole people, and of the whole world, should go up to heaven in praise, and supplication, and thankfulness.

> " The Moorish king rides up and down
> Through Granada's royal town;
> From Elvira's gates to those
> Of Bivarambla on he goes.
> Woe is me, Alhama!"

Thus commences one of the fine old Spanish ballads, commemorating the downfall of the city of Alhama, where we have stopped to rest our horses on their fatiguing march from Velez-Málaga to Granada. Alhama was one of the last strongholds of the Moslem power in Spain. Its fall opened the way for the Christian army across the Sierra Nevada, and spread consternation and despair through the city of Granada. The description in the old ballad is highly graphic and beautiful; and its beauty is well preserved in the spirited English translation by Lord Byron.

As we crossed the Sierra Nevada, the snowy mountains that look down upon the luxuriant Vega of Granada, we overtook a solitary rider, who was singing a wild national song, to cheer the loneliness of his journey. He was an athletic man, and rode a spirited horse of the Arab breed. A black bearskin jacket covered his broad shoulders, and around his waist was wound the crimson *faja*, so universally worn by the Spanish peasantry. His velvet breeches reached below his knee, just meeting a pair of leather gaiters of elegant workmanship. A gay silken handkerchief was tied around his head, and over this he wore the little round Andalusian hat, decked out with a profusion of tassels of silk and bugles of silver. The steed he mounted was dressed no less gayly than his rider. There was a silver star upon his forehead, and a bright-colored woollen tassel between his ears; a blanket striped with blue and red covered the saddle, and even the Moorish stirrups were ornamented with brass studs.

This personage was a *contrabandista*, — a smuggler between Granada and the seaport of Velez-Málaga. The song he sung was one of the popular ballads of the country.

> " Worn with speed is my good steed,
> And I march me hurried, worried;
> Onward! caballito mio,
> With the white star in thy forehead!
> Onward! for here comes the Ronda,
> And I hear their rifles crack!
> Ay, jaleo! Ay, ay, jaleo!
> Ay, jaleo! they cross our track!"[1]

[1] I here transcribe the original of which this is a single stanza. Its only merit is simplicity, and a certain grace

The air to which these words are sung is wild and high ; and the prolonged and mournful cadence gives it the sound of a funeral wail, or a cry for help. To have its full effect upon the mind, it should be heard by night, in some wild mountain-pass, and from a distance. Then the harsh tones come softened to the ear, and, in unison with the hour and the scene, produce a pleasing melancholy.

The contrabandista accompanied us to Granada. The sun had already set when we entered the Vega, — those luxuriant meadows which stretch away to the south and west of the city, league after league of rich, unbroken verdure. It was Saturday night ; and, as the gathering twilight fell around us, and one by one the lamps of the city twinkled in the distance, suddenly kindling here and there, as the stars start to their places in the evening sky, a loud peal of bells rang forth its glad welcome to the day of rest, over the meadows to the distant hills, "swinging slow, with solemn roar."

————

Is this reality and not a dream ? Am I indeed in Granada ? Am I indeed within the walls of that earthly paradise of the Moorish kings ? How my spirit is stirred within me ! How my heart is lifted up ! How my thoughts are rapt away in the visions of other days !

Ave, Maria purissima ! It is midnight. The bell has tolled the hour from the watch-tower of the Alhambra ; and the silent street echoes only to the watchman's cry, *Ave, Maria purissima !* I am alone in my chamber, — sleepless, — spell-bound by the genius of the place, — entranced by the beauty of the starlit night. As I gaze from my window, a sudden radiance which belongs to its provincial phraseology, and which would be lost in a translation.

> "Yo que soy contrabandista,
> Y campo por mi respeto,
> Á todos los desafío,
> Porque á naide tengo mieo.
> ¡Ay, jaleo! ¡Muchachas, jaleo!
> ¿ Quien me compra jilo negro ?

> "Mi caballo está cansao,
> Y yo me marcho corriendo.
> ¡Anda, caballito mio,

139

brightens in the east. It is the moon, rising behind the Alhambra. I can faintly discern the dusky and indistinct outline of a massive tower, standing amid the uncertain twilight, like a gigantic shadow. It changes with the rising moon, as a palace in the clouds, and other towers and battlements arise, — every moment more distinct, more palpable, till now they stand between me and the sky, with a sharp outline, distant, and yet so near that I seem to sit within their shadow.

Majestic spirit of the night, I recognize thee ! Thou hast conjured up this glorious vision for thy votary. Thou hast baptized me with thy baptism. Thou hast nourished my soul with fervent thoughts and holy aspirations, and ardent longings after the beautiful and the true. Majestic spirit of the past, I recognize thee ! Thou hast bid the shadow go back for me upon the dial-plate of time. Thou hast taught me to read in thee the present and the future, — a revelation of man's destiny on earth. Thou hast taught me to see in thee the principle that unfolds itself from century to century in the progress of our race, — the germ in whose bosom lie unfolded the bud, the leaf, the tree. Generations perish, like the leaves of the forest, passing away when their mission is completed ; but at each succeeding spring, broader and higher spreads the human mind unto its perfect stature, unto the fulfilment of its destiny, unto the perfection of its nature. And in these high revelations, thou hast taught me more, — thou hast taught me to feel that I, too, weak, humble, and unknown, feeble of purpose and irresolute of good, have something to accomplish upon earth, — like the falling leaf, like the passing wind, like the drop of rain. O glorious thought ! that lifts me above the power

> Caballo mio careto!
> ¡Anda, que viene la ronda,
> Y se mueve el tiroteo!
> ¡Ay, jaleo! ¡Ay, ay, jaleo!
> ¡Ay, jaleo, que nos cortan!
> Sácame de aqueste aprieto.

> "Mi caballo ya no corre,
> Ya mi caballo paró.
> Todo para en este mundo,
> Tambien he de parar yo.
> ¡Ay, jaleo! ¡Muchachas, jaleo!
> ¿ Quien me compra jilo negro ? "

of time and chance, and tells me that I cannot pass away, and leave no mark of my existence. I may not know the purpose of my being, — the end for which an all-wise Providence created me as I am, and placed me where I am; but I do know — for in such things faith is knowledge — that my being has a purpose in the omniscience of my Creator, and that all my actions tend to the completion, to the full accomplishment of that purpose. Is this fatality? No. I feel that I am free, though an infinite

These are manifestations of the human mind at a remote period of its history, and among a people who came from another clime, — the children of the desert. Their mission is accomplished, and they are gone; yet leaving behind them a thousand records of themselves and of their ministry, not as yet fully manifest, but "seen through a glass darkly," dimly shadowed forth in the language, and character, and manners, and history of the nation, that was by turns the conquered and the conquering. The

and invisible power overrules me. Man proposes, and God disposes. This is one of the many mysteries in our being which human reason cannot find out by searching.

Yonder towers, that stand so huge and massive in the midnight air, the work of human hands that have long since forgotten their cunning in the grave, and once the home of human beings immortal as ourselves, and filled like us with hopes and fears, and powers of good and ill, — are lasting memorials of their builders; inanimate material forms, yet living with the impress of a creative mind. These are landmarks of other times. Thus from the distant past the history of the human race is telegraphed from generation to generation, through the present to all succeeding ages.

Goth sat at the Arab's feet; and athwart the cloud and storm of war, streamed the light of Oriental learning upon the Western world, —

> " As when the autumnal sun,
> Through travelling rain and mist,
> Shines on the evening hills."

This morning I visited the Alhambra; an enchanted palace, whose exquisite beauty baffles the power of language to describe. Its outlines may be drawn, — its halls and galleries, its court-yards and its fountains, numbered; but what skilful limner shall portray in words its curious architecture, the grotesque ornaments, the quaint devices, the rich tracery of the walls, the ceilings inlaid with pearl and

ARTIST: H. BOLTON JONES.

AT THE ALHAMBRA.

tortoise-shell? what language paint the magic hues of light and shade, the shimmer of the sunbeam as it falls upon the marble pavement, and the brilliant panels inlaid with many-colored stones? Vague recollections fill my mind, — images dazzling but undefined, like the memory of a gorgeous dream. They crowd my brain confusedly, but they will not stay; they change and mingle, like the tremulous sunshine on the wave, till imagination itself is dazzled, — bewildered, — overpowered!

What most arrests the stranger's foot within the walls of the Alhambra is the refinement of luxury which he sees at every step. He lingers in the deserted bath, — he pauses to gaze upon the now vacant saloon, where, stretched upon his gilded couch, the effeminate monarch of the East was wooed to sleep by softly-breathing music. What more delightful than this secluded garden, green with the leaf of the myrtle and the orange, and freshened with

the gush of fountains, beside whose basin the nightingale still wooes the blushing rose? What more fanciful, more exquisite, more like a creation of Oriental magic, than the lofty tower of the Tocador, — its airy sculpture resembling the fretwork of wintry frost, and its windows overlooking the romantic valley of the Darro; and the city, with its gardens, domes, and spires, far, far below? Cool through this lattice comes the summer wind from the icy summits of the Sierra Nevada. Softly in yonder fountain falls the crystal water, dripping from its marble vase with never-ceasing sound. On every side comes up the fragrance of a thousand flowers, the murmur of innumerable leaves; and overhead is a sky where not a vapor floats, — as soft, and blue, and radiant as the eye of childhood!

Such is the Alhambra of Granada; a fortress, — a palace, — an earthly paradise, — a ruin, wonderful in its fallen greatness!

THE JOURNEY INTO ITALY.

What I catch is at present only sketch-ways, as it were; but I prepare myself betimes for the Italian journey.

GOETHE'S FAUST.

ON the afternoon of the 15th of December, in the year of grace one thousand eight hundred and twenty-seven, I left Marseilles for Genoa, taking the sea-shore road through Toulon, Draguignan, and Nice. This journey is written in my memory with a sunbeam. We were a company whom chance had thrown together, — different in ages, humors, and pursuits, — and yet so merrily the days went by, in sunshine, wind, or rain, that methinks some lucky star must have ruled the hour that brought us five so auspiciously together. But where is now that merry company? One sleeps in his youthful grave; two sit in their fatherland, and "coin their brain for their daily bread;" and the others, — where are they? If still among the living, I beg them to remember in their prayers the humble historian of their journey into Italy.

At Toulon we took a private carriage in order to pursue our journey more leisurely and more at ease. I well remember the strange,

outlandish vehicle, and our vetturino Joseph, with his *blouse*, his short-stemmed pipe, his limping gait, his comical phiz, and the lowland dialect his mother taught him at Avignon. Every scene, every incident of the journey is now before me as if written in a book. The sunny landscapes of the Var, — the peasant girls, with their broad-brimmed hats of straw, — the inn at Draguignan, with its painting of a lady on horseback, underwritten in French and English, " *Une jeune dame à la promenade*, — A young ladi taking a walk," — the mouldering arches of the Roman aqueducts at Fréjus, standing in the dim twilight of morning like shadowy apparitions of the past, — the wooded bridge across the Var, — the glorious amphitheatre of hills that half encircle Nice, — the midnight scene at the village inn of Monaco, — the mountain-road overhanging the sea at a dizzy height, and its long, dark passages cut through the solid rock, — the tumbling mountain-torrent, — and a fortress perched on a jutting spur of the Alps ; these, and a thousand varied scenes and landscapes of this journey, rise before me, as if still visible to the eye of sense, and not to that of memory only. And yet I will not venture upon a minute description of them. I have not colors bright enough for such landscapes ; and besides, even the most determined lovers of the picturesque grow weary of long descriptions ; though, as the French guide-book says of these scenes, " *Tout cela fait sans doute un spectacle admirable !* "

———

On the tenth day of our journey, we reached Genoa, the city of palaces, — the superb city. The writer of an old book, called " Time's Storehouse," thus poetically describes its situation : " This cittie is most proudly built upon the seacoast and the downefall of the Appenines, at the foot of a mountaine ; even as if she were descended downe the mount, and come to repose herselfe uppon a plaine."

It was Christmas eve, — a glorious night ! I stood at midnight on the wide terrace of our hotel, which overlooks the sea, and, gazing on the tiny and crisping waves that broke in pearly light beneath the moon, sent back my wandering thoughts far over the sea, to a distant home. The jangling music of church-bells aroused me from my dream. It was the sound of jubilee at the approaching festival of the Nativity, and summoned alike the pious devotee, the curious stranger, and the gallant lover to the church of the Annunziata.

I descended from the terrace, and, groping my way through one of the dark and narrow lanes which intersect the city in all directions, soon found myself in the Strada Nuova. The long line of palaces lay half in shadow, half in light, stretching before me in magical perspective, like the long vapory opening of a cloud in the summer sky. Following the various groups that were passing onward towards the public square, I entered the church, where midnight mass was to be chanted. A dazzling blaze of light from the high altar shone upon the red marble columns which support the roof, and fell with a solemn effect upon the kneeling crowd that filled the body of the church. All beyond was in darkness ; and

from that darkness at intervals burst forth the deep voice of the organ and the chanting of the choir, filling the soul with solemnity and awe. And yet, among that prostrate crowd, how many had been drawn thither by unworthy motives, — motives even more unworthy than mere idle curiosity ! How many sinful purposes arose in souls unpurified, and mocked at the bended knee ! How many a heart beat wild with earthly passion, while the unconscious lip repeated the accustomed prayer ! Immortal spirit ! canst thou so heedlessly resist the imploring voice that calls thee from thine errors and pollutions ? Is not the long day long enough, is not the wide world wide enough, has not society frivolity enough for thee, that thou shouldst seek out this midnight hour, this holy place, this solemn sacrifice, to add irreverence to thy folly ?

In the shadow of a column stood a young man wrapped in a cloak, earnestly conversing in a low whisper with a female figure, so veiled as to hide her face from the eyes of all but her companion. At length they separated. The young man continued leaning against the column, and the girl, gliding silently along the dimly lighted aisle, mingled with the crowd, and threw herself upon her knees. Beware, poor girl, thought I, lest thy gentle nature prove thy undoing ! Perhaps, alas, thou art already undone ! And I almost heard the evil spirit whisper, as in the Faust, " How different was it with thee, Margaret, when, still full of innocence, thou camest to the altar here, — out of the well-worn little book lispedst prayers, half child-sport, half God in the heart ! Margaret, where is thy head ? What crime in thy heart ! "

The city of Genoa is magnificent in parts, but not as a whole. The houses are high, and the streets in general so narrow that in many of them you may almost step across from side to side. They are built to receive the cool sea-breeze, and shut out the burning sun. Only three of them — if my memory serves me — are wide enough to admit the passage of carriages ; and these three form but one continuous street, — the street of palaces. They are the Strada Nuova, the Strada Novissima, and the Strada Balbi, which connect the Piazza

Amorosa with the Piazza dell' Annunziata. These palaces, the Doria, the Durazzo, the Ducal Palace, and others of less munificence, — with their vast halls, their marble staircases, vestibules, and terraces, and the aspect of splendor and munificence they wear, — have given this commercial city the title of Genoa the Superb. And, as if to humble her pride, some envious rival among the Italian cities has launched at her a biting sarcasm in the well known proverb, "*Mare senza pesce, uomini senza fede, e donne senza vergogna,*" — A sea without fish, men without faith, and women without shame !

The road from Genoa to Lucca strongly resembles that from Nice to Genoa. It runs along the seaboard, now dipping to the water's edge, and now climbing the zigzag mountain-pass, with toppling crags, and yawning chasms, and verdant terraces of vines and olive-trees. Many a sublime and many a picturesque landscape catches the traveller's eye, now almost weary with gazing; and still brightly painted upon my mind lies a calm evening scene on the borders of the Gulf of Spezia, with its broad sheet of crystal water, — the blue-tinted hills that form its oval basin, — the crimson sky above. and its bright reflection, —

> "Where it lay
> Deep bosomed in the still and quiet bay,
> The sea reflecting all that glowed above,
> Till a new sky, softer but not so gay,
> Arched in its bosom, trembled like a dove."

Pisa, the melancholy city, with its Leaning Tower, its Campo Santo, its bronze-gated cathedral, and its gloomy palaces, — Florence the Fair, with its magnificent Duomo, its gallery of ancient art, its gardens, its gay society, and its delightful environs, — Fiesole, Camaldoli, Vallombrosa, and the luxuriant Val d'Arno; — these have been so often and so beautifully described by others, that I need not repeat the twice-told tale.

At Florence I took lodgings in a house which looks upon the Piazza Novella. In front of my windows was the venerable church of Santa Maria Novella, in whose gloomy aisles Boccaccio has placed the opening scene of his Decamerone. There, when the plague was raging in the city, one Tuesday morning, after mass, the "seven ladies, young and fair," held counsel together, and resolved to leave the infected city, and flee to their rural villas in the environs, where they might ·hear the birds sing, and see the green hills, and the plains, and the fields covered with grain and undulating like the sea, and trees of species manifold."

In the Florentine museum is a representation in wax of some of the appalling scenes of the plague which desolated this city about the middle of the fourteenth century, and which Boccaccio has described with such simplicity and power in the introduction of his Decamerone. It is the work of a Sicilian artist, by the name of Zumbo. He must have been a man of the most gloomy and saturnine imagination, and more akin to the worm than most of us, thus to have revelled night and day in the hideous mysteries of death, corruption, and the charnel-house. It is strange how this representation haunts one. It is like a dream of the sepulchre, with its loathsome corses, with "the blackening, the swelling, the bursting of the trunk, — the worm, the rat, and the tarantula at work." You breathe more freely as you step out into the open air again ; and when the bright sunshine and the crowded busy streets next meet your eye, you are ready to ask, Is this indeed a representation of reality ? Can this pure air have been laden with pestilence ? Can this gay city have ever been a city of the plague ?

The work of the Sicilian artist is admirable as a piece of art; the description of the Florentine prose-poet equally admirable as a piece of eloquence. "How many vast palaces," he exclaims, " how many beautiful houses, how many noble dwellings, aforetime filled with lords and ladies and trains of servants, were now untenanted even by the lowest menial ! How many memorable families, how many ample heritages, how many renowned possessions, were left without an heir ! How many valiant men, how many beautiful women, how many gentle youths breakfasted in the morning with their relatives, companions, and friends, and, when the evening came, supped with their ancestors in the other world!"

———

I met with an odd character at Florence, — a complete humorist. He was an Englishman of some forty years of age, with a round good-humored countenance, and a nose that wore the livery of good company. He was making the grand tour through France and Italy, and home again by the way of the Tyrol and the Rhine. He travelled post, with a double-bar-relled gun, two pairs of pistols, and a violin without a bow. He had been in Rome with-out seeing St. Peter's, — he did not care about it; he had seen St. Paul's in London. He had been in Naples without visiting Pompeii, be-cause "they told him it was hardly worth see-ing, — nothing but a parcel of dark streets and old walls." The principal object he seemed to have in view was to complete the grand tour.

I afterward met with his counterpart in a countryman of my own, who made it a point to see everything which was mentioned in the guide-books; and boasted how much he could accomplish in a day. He would dis-patch a city in an incredibly short space of time. A Roman aqueduct, a Gothic cathedral, two or three modern churches, and an ancient ruin or so, were only a breakfast for him. Nothing came amiss; not a stone was left un-turned. A city was like a Chinese picture to him, — it had no perspective. Every object seemed of equal magnitude and importance. He saw them all; they were all wonderful.

"Life is short, and art is long," says Hippo-crates; yet spare me from thus travelling with the speed of thought, and trotting, from day-light until dark, at the heels of a cicerone, with an umbrella in one hand, and a guide-book and plan of the city in the other.

———

I copied the following singular inscription from a tombstone in the Protestant cemetery at Leghorn. It is the epitaph of a lady, writ-ten by herself, and engraven upon her tomb at her own request.

"Under this stone lies the victim of sorrow,
 Fly, wandering stranger, from her mouldering dust,
 Lest the rude wind, conveying a particle thereof unto
    thee,
 Should communicate that venom melancholy
 That has destroyed the strongest frame and liveliest
    spirit.
 With joy of heart has she resigned her breath,
 A living martyr to sensibility!"

How inferior in true pathos is this inscription to one in the cemetery of Bologna: —

"Lucrezia Picini
    Implora eterna pace."

Lucretia Picini implores eternal peace!

From Florence to Rome I travelled with a vetturino, by the way of Siena. We were six days upon the road, and, like Peter Rugg in the story-book, were followed constantly by clouds and rain. At times, the sun, not all-forgetful of the world, peeped from beneath his cowl of mist, and kissed the swarthy face of his beloved land; and then, like an anchorite, withdrew again from earth, and gave him-self to heaven. Day after day the mist and the rain were my fellow-travellers; and as I sat wrapped in the thick folds of my Spanish cloak, and looked out upon the misty land-scape and the leaden sky, I was continually saying to myself, " Can this be Italy?" and smiling at the untravelled credulity of those who, amid the storms of a northern winter, give way to the illusions of fancy, and dream of Italy as a sunny land, where no wintry tem-pest beats, and where, even in January, the pale invalid may go about without his umbrella, or his India-rubber walk-in-the-waters.

Notwithstanding all this, with the help of a good constitution and a thick pair of boots, I contrived to see all that was to be seen upon the road. I walked down the long hillside at San Lorenzo, and along the border of the Lake of Bolsena, which, veiled in the driving mist, stretched like an inland sea beyond my ken; and through the sacred forest of oak, held in superstitious reverence by the peasant, and in-violate from his axe. I passed a night at Montefiascone, renowned for a delicate Muscat wine, which bears the name of Est, and made a midnight pilgrimage to the tomb of the

Bishop John Defoucris, who died a martyr to his love of this wine of Montefiascone.

> " Propter nimium Est, Est, Est,
> Dominus meus mortuus est."

A marble slab in the pavement, worn by the footsteps of pilgrims like myself, covers the dominie's ashes. There is a rude figure carved upon it, at whose feet I traced out the cabalistic words, " Est, Est, Est." The remainder of the inscription was illegible by the flickering light of the sexton's lantern.

At Baccano I first caught sight of the dome of Saint Peter's. We had entered the desolate Campagna ; we passed the tomb of Nero, — we approached the Eternal City ; but no sound of active life, no thronging crowds, no hum of busy men, announced that we were near the gates of Rome. All was silence, solitude, and desolation.

ROME IN MIDSUMMER.

She who tamed the world seemed to tame herself at last, and, falling under her own weight, grew to be a prey to Time, who with his iron teeth consumes all bodies at last, making all things, both animate and inanimate, which have their being under that changeling, the moon, to be subject unto corruption and desolation.

HOWELL'S SIGNORIE OF VENICE.

THE masks and mummeries of Carnival are over ; the imposing ceremonies of Holy Week have become a tale of the times of old ; the illumination of St. Peter's and the Girandola are no longer the theme of gentle and simple ; and finally, the barbarians of the North have retreated from the gates of Rome, and left the Eternal City silent and deserted. The cicerone stands at the corner of the street with his hands in his pockets ; the artist has shut himself up in his studio to muse upon antiquity ; and the idle facchino lounges in the marketplace, and plays at *mora* by the fountain. Midsummer has come ; and you may now hire a palace for what, a few weeks ago, would hardly have paid your night's lodging in its garret.

I am still lingering in Rome, — a student, not an artist, — and have taken lodgings in the Piazza Navona, the very heart of the city, and one of the largest and most magnificent squares of modern Rome. It occupies the site of the ancient amphitheatre of Alexander Severus ; and the churches, palaces, and shops that now surround it are built upon the old foundations of the amphitheatre. At each extremity of the square stands a fountain ; the one with a simple jet of crystal water, the other with a triton holding a dolphin by the tail. In the centre rises a nobler work of art ; a fountain with a marble basin more than two hundred feet in circumference. From the midst uprises a huge rock pierced with grottoes, wherein sit a rampant sea-horse, and a lion couchant. On the sides of the rock are four colossal statues, representing the four principal rivers of the world ; and from its summit, forty feet from the basin below, shoots up an obelisk of red granite, covered with hieroglyphics, and fifty feet in height, — a relic of the amphitheatre of Caracalla.

In this quarter of the city I have domiciliated myself in a family of whose many kindnesses I shall always retain the most lively and grateful remembrance. My mornings are spent in visiting the wonders of Rome, in studying the miracles of ancient and modern art, or in reading at the public libraries. We breakfast at noon, and dine at eight in the evening. After dinner comes the conversazione, enlivened with music, and the meeting of travellers, artists, and literary men from every quarter of the globe. At midnight, when the crowd is gone, I retire to my chamber, and, poring over the gloomy pages of Dante, or "Bandello's laughing tale," protract my nightly vigil till the morning star is in the sky.

Our windows look out upon the square, which circumstance is a source of infinite enjoyment to me. Directly in front, with its fantastic belfries and swelling dome, rises the church of St. Agnes; and sitting by the open window, I note the busy scene below, enjoy the cool air of morning and evening, and even feel the freshness of the fountain, as its waters leap in mimic cascades down the sides of the rock.

———

The Piazza Navona is the chief market-place of Rome; and on market-days is filled with a noisy crowd of the Roman populace, and the peasantry from the neighboring villages of Albano and Frascati. At such times the square presents an animated and curious scene. The gayly-decked stalls, — the piles of fruits and vegetables, — the pyramids of flowers, — the various costumes of the peasantry, — the constant movement of the vast, fluctuating crowd, and the deafening clamor of their discordant voices, that rise louder than the roar of the loud ocean, — all this is better than a play to me, and gives me amusement when naught else has power to amuse.

Every Saturday afternoon in the sultry month of August, this spacious square is converted into a lake, by stopping the conduit-pipes which carry off the water of the fountains. Vehicles of every description, axle deep, drive to and fro across the mimic lake; a dense crowd gathers around its margin, and a thousand tricks excite the loud laughter of the idle populace. Here is a fellow groping with a stick after his seafaring hat; there another splashing in the water in pursuit of a mischievous spaniel, who is swimming away with his shoe; while from a neighboring balcony a noisy burst of military music fills the air, and gives fresh animation to the scene of mirth. This is one of the popular festivals of midsummer in Rome, and the merriest of them all. It is a kind of carnival unmasked; and many a popular bard, many a *Poeta di dozzina*, invokes this day the plebeian Muse of the market-place to sing in high-sounding rhyme, " *Il Lago di Piazza Navona.*"

I have before me one of these sublime effusions. It describes the square, — the crowd, — the rattling carriages, — the lake, — the fountain, raised by "the superhuman genius of Bernini," — the lion, — the sea-horse, and the triton grasping the dolphin's tail. "Half the grand square," thus sings the poet, "where Rome with food is satiate, was changed into a lake, around whose margin stood the Roman people, pleased with soft idleness and merry holiday, like birds upon the margin of a limpid brook. Up and down drove car and chariot; and the women trembled for fear of the deep water; though merry were the young, and well I ween, had they been borne away to unknown shores by the bull that bore away Europa, they would neither have wept nor screamed!"

———

On the eastern slope of the Janiculum, now called, from its yellow sands, Montorio, or the Golden Mountain, stands the fountain of Acqua Paola, the largest and most abundant of the Roman fountains. It is a small Ionic temple, with six columns of reddish granite in front, a spacious hall and chambers within, and a garden with a terrace in the rear. Beneath the pavement, a torrent of water from the ancient aqueducts of Trajan, and from the lakes of Bracciano and Martignano, leaps forth in three beautiful cascades, and from the overflowing basin rushes down the hillside to turn the busy wheels of a dozen mills.

The key of this little fairy palace is in our hands, and as often as once a week we pass the day there, amid the odor of its flowers, the rushing sound of its waters, and the enchantments of poetry and music. How pleasantly the sultry hours steal by! Cool comes the summer wind from the Tiber's mouth at Ostia. Above us is a sky without a cloud; beneath us the magnificent panorama of Rome and the Campagna, bounded by the Abruzzi and the sea. Glorious scene! one glance at thee would move the dullest soul, — one glance can melt the painter and the poet into tears!

In the immediate neighborhood of the fountain are many objects worthy of the stranger's notice. A bowshot down the hillside towards the city stands the convent of San Pietro in Montorio; and in the cloister of this convent is a small, round Doric temple, built upon the spot which an ancient tradition points out as the scene of St. Peter's martyrdom. In the opposite direction the road leads you over the shoulder of the hill, and out through the city-gate to gardens and villas beyond. Passing beneath a lofty arch of Trajan's aqueduct, an ornamented gateway on the left admits you to the Villa Pamfili-Doria, built on the western declivity of the hill. This is the largest and most magnificent of the numerous villas that crowd the immediate environs of Rome. Its spacious terraces, its marble statues, its woodlands and green alleys, its lake and waterfalls and fountains, give it an air of courtly splendor and of rural beauty, which realizes the beau ideal of a suburban villa.

This is our favorite resort, when we have passed the day at the fountain, and the afternoon shadows begin to fall. There we sit on the broad marble steps of the terrace, gaze upon the varied landscape stretching to the misty sea, or ramble beneath the leafy dome of the woodland and along the margin of the lake,

> " And drop a pebble to see it sink
> Down in those depths so calm and cool."

Oh, did we but know when we are happy! Could the restless, feverish, ambitious heart be still, but for a moment still, and yield itself, without one farther-aspiring throb, to its enjoyment, — then were I happy, — yes, thrice happy! But no; this fluttering, struggling, and imprisoned spirit beats the bars of its golden cage, — disdains the silken fetter; it will not close its eye and fold its wings; as if time were not swift enough, its swifter thoughts outstrip his rapid flight, and onward, onward do they wing their way to the distant mountains, to the fleeting clouds of the future; and yet I know, that ere long, weary, and wayworn, and disappointed, they shall return to nestle in the bosom of the past!

This day, also, I have passed at Acqua Paola. From the garden terrace I watched the setting sun, as, wrapped in golden vapor, he passed to other climes. A friend from my native land was with me; and as we spake of home, a liquid star stood trembling like a tear upon the closing eyelid of the day. Which of us wrote these lines with a pencil upon the cover of Julia's Corinna?

> Bright star! whose soft, familiar ray,
>   In colder climes and gloomier skies,
> I 've watched so oft when closing day
>   Had tinged the west with crimson dyes;
> Perhaps to-night some friend I love,
>   Beyond the deep, the distant sea,
> Will gaze upon thy path above,
>   And give one lingering thought to me.

TORQUATI TASSO OSSA HIC JACENT, — Here lie the bones of Torquato Tasso, — is the simple inscription upon the poet's tomb, in the church of St. Onofrio. Many a pilgrimage is made to this grave. Many a bard from distant lands comes to visit the spot, — and, as he paces the secluded cloisters of the convent where the poet died, and where his ashes rest, muses on the sad vicissitudes of his life, and breathes a prayer for the peace of his soul. He sleeps midway between his cradle at Sorrento and his dungeon at Ferrara.

The monastery of St. Onofrio stands on the Janiculum, overlooking the Tiber and the city of Rome; and in the distance rise the towers of the Roman Capitol, where after long years of sickness, sorrow, and imprisonment, the laurel crown was prepared for the great epic poet of Italy. The chamber in which Tasso died is still shown to the curious traveller; and the

140

tree in the garden, under whose shade he loved to sit. The feelings of the dying man, as he reposed in this retirement, are not the vague conjectures of poetic revery. He has himself recorded them in a letter which he wrote to his friend Antonio Constantini, a few days only before his dissolution. These are his melancholy words: —

"What will my friend Antonio say, when he hears the death of Tasso? Erelong, I think, the news will reach him; for I feel that the end of my life is near; being able to find no remedy for this wearisome indisposition which is superadded to my customary infirmities, and by which, as by a rapid torrent, I see myself swept away, without a hand to save. It is no longer time to speak of my unyielding destiny, not to say the ingratitude of the world, which has longed even for the victory of driving me a beggar to my grave; while I thought that the glory which, in spite of those who will it not, this age shall receive from my writings was not to leave me thus without reward. I have come to this monastery of St. Onofrio, not only because the air is commended by physicians as more salubrious than in any other part of Rome, but that I may, as it were, commence, in this high place, and in the conversation of these devout fathers, my conversation in heaven. Pray God for me; and be assured that as I have loved and honored you in this present life so in that other and more real life will I do for you all that belongs to charity unfeigned and true. And to the divine mercy I commend both you and myself."

The modern Romans are a very devout people. The Princess Doria washes the pilgrims' feet in Holy Week; every evening, foul or fair, the whole year round, there is a rosary sung before an image of the Virgin, within a stone's throw of my window; and the young ladies write letters to St. Louis Gonzaga, who in all paintings and sculpture is represented as young and angelically beautiful. I saw a large pile of these letters a few weeks ago in Gonzaga's chapel, at the church of St. Ignatius. They were lying at the foot of the altar, prettily written on smooth paper, and tied with silken ribands of various colors. Leaning over the marble balustrade, I read the following superscription upon one of them: "*All' Angelico Giovane S. Luigi Gonzaga, Paradiso,* — To the angelic youth St. Louis Gonzaga, Paradise." A soldier, with a musket, kept guard over this treasure; and I had the audacity to ask him at what hour the mail went out; for which heretical impertinence he cocked his mustache at me with the most savage look imaginable, as much as to say, "Get thee gone:" —

"Andate,
Niente pigliate,
E mai ritornate."

The modern Romans are likewise strongly given to amusements of every description. *Panem et circenses*, says the Latin satirist, when chiding the degraded propensities of his countrymen; *Panem et circenses*, — they are content with bread and the sports of the circus. The same may be said at the present day. Even in this hot weather, when the shops are shut at noon, and the fat priests waddle about the streets with fans in their hands, the people crowd to the Mausoleum of Augustus, to be choked with the smoke of fireworks, and see deformed and humpback dwarfs tumbled into the dirt by the masked horns of young bullocks. What a refined amusement for the inhabitants of "pompous and holy Rome!"

The Sirocco prevails to-day, — a hot wind from the burning sands of Africa, that bathes its wings in the sea, and comes laden with fogs and vapors to the shores of Italy. It is oppressive and dispiriting, and quite unmans one, like the dog-days of the North. There is a scrap of an old English song running in my mind, in which the poet calls it a cool wind; though ten to one I misquote.

"When the cool Sirocco blows,
And daws and pies and rooks and crows
Sit and curse the wintry snows,
Then give me ale!"

I should think that stark English beer might have a potent charm against the powers of the foul fiend that rides this steaming, reeking wind. A flask of Montefiascone, or a bottle of Lacrima Christi does very well.

———

Beggars all, — beggars all! The Papal city is full of them; and they hold you by the button through the whole calendar of saints. You cannot choose but hear. I met an old woman yesterday who pierced my ear with this alluring petition: —

"*Ah signore! Qualche piccola cosa, per carità! Vi dirò la buona ventura! C' è una bella signorina, che vi ama molto! Per il Sacro Sacramento! Per la Madonna!*"

Which being interpreted, is, "Ah, sir, a trifle, for charity's sake! I will tell your fortune for you! There is a beautiful young lady who loves you well! For the Holy Sacrament, — for the Madonna's sake!"

Who could resist such an appeal?

I made a laughable mistake this morning in giving alms. A man stood on the shady side of the street with his hat in his hand, and as I passed he gave me a piteous look, though he said nothing. He had such a woe-begone face, and such a threadbare coat, that I at once took him for one of those mendicants who bear the title of *poveri vergognosi*, — bashful beggars; persons whom pinching want compels to receive the stranger's charity, though pride restrains them from asking it. Moved with compassion, I threw into the hat the little I had to give; when, instead of thanking me with a blessing, my man with the threadbare coat showered upon me the most sonorous maledictions of his native tongue, and, emptying his greasy hat upon the pavement, drew it down over his ears with both hands, and stalked away with all the dignity of a Roman senator in the best days of the republic, — to the infinite amusement of a green-grocer, who stood at his shop-door bursting with laughter. No time was given me for an apology; but I resolved to be for the future more discriminating in my charities, and not to take for a beggar every poor gentleman who chose to stand in the shade with his hat in his hand on a hot summer's day.

———

There is an old fellow who hawks pious legends and the lives of saints through the streets of Rome, with a sharp, cracked voice, that knows no pause nor division in the sentences it utters. I just heard him cry at a breath: —

"*La Vita di San Giuseppe quel fidel servitor di Dio santo e maraviglioso mezzo bajocco,* — The Life of St. Joseph that faithful servant of God holy and wonderful ha'penny!*"

This is the way with some people; everything helter-skelter, — heads and tails, — prices current and the lives of saints!

———

It has been a rainy day, — a day of gloom. The church-bells never rang in my ears with so melancholy a sound; and this afternoon I saw a mournful scene, which still haunts my imagination. It was the funeral of a monk. I was drawn to the window by the solemn chant, as the procession came from a neighboring street, and crossed the square. First came a long train of priests, clad in black, and bearing in their hands large waxen tapers, which flared in every gust of wind, and were now and then extinguished by the rain. The bier followed, borne on the shoulders of four barefooted Carmelites; and upon it, ghastly and grim, lay the body of the dead monk, clad in his long gray kirtle, with the twisted cord about his waist. Not even a shroud was thrown over him. His head and feet were bare, and his hands were placed upon his bosom, palm to palm, in the attitude of prayer. His face was emaciated, and of a livid hue; his eyes unclosed; and at every movement of the bier, his head nodded to and fro, with an unearthly and hideous aspect. Behind walked the monastic brotherhood, a long and melancholy procession, with their cowls thrown back, and their eyes cast upon the ground; and last of all came a man with a rough, unpainted coffin upon his shoulders, closing the funeral train.

———

Many of the priests, monks, monsignori, and cardinals of Rome have a bad reputation, even after deducting a tithe or so from the tales of gossip. To some of them may be applied the rhyming Latin distich, written for the monks of old : —

> " O Monachi,
> Vestri stomachi
> Sunt amphora Bacchi;
> Vos estis,
> Deus est testis,
> Turpissima pestis."

The graphic description which Thomson gives in his " Castle of Indolence " would readily find an impersonation among the Roman priesthood : —

> " Full oft by holy feet our ground was trod, —
> Of clerks good plenty here you mote espy; —
> A little, round, fat, oily man of God
> Was one I chiefly marked among the fry;
> He had a roguish twinkle in his eye,
> Which shone all glittering with ungodly dew,
> When a tight damsel chanced to trippen by;
> But when observed, would shrink into his mew,
> And straight would recollect his piety anew."

Yonder across the square goes a *Minente* of Trastevere; a fellow who boasts the blood of the old Romans in his veins. He is a plebeian exquisite of the western bank of the Tiber, with a swarthy face and the step of an emperor. He wears a slouched hat, and blue velvet jacket and breeches, and has enormous silver buckles in his shoes. As he marches along, he sings a ditty in his own vulgar dialect : —

> " Uno, due, e tre,
> E lo Papa non è Re."

Now he stops to talk with a woman with a pan of coals in her hand. What violent gestures! what expressive attitudes! Head, hands, and feet are all in motion, — not a muscle is still! It must be some interesting subject that excites him so much, and gives such energy to his gestures and his language. No; he only wants to light his pipe!

It is now past midnight. The moon is full and bright, and the shadows lie so dark and massive in the street that they seem a part of the walls that cast them. I have just returned from the Coliseum, whose ruins are so marvellously beautiful by moonlight. No stranger at

Rome omits this midnight visit; for though there is something unpleasant in having one's admiration forestalled, and being as it were romantic aforethought, yet the charm is so powerful, the scene so surpassingly beautiful and sublime, — the hour, the silence, and the colossal ruin have such a mastery over the soul, — that you are disarmed when most upon your guard, and betrayed into an enthusiasm which perhaps you had silently resolved you would not feel.

On my way to the Coliseum, I crossed the Capitoline Hill, and descended into the Roman Forum by the broad staircase that leads to the triumphal arch of Septimius Severus. Close upon my right hand stood the three remaining columns of the Temple of the Thunderer, and the beautiful Ionic portico of the Temple of Concord, — their base in shadow, and the bright moonbeam striking aslant upon the broken entablature above. Before me rose the Phocian Column, — an isolated shaft, like a thin vapor hanging in the air scarce visible; and far to the left, the ruins of the Temple of Antonio and Faustina, and the three colossal arches of the Temple of Peace, — dim, shadowy, indistinct, — seemed to melt away and mingle with the sky. I crossed the Forum to the foot of the Palatine, and, ascending the Via Sacra, passed beneath the Arch of Titus. From this point, I saw below me the gigantic outline of the Coliseum, like a cloud resting upon the earth. As I descended the hillside, it grew more broad and high, — more definite in its form, and yet more grand in its dimensions, — till, from the vale from which it stands encompassed by three of the Seven Hills of Rome, — the Palatine, the Cœlian, and the Esquiline, — the majestic ruin in all its solitary grandeur " swelled vast to heaven."

A single sentinel was pacing to and fro beneath the arched gateway which leads to the interior, and his measured footsteps were the only sound that broke the breathless silence of the night. What a contrast with the scene which that same midnight hour presented, when, in Domitian's time, the eager populace began to gather at the gates, impatient for the morning sports! Nor was the contrast within less striking. Silence, and the quiet moonbeams, and the broad, deep shadows of the ruined wall! Where were the senators of Rome, her matrons, and her virgins? where the ferocious populace that rent the air with shouts, when, in the hundred holidays that marked the dedication of this imperial slaughter-house, five thousand wild beasts from the Libyan deserts and the forests of Anatolia made the arena sick with blood? Where were the Christian martyrs, that died with prayers upon their lips, amid the jeers and imprecations of their fellow-men? where the barbarian gladiators, brought forth to the festival of blood, and "butchered to make a Roman holiday"? The awful silence answered, "They are mine!" The dust beneath me answered, "They are mine!"

I crossed to the opposite extremity of the amphitheatre. A lamp was burning in the little chapel, which has been formed from what was once a den for the wild beasts of the Roman festivals. Upon the steps sat the old beadsman, the only tenant of the Coliseum, who guides the stranger by night through the long galleries of this vast pile of ruins. I followed him up a narrow wooden staircase, and entered one of the long and majestic corridors, which in ancient times ran entirely round the amphitheatre. Huge columns of solid mason-work, that seem the labor of Titans, support the flattened arches above; and though the iron clamps are gone, which once fastened the

hewn stones together, yet the columns stand majestic and unbroken, amid the ruin around them, and seem to defy "the iron tooth of time." Through the arches at the right, I could faintly discern the ruins of the baths of Titus on the Esquiline; and from the left, through every chink and cranny of the wall, poured in the brilliant light of the full moon, casting gigantic shadows around me, and diffusing a soft, silvery twilight through the long arcades. At length I came to an open space, where the arches above had crumbled away, leaving the pavement an unroofed terrace high in air. From this point, I could see the whole interior of the amphitheatre spread out beneath me, with such a soft and indefinite outline that it seemed less an earthly reality than a reflection in the bosom of a lake. The figures of several persons below were just perceptible, mingling grotesquely with their foreshortened shadows. The sound of their voices reached me in a whisper; and the cross that stands in the centre of the arena looked like a dagger thrust into the sand. I did not conjure up the past, for the past had already become identified with the present. It was before me in one of its visible and most majestic forms. The arbitrary distinctions of time, years, ages, centuries were annihilated. I was a citizen of Rome! This was the amphitheatre of Flavius Vespasian! Mighty is the spirit of the past, amid the ruins of the Eternal City!

THE VILLAGE OF LA RICCIA.

Egressum magnâ me excepit Aricia Româ,
Hospitio modico.

HORACE.

I PASSED the month of September at the village of La Riccia, which stands upon the western declivity of the Albanian hills, looking towards Rome. Its situation is one of the most beautiful which Italy can boast. Like a mural crown, it encircles the brow of a romantic hill; woodlands of the most luxuriant foliage whisper around it; above rise the rugged summits of the Abruzzi, and beneath lies the level floor of the Campagna, blotted with ruined tombs, and marked with broken but magnificent aqueducts that point the way to Rome. The whole region is classic ground. The Appian Way leads you from the gate of Rome to the gate of La Riccia. On one hand you have the Alban Lake, on the other the Lake of Nemi; and the sylvan retreats around were once the dwellings of Hippolytus and the nymph Egeria.

The town itself, however, is mean and dirty. The only inhabitable part is near the northern gate, where the two streets of the village meet. There, face to face, upon a square terrace, paved with large, flat stones, stand the Chigi palace and the village church with a dome and portico. There, too, stands the village inn, with its beds of cool, elastic maize-husks, its little dormitories, six feet square, and its spacious saloon, upon whose walls the melancholy story of Hippolytus is told in gorgeous frescoes. And there, too, at the union of the streets, just peeping through the gateway, rises the wedge-shaped Casa Antonini, within whose dusty chambers I passed the month of my *villeggiatura*, in company with two much-esteemed friends from the Old Dominion, — a fair daughter of that generous clime, and her husband, an artist, an enthusiast, and a man of "infinite jest."

My daily occupations in this delightful spot were such as an idle man usually whiles away his time withal in such a rural residence. I read Italian poetry, — strolled in the Chigi park, — rambled about the wooded environs of the village, — took an airing on a jackass, — threw stones into the Alban Lake, — and, being seized at intervals with the artist-mania, that came upon me like an intermittent fever, sketched — or thought I did — the trunk of a hollow tree, or the spire of a distant church, or a fountain in the shade.

At such seasons, the mind is "tickled with a straw," and magnifies each trivial circumstance into an event of some importance. I recollect one morning, as I sat at breakfast in the village coffee-house, a large and beautiful spaniel came into the room, and placing his head upon my knee looked up into my face with a most piteous look, poor dog! as much as to say that he had not breakfasted. I gave him a morsel of bread, which he swallowed without so much as moving his long silken ears; and keeping his soft, beautiful eyes still fixed upon mine, he thumped upon the floor with his bushy tail, as if knocking for the waiter. He was a very beautiful animal, and so gentle and affectionate in his manner, that I asked the waiter who his owner was.

"He has none now," said the boy.

"What!" said I, "so fine a dog without a master?"

"Ah, sir, he used to belong to Gasparoni, the famous robber of the Abruzzi mountains, who murdered so many people, and was caught at last and sent to the galleys for life. There's his portrait on the wall."

It hung directly in front of me; a coarse print, representing the dark, stern countenance of that sinful man, a face that wore an expression of savage ferocity and coarse sensuality. I had heard his story told in the village; the accustomed tale of outrage, violence, and murder. And is it possible, thought I, that this man of blood could have chosen so kind and gentle a companion? What a rebuke must he have met in those large, meek eyes, when he patted his favorite on the head, and dappled his long ears with blood! Heaven seems in mercy to have ordained that none — no, not even the most depraved — should be left entirely to his evil nature, without one patient monitor, — a wife, — a daughter, — a fawning, meek-eyed dog, whose silent, supplicating look may rebuke the man of sin! If this mute, playful creature, that licks the stranger's hand, were gifted with the power of articulate speech, how many a tale of midnight storm, and mountain-pass, and lonely glen, would — but these reflections are commonplace!

On another occasion, I saw an overladen ass fall on the steep and slippery pavement of the street. He made violent but useless efforts to get upon his feet again; and his brutal driver — more brutal than the suffering beast of burden — beat him unmercifully with his heavy whip. Barbarian! is it not enough that you have laid upon your uncomplaining servant a burden greater than he can bear? Must you scourge this unresisting slave, because his strength has failed him in your hard service? Does not that imploring look disarm you? Does not — and here was another theme for commonplace reflection!

Again. A little band of pilgrims, clad in white, with staves, and scallop-shells, and sandal shoon, have just passed through the village gate, wending their toilsome way to the holy shrine of Loretto. They wind along the brow of the hill with slow and solemn pace, — just as they ought to do, to agree with my notion of a pilgrimage drawn from novels. And now they disappear behind the hill; and hark! they are singing a mournful hymn, like Christian and Hopeful on their way to the Delectable Mountains. How strange it seems to me, that I should ever behold a scene like this! a pilgrimage to Loretto! Here was another outline for the imagination to fill up.

But my chief delight was in sauntering along the many woodland walks, which diverge in every direction from the gates of La Riccia. One of these plunges down the steep declivity of the hill, and, threading its way through a most romantic valley, leads to the shapeless tomb of the Horatii and the pleasant village of Albano. Another conducts you over swelling uplands and through wooded hollows to Genzano and the sequestered Lake of Nemi, which lies in its deep crater, like the waters of a well, "all coiled into itself and round, as sleeps the snake." A third, and the most beautiful of all, runs in an undulating line along the crest of the last and lowest ridge of the Albanian Hills, and leads to the borders of the Alban Lake. In parts it hides itself in thick-leaved hollows, in parts climbs the open hillside and overlooks the Campagna. Then it winds along the brim of the deep, oval basin of the lake, to the village of Castel Gandolfo, and thence onward to Marino, Grotta-Ferrata, and Frascati.

That part of the road which looks down upon the lake passes through a magnificent gallery of thick embowering trees, whose dense and luxuriant foliage completely shuts out the noonday sun, forming

> "A greensward wagon-way, that, like
> Cathedral aisle, completely roofed with branches,
> Runs through the gloomy wood from top to bottom,
> And has at either end a Gothic door
> Wide open."

This long sylvan arcade is called the *Galleria-di-sopra*, to distinguish it from the *Galleria-di-sotto*, a similar, though less beautiful avenue, leading from Castel Gandolfo to Albano, under the brow of the hill. In this upper gallery, and almost hidden amid its old and leafy trees, stands a Capuchin convent, with a little esplanade in front, from which the eye enjoys a beautiful view of the lake, and the swelling hills beyond. It is a lovely spot, — so lonely, cool, and still; and was my favorite and most frequented haunt.

Another pathway conducts you round the southern shore of the Alban Lake, and, after passing the site of the ancient Alba Longa, and the convent of Palazzuolo, turns off to the right through a luxuriant forest, and climbs the rugged precipice of Rocca di Papa. Behind this village swells the rounded peak of Monte Cavo, the highest pinnacle of the Albanian Hills, rising three thousand feet above the level of the sea. Upon its summit once stood a temple of Jupiter, and the Triumphal Way, by which the Roman conquerors ascended once a year in solemn procession to offer sacrifices, still leads you up the side of the hill. But a convent has been built upon the ruins of the ancient temple, and the disciples of Loyola are now the only conquerors that tread the pavement of the Triumphal Way.

The view from the windows of the convent is vast and magnificent. Directly beneath you, the sight plunges headlong into a gulf of dark-green foliage, — the Alban Lake seems so near that you can almost drop a pebble into it, — and Nemi, embosomed in a green and cup-like valley, lies like a dew-drop in the hollow of a leaf. All around you, upon every swell of the landscape, the white walls of rural towns and villages peep from their leafy coverts, — Genzano, La Riccia, Castel Gandolfo, and Albano; and beyond spreads the flat and desolate Campagna, with Rome in its centre and seamed by the silver thread of the Tiber, that at Ostia, "with a pleasant stream, whirling in rapid eddies, and yellow with much sand, rushes forward into the sea." The scene of half the Æneid is spread beneath you like a map; and it would need volumes to describe each point that arrests the eye in this magnificent panorama.

As I stood leaning over the balcony of the convent, giving myself up to those reflections which the scene inspired, one of the brotherhood came from a neighboring cell, and entered into conversation with me. He was an old man, with a hoary head, and a trembling hand; yet his voice was musical and soft, and his eye still beamed with the enthusiasm of youth.

"How wonderful," said he, "is the scene before us! I have been an inmate of these walls for thirty years, and yet this prospect is as beautiful to my eye as when I gazed upon it for the first time. Not a day passes that I do not come to this window to behold and to admire. My heart is still alive to the beauties of the scene, and to all the classic associations it inspires."

"You have never, then, been whipped by an angel for reading Cicero and Plautus, as St. Jerome was?"

"No," said the monk, with a smile. "From my youth up I have been a disciple of Chrysostom, who often slept with the comedies of

Aristophanes beneath his pillow; and yet I confess that the classic associations of Roman history and fable are not the most thrilling which this scene awakens in my mind. Yonder is the bridge from which Constantine beheld the miraculous cross of fire in the sky; and I can never forget that this convent is built upon the ruins of a pagan temple. The town of Ostia, which lies before us on the seashore, is renowned as the spot where the Trojan fugitive first landed on the coast of Italy. But other associations than this have made the spot holy in my sight. Marcus Minutius Felix, a Roman lawyer, who flourished in the third century, a convert to our blessed faith, and one of the purest writers of the Latin Church, here places the scene of his 'Octavius.' This work has probably never fallen into your hands; for you are too young to have pushed your studies into the dusty tomes of the early Christian fathers."

I replied that I had never so much as heard the book mentioned before; and the monk continued: —

"It is a dialogue upon the vanity of pagan idolatry and the truth of the Christian religion, between Cæcilius, a heathen, and Octavius, a Christian. The style is rich, flowing, and poetical; and if the author handles his weapons with less power than a Tertullian, yet he exhibits equal adroitness and more grace. He has rather the studied elegance of the Roman lawyer, than the bold spirit of a Christian martyr. But the volume is a treasure to me in my solitary hours, and I love to sit here upon the balcony, and con its poetic language and sweet imagery. You shall see the volume; I carry it in my bosom."

With these words, the monk drew from the folds of his gown a small volume, bound in parchment, and clasped with silver; and, turning over its well worn leaves, continued: —

"In the introduction, the author describes himself as walking upon the sea-shore at Ostia, in company with his friends Octavius and Cæcilius. Observe in what beautiful language he describes the scene."

Here he read to me the following passage, which I transcribe, not from memory, but from the book itself.

"It was vacation-time, and that gave me aloose from my business at the bar; for it was the season after the summer's heat, when autumn promised fair, and put on the face of temperate. We set out, therefore, in the morning early, and as we were walking upon the sea-shore, and a kindly breeze fanned and refreshed our limbs, and the yielding sand softly submitted to our feet and made it delicious travelling, Cæcilius on a sudden espied the statue of Serapis, and, according to the vulgar mode of superstition, raised his hand to his mouth, and paid his adoration in kisses. Upon which, Octavius, addressing himself to me, said, — 'It is not well done, my brother Marcus, thus to leave your inseparable companion in the depth of vulgar darkness, and to suffer him, in so clear a day, to stumble upon stones; stones, indeed, of figure, and anointed with oil, and crowned; but stones, however, still they are; — for you cannot but be sensible that your permitting so foul an error in your friend redounds no less to your disgrace than his.' This discourse of his held us through half the city; and now we began to find ourselves upon the free and open shore. There the gently washing waves had spread the extremest sands into the order of an artificial walk; and as the sea always expresses some roughness in his looks, even when the winds are still, although he did not roll in foam and angry surges to the shore, yet were we much delighted, as we walked upon the edges of the water, to see the crisping, frizzly waves glide in snaky folds, one while playing against our feet, and then again retiring and lost in the devouring ocean. Softly then, and calmly as the sea about us, we travelled on, and kept upon the brim of the gently declining shore, beguiling the way with our stories."

Here the sound of the convent-bell interrupted the reading of the monk, and, closing the volume, he replaced it in his bosom, and bade me farewell, with a parting injunction to read the " Octavius " of Minutius Felix as soon as I should return to Rome.

During the summer months, La Riccia is a favorite resort of foreign artists who are pursuing their studies in the churches and galleries of Rome. Tired of copying the works of art, they go forth to copy the works of nature; and you will find them perched on their camp-stools at every picturesque point of view, with white umbrellas to shield them from the sun, and paint-boxes upon their knees, sketching with busy hands the smiling features of the landscape. The peasantry, too, are fine models for their study. The women of Genzano are noted for their beauty, and almost every village in the neighborhood has something peculiar in its costume.

The sultry day was closing, and I had reached, in my accustomed evening's walk, the woodland gallery that looks down upon the Alban Lake. The setting sun seemed to melt away in the sky, dissolving into a golden rain, that bathed the whole Campagna with unearthly splendor; while Rome in the distance, half-hidden, half-revealed, lay floating like a mote in the broad and misty sunbeam. The woodland walk before me seemed roofed with gold and emerald; and at intervals across its leafy arches shot the level rays of the sun, kindling, as they passed, like the burning shaft of Acestes. Beneath me the lake slept quietly. A blue, smoky vapor floated around its overhanging cliffs; the tapering cone of Monte Cavo hung reflected in the water; a little boat skimmed along its glassy surface, and I could even hear the sound of the laboring oar, so motionless and silent was the air around me.

I soon reached the convent of Castel Gandolfo. Upon one of the stone benches of the esplanade sat a monk with a book in his hand. He saluted me, as I approached, and some trivial remarks upon the scene before us led us into conversation. I observed by his accent that he was not a native of Italy, though he spoke Italian with great fluency. In this opinion I was confirmed by his saying that he should soon bid farewell to Italy and return to his native lakes and mountains in the north of Ireland. I then said to him in English, —

" How strange, that an Irishman and an Anglo-American should be conversing together in Italian upon the shores of Lake Albano!"

"It is strange," said he, with a smile; "though stranger things have happened. But I owe the pleasure of this meeting to a circumstance which changes that pleasure into pain. I have been detained here many weeks beyond the time I had fixed for my departure by the illness of a friend, who lies at the point of death within the walls of this convent."

"Is he, too, a Capuchin friar like yourself?"

"He is. We came together from our native land, some six years ago, to study at the Jesuit College in Rome. This summer we were to have returned home again; but I shall now make the journey alone."

"Is there, then, no hope of his recovery?"

"None whatever," answered the monk, shaking his head. "He has been brought to this convent from Rome, for the benefit of a purer air; but it is only to die, and be buried near the borders of this beautiful lake. He is a victim of consumption. But come with me to his cell. He will feel it a kindness to have you visit him. Such a mark of sympathy in a stranger will be grateful to him in this foreign land, where friends are so few."

We entered the chapel together, and, ascending a flight of steps beside the altar, passed into the cloisters of the convent. Another flight of steps led us to the domitories above, in one of which the sick man lay. Here my guide left me for a moment, and softly entered a neighboring cell. He soon returned and beckoned me to come in. The room was dark and hot; for the window-shutters had been closed to keep out the rays of the sun, that in the after part of the day fell unobstructed upon the western wall of the convent. In one corner of the little room, upon a pallet of straw, lay the sick man, with his face towards the wall. As I entered, he raised himself upon his elbow, and, stretching out his hand to me, said, in a faint voice, — "I am glad to see you. It is kind in you to make me this visit."

Then speaking to his friend, he begged him to open the shutters and let in the light and air; and as the bright sunbeam through the wreathing vapors of evening played upon the wall and ceiling, he said, with a sigh, — "How beautiful is an Italian sunset! Its splendor is all around us, as if we stood in the horizon itself and could touch the sky. And yet, to a sick man's feeble and distempered sight, it has a wan and sickly hue. He turns away with an aching heart from the splendor he cannot en-

joy. The cool air seems the only friendly thing that is left for him."

As he spake, a deeper shade of sadness stole over his pale countenance, sallow and attenuated by long illness. But it soon passed off: and as the conversation changed to other topics, he grew cheerful again. He spoke of his return to his native land with childish delight. This hope had not deserted him. It seemed never to have entered his mind that even this consolation would be denied him, — that death would thwart even these fond anticipations.

"I shall soon be well enough," said he, "to undertake the journey; and, oh, with what delight shall I turn my back upon the Apennines! We shall cross the Alps into Switzerland, then go down the Rhine to England, and soon, soon we shall see the shores of the Emerald Isle, and once more embrace father, mother, sisters! By my profession, I have renounced the world, but not those holy emotions of love which are one of the highest attributes of the soul, and which, though sown in corruption here, shall hereafter be raised in incorruption. No; even he that died for us upon the cross, in the last hour, in the unutterable agony of death, was mindful of his mother; as if to teach us that this holy love should be our last worldly thought, the last point of earth from which the soul should take its flight for heaven."

He ceased to speak. His eyes were fastened upon the sky with a fixed and steady gaze, though all unconsciously, for his thoughts were far away amid the scenes of his distant home. As I left his cell, he seemed sinking to sleep, and hardly noticed my departure. The gloom of twilight had already filled the cloisters; the monks were chanting their evening hymn in the chapel; and one unbroken shadow spread through the long cathedral aisle of forest-trees which led me homeward. There, in the silence of the hour, and amid the almost sepulchral gloom of the woodland scene, I tried to impress upon my careless heart the serious and affecting lesson I had learned.

I saw the sick monk no more; but a day or two afterward I heard in the village that he had departed, — not for an earthly, but for a heavenly home.

VENICE BY MOONLIGHT.

ARTIST: ROSS TURNER.

NOTE-BOOK.

Once more among the old, gigantic hills,
    With vapors clouded o'er,
The vales of Lombardy grow dim behind,
    And rocks ascend before.
They beckon me, — the giants, — from afar,
    They wing my footsteps on;
Their helms of ice, their plumage of the pine,
    Their cuirasses of stone.

OEHLENSCHLÄGER.

THE glorious autumn closed. From the Abruzzi Mountains came the Zampognari, playing their rustic bagpipes beneath the images of the Virgin in the streets of Rome, and hailing with rude minstrelsy the approach of merry Christmas. The shops were full of dolls and playthings for the Bifana, who enacts in Italy the same merry interlude for children that Santiclaus does in the North ; and travellers from colder climes began to fly southward, like sun-seeking swallows.

I left Rome for Venice, crossing the Apennines by the wild gorge of the Strettura, in a drenching rain. At Fano we struck into the sands of the Adriatic, and followed the seashore northward to Rimini, where in the market-place stands a pedestal of stone, from which, as an officious cicerone informed me, "Julius Cæsar preached to his army, before crossing the Rubicon." Other principal points in my journey were Bologna, with its Campo Santo, its gloomy arcades, and its sausages ; Ferrara, with its ducal palace and the dungeon of Tasso ; Padua the Learned, with its sombre and scholastic air, and its inhabitants "apt for pike or pen."

—————

I first saw Venice by moonlight, as we skimmed by the island of St. George in a felucca, and entered the Grand Canal. A thousand lamps glittered from the square of St. Mark, and along the water's edge. Above rose the cloudy shapes of spires, domes, and palaces, emerging from the sea ; and occasionally the twinkling lamp of a gondola darted across the water like a shooting star, and suddenly disappeared, as if quenched in the wave. There was something so unearthly in the scene, — so visionary and fairy-like, — that I almost expected to see the city float away like a cloud, and dissolve into thin air. Howell, in his " Signorie of Venice," says, " It is the water, wherein she lies like a swan's nest, that doth both fence and feed her." Again: "She swims in wealth and wantonness, as well as she doth in the waters ; she melts in softness and sensuality, as much as any other whatsoever." And still further : " Her streets are so neat and evenly paved, that in the dead of winter one may walk up and down in a pair of satin pantables and crimson silk stockings, and not be dirtied." And the old Italian proverb says, —

" Venegia, Venegia,
    Chi non ti vede non ti pregia;
    Ma chi t' ha troppo veduto
    Ti dispregia!"

Venice, Venice, who sees thee not doth not prize thee ; but who hath too much seen thee doth despise thee !

Should you ever want a gondolier at Venice to sing you a passage from Tasso by moonlight, inquire for Toni Toscan. He has a voice like a raven. I sketched his portrait in my note-book ; and he wrote beneath it this inscription : —

" Poeta Natural che Venizian,
    Ch' el so nome xe un tal Toni Toscan."

—————

The road from Venice to Trieste traverses a vast tract of level land, with the Friulian Mountains on the left, and the Adriatic on the right. You pass through long avenues of trees, and the road stretches in unbroken perspective before and behind. Trieste is a busy, commercial city, with wide streets intersecting each other at right angles. It is a mart for all nations. Greeks, Turks, Italians, Germans, French, and English meet you at every corner and in every coffee-house; and the ever-changing variety of national countenance and costume affords an amusing and instructive study for a traveller.

Trieste to Vienna. Daybreak among the Carnic Alps. Above and around me huge snow-covered pinnacles, shapeless masses in the pale starlight, — till touched by the morning sunbeam, as by Ithuriel's spear, they assume their natural forms and dimensions. A long, winding valley beneath, sheeted with spotless snow. At my side a yawning and rent chasm; — a mountain brook, — seen now and then through the chinks of its icy bridge, — black and treacherous, — and tinkling along its frozen channel with a sound like a distant clanking of chains.

Magnificent highland scenery between Grätz and Vienna in the Steiermark. The wild mountain-pass from Meerzuschlag to Schottwien. A castle built like an eagle's nest upon the top of a perpendicular crag. A little hamlet at the base of the mountain. A covered wagon, drawn by twenty-one horses, slowly toiling up the slippery, zigzag road. A snowstorm. Reached Vienna at midnight.

On the southern bank of the Danube, about sixteen miles above Vienna, stands the ancient castle of Greifenstein, where — if the tale be true, though many doubt, and some deny it — Richard the Lion-heart of England was imprisoned, when returning from the third crusade. It is built upon the summit of a steep and rocky hill, that rises just far enough from the river's brink to leave a foothold for the highway. At the base of the hill stands the village of Greifenstein, from which a winding pathway leads you to the old castle. You pass through an arched gate into a narrow courtyard, and thence onward to a large, square tower. Near the doorway, and deeply cut into the solid rock, upon which the castle stands, is the form of a human hand, so perfect that your

own lies in it as in a mould. And hence the name of Greifenstein. In the square tower is Richard's prison, completely isolated from the rest of the castle. A wooden staircase leads up on the outside to a light balcony, running entirely round the tower, not far below its turrets. From this balcony you enter the prison, — a small, square chamber, lighted by two Gothic windows. The walls of the tower are some five feet thick; and in the pavement is a trap-door, opening into a dismal vault, — a vast dungeon which occupies all the lower part of the tower, quite down to its rocky foundations, and which formerly had no entrance but the trap-door above. In one corner of the chamber stands a large cage of oaken timber, in which the royal prisoner is said to have been shut up; — the grossest lie that ever cheated the gaping curiosity of a traveller.

The balcony commands some fine and picturesque views. Beneath you winds the lordly Danube, spreading its dark waters over a wide tract of meadow-land, and forming numerous little islands; and all around, the landscape is bounded by forest-covered hills, topped by the mouldering turrets of a feudal castle or the tapering spire of a village church. The spot is well worth visiting, though German antiquaries say that Richard was not imprisoned there; this story being at best a bold conjecture of what is possible, though not probable.

From Vienna I passed northward, visiting Prague, Dresden, and Leipsic, and then folding my wings for a season in the scholastic shades of Göttingen. Thence I passed through Cassel to Frankfort-on-the-Maine; and thence to Mayence, where I took the steamboat down the Rhine. These several journeys I shall not describe, for as many several reasons. First, — but no matter, — I prefer thus to stride across the earth like the Saturnian in Micromegas, making but one step from the Adriatic to the German Ocean. I leave untold the wonders of the wondrous Rhine, a fascinating theme. Not even the beauties of the Vautsburg and the Bingenloch shall detain me. I hasten, like the blue waters of that romantic river, to lose myself in the sands of Holland.

THE PILGRIM'S SALUTATION.

Ye who have traced the Pilgrim to the scene
Which is his last, if in your memories dwell
A thought which once was his, if on ye swell
A single recollection, not in vain
He wore his sandal-shoon and scallop-shell.
      Childe Harold.

THESE, fair dames and courteous gentlemen, are some of the scenes and musings of my pilgrimage, when I journeyed away from my kith and kin into the land of Outre-Mer. And yet amid these scenes and musings, — amid all the novelties of the Old World, and the quick succession of images that were continually calling my thoughts away, there were always fond regrets and longings after the land of my birth lurking in the secret corners of my heart. When I stood by the sea-shore, and listened to the melancholy and familiar roar of its waves, it seemed but a step from the threshold of a foreign land to the fireside of home; and when I watched the out-bound sail, fading over the water's edge, and losing itself in the blue mists of the sea, my heart went with it and I turned away fancy-sick with the blessings of home and the endearments of domestic love.

> " I know not how, — but in yon land of roses
> My heart was heavy still;
> I startled at the warbling nightingale,
> The zephyr on the hill.
> They said the stars shone with a softer gleam:
> It seemed not so to me!
> In vain a scene of beauty beamed around, —
> My thoughts were o'er the sea."

At times I would sit at midnight in the solitude of my chamber, and give way to the recollection of distant friends. How delightful it is thus to strengthen within us the golden threads that unite our sympathies with the past,

— to fill up, as it were, the blanks of existence with the images of those we love! How sweet are these dreams of home in a foreign land! How calmly across life's stormy sea blooms that little world of affection, like those Hesperian isles where eternal summer reigns, and the olive blossoms all the year round, and honey distils from the hollow oak! Truly, the love of home is interwoven with all that is pure, and deep, and lasting in earthly affection. Let us wander where we may, the heart looks back with secret longing to the paternal roof. There the scattered rays of affection concentrate. Time may enfeeble them, distance overshadow them, and the storms of life obstruct them for a season; but they will at length break through the cloud and storm, and glow, and burn, and brighten around the peaceful threshold of home.

And now, farewell! The storm is over, and through the parting clouds the radiant sunshine breaks upon my path. God's blessing upon you for your hospitality. I fear I have but poorly repaid it by these tales of my pilgrimage; and I bear your kindness meekly, for I come not like Theudas of old, " boasting myself to be somebody."

Farewell! My prayer is that I be not among you as the stranger at the court of Busiris; that your God-speed be not a thrust that kills.

The Pilgrim's benison upon this honorable company. *Pax vobiscum!*

COLOPHON.

My pilgrimage is ended. I have come home to rest; and, recording the time past, I have fulfilled these things, and written them in this book, as it would come into my mind, — for the most part, when the duties of the day were over, and the world around me was hushed in sleep. The pen wherewith I write most easily is a feather stolen from the sable wing of night. Even now, as I record these parting words, it is long past midnight. The morning watches have begun. And as I write, the melancholy thought intrudes upon me, — To what end is all this toil? Of what avail these midnight vigils? Dost thou covet fame? Vain dreamer! A few brief days, — and what will the busy world know of thee? Alas! this little book is but a bubble on the stream; and although it may catch the sunshine for a moment, yet it will soon float down the swift-rushing current, and be seen no more!

Heart, take thine ease, —
Men hard to please
  Thou haply mightst offend.
Though some speak ill
Of thee, some will
  Say better; — there 's an end.
                              Heylin.

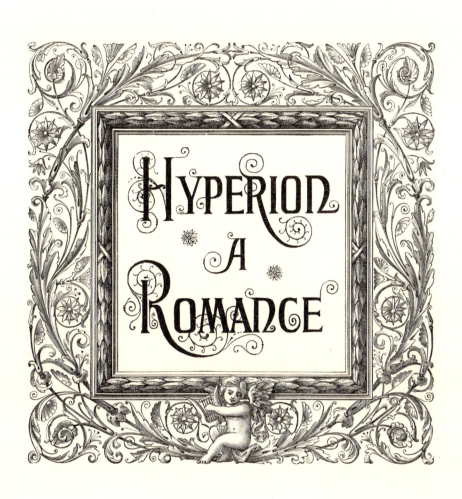

Hyperion

A

Romance

"Look not mournfully into the Past. It comes not back again. Wisely improve the Present. It is thine. Go forth to meet the shadowy Future, without fear, and with a manly heart."

BOOK THE FIRST.

CHAPTER I.

THE HERO.

IN John Lyly's "Endymion," Sir Topas is made to say: "Dost thou know what a poet is? Why, fool, a poet is as much as one should say, — a poet!" And thou, reader, dost thou know what a hero is? Why, a hero is as much as one should say, — a hero! Some romance-writers, however, say much more than this. Nay, the old Lombard, Matteo Maria Bojardo, set all the church-bells in Scandiano ringing, merely because he had found a name for one of his heroes. Here, also, shall church-bells be rung, but more solemnly.

The setting of a great hope is like the setting of the sun. The brightness of our life is gone. Shadows of evening fall around us, and the world seems but a dim reflection, — itself a broader shadow. We look forward into the coming lonely night. The soul withdraws into itself. Then stars arise, and the night is holy.

Paul Flemming had experienced this, though still young. The friend of his youth was dead. The bough had broken "under the burden of the unripe fruit." And when, after a season, he looked up again from the blindness of his sorrow, all things seemed unreal. Like the man whose sight had been restored by miracle, he beheld men, as trees, walking. His household gods were broken. He had no home. His sympathies cried aloud from his desolate soul, and there came no answer from the busy, turbulent world around him. He did not willingly give way to grief. He struggled to be cheerful, — to be strong. But he could no longer look into the familiar faces of his friends. He could no longer live alone, where he had lived with her. He went abroad, that the sea might be between him and the grave. Alas! between him and his sorrow there could be no sea, but that of time.

He had already passed many months in lonely wandering, and was now pursuing his way along the Rhine, to the South of Germany. He had journeyed the same way before, in brighter days and a brighter season of the year, in the May of life and in the month of May. He knew the beautiful river all by heart, — every rock and ruin, every echo, every legend. The ancient castles, grim and hoar, that had taken root as it were on the cliffs, — they were all his; for his thoughts dwelt in them, and the wind told him tales.

He had passed a sleepless night at Roland-seck, and had risen before daybreak. He opened the window of the balcony to hear the rushing of the Rhine. It was a damp December morning; and clouds were passing over the sky, — thin, vapory clouds, whose snow-white skirts were "often spotted with golden tears, which men call stars." The day dawned slowly; and, in the mingling of daylight and starlight, the island and cloister of Nonnenwerth made together but one broad, dark shadow on the silver breast of the river. Beyond, rose the summits of the Siebengebirg. Solemn and dark, like a monk, stood the Drachenfels, in his hood of mist; and rearward extended the curtain of mountains, back to the Wolkenburg, — the Castle of Clouds.

But Flemming thought not of the scene before him.   Sorrow unspeakable was upon his spirit in that lonely hour; and, hiding his face in his hands, he exclaimed aloud: —

"Spirit of the past! look not so mournfully at me with thy great tearful eyes!   Touch me not with thy cold hand!   Breathe not upon me with the icy breath of the grave!   Chant no more that dirge of sorrow, through the long and silent watches of the night!"

Mournful voices from afar seemed to answer, "Treuenfels!" and he remembered how others had suffered, and his heart grew still.

Slowly the landscape brightened.   Down the rushing stream came a boat, with its white wings spread, and darted like a swallow through the narrow pass of God's-Help.   The boatmen were singing, — but not the song of Roland the Brave, which was heard of old by the weeping Hildegund, as she sat within the walls of that cloister which now looked forth in the pale morning from amid the leafless lin-den-trees.   The dim traditions of those gray old times rose in the traveller's memory; for the ruined tower of Rolandseck was still looking down upon the Kloster Nonnenwerth, as if the sound of the funeral bell had changed the faithful paladin to stone and he were watching still to see the form of his beloved one come forth, not from her cloister, but from her grave.   Thus the brazen clasps of the book of legends were opened, and, on the page illuminated by the misty rays of the rising sun, he read again the tales of Liba, and the mournful bride of Argenfels, and Siegfried, the mighty slayer of the dragon.   Meanwhile the mists had risen from the Rhine, and the whole air was filled with golden vapor, through which he beheld the sun, hanging in heaven like a drop of blood.   Even thus shone the sun within him, amid the wintry vapors uprising from the valley of the shadow of death, through which flowed the stream of his life, — sighing, sighing!

CHAPTER II.

THE CHRIST OF ANDERNACH.

PAUL FLEMMING resumed his solitary journey.   The morning was still misty, but not cold.   Across the Rhine the sun came wading through the reddish vapors; and soft and silver-white outspread the broad river, without a ripple upon its surface, or visible motion of the ever-moving current.   A little vessel, with one loose sail, was riding at anchor, keel to keel with another that lay beneath it, its own apparition — and all was silent, and calm, and beautiful.

The road was for the most part solitary; for there are few travellers upon the Rhine in winter.   Peasant-women were at work in the vineyards, climbing up the slippery hillsides, like beasts of burden, with large baskets upon their backs.   And once during the morning a band of apprentices, with knapsacks, passed by, singing, "The Rhine! the Rhine! a blessing on the Rhine!"

Oh, the pride of the German heart in this noble river!   And right it is; for, of all the rivers of this beautiful earth, there is none so beautiful as this.   There is hardly a league of its whole course, from its cradle in the snowy Alps to its grave in the sands of Holland, which boasts not its peculiar charms. By heavens!   If I were a German, I would be proud of it too; and of the clustering grapes that hang about its temples, as it reels onward through vineyards in a triumphal march, like Bacchus crowned and drunken.

But I will not attempt to describe the Rhine; it would make this chapter much too long. And to do it well, one should write like a god; and his language flow onward royally with breaks and dashes, like the waters of that royal river, and antique, quaint, and Gothic times be reflected in it.   Alas! this evening mine flows not at all.   Flow, then, into this smoke-colored goblet, thou blood of the Rhine! out of thy prison-house, — out of thy long-necked, tapering flask, in shape not unlike a church-spire among thy native hills; and from the crystal belfry loud ring the merry tinkling bells, while I drink a health to

ARTIST: FREDERIC CROWNINSHIELD.

"Spirit of the past! look not so mournfully at me with thy great tearful eyes!"

my hero, in whose heart is sadness, and in whose ears the bells of Andernach are ringing noon.

He is threading his way alone through a narrow alley, and now up a flight of stone steps, and along the city wall, towards that old round tower built by the Archbishop Frederick of Cologne in the twelfth century. It has a romantic interest in his eyes; for he has still in his mind and heart that beautiful sketch of Carové, in which is described a day on the tower of Andernach. He finds the old keeper and his wife still there; and the old keeper closes the door behind him slowly, as of yore, lest he should jam too hard the poor souls in purgatory, whose fate it is to suffer in the cracks of doors and hinges. But, alas! alas! the daughter, the maiden with long, dark eyelashes! she is asleep in her little grave, under the linden-trees of Feldkirche, with rosemary in her folded hands!

Flemming returned to the hotel disappointed. As he passed along the narrow streets, he was dreaming of many things; but mostly of the keeper's daughter, asleep in the churchyard of Feldkirche. Suddenly, on turning the corner of an ancient, gloomy church, his attention was arrested by a little chapel in an angle of the wall. It was only a small thatched roof, like a bird's nest; under which stood a rude wooden image of the Saviour on the cross. A real crown of thorns was upon his head, which was bowed downward, as if in the death agony; and drops of blood were falling down his cheeks, and from his hands and feet and side. The face was haggard and ghastly beyond expression, and wore a look of unutterable bodily anguish. The rude sculptor had given it this, but his art could go no further. The sublimity of death in a dying Saviour, the expiring Godlikeness of Jesus of Nazareth, was not there. The artist had caught no heavenly inspiration from his theme. All was coarse, harsh, and revolting to a sensitive mind; and Flemming turned away with a shudder, as he saw this fearful image gazing at him with its fixed and half-shut eyes.

He soon reached the hotel, but that face of agony still haunted him. He could not refrain from speaking of it to a very old woman, who sat knitting by the window of the dining-room, in a high-backed, old-fashioned arm-chair. I believe she was the inn-keeper's grandmother. At all events, she was old enough to be so. She took off her owl-eyed spectacles, and, as she wiped the glasses with her handkerchief, said : —

"Thou dear Heaven! Is it possible? Did you never hear of the Christ of Andernach?"

Flemming answered in the negative.

"Thou dear Heaven!" continued the old woman. "It is a very wonderful story; and a true one, as every good Christian in Andernach will tell you. And it all happened before the death of my blessed man, four years ago; let me see, — yes, four years ago, come Christmas."

Here the old woman stopped speaking, but went on with her knitting. Other thoughts seemed to occupy her mind. She was thinking, no doubt, of her blessed man, as German widows call their dead husbands. But Flemming having expressed an ardent wish to hear the wonderful story, she told it, in nearly the following words.

"There was once a poor old woman in Andernach whose name was Frau Martha, and she lived all alone in a house by herself, and loved all the Saints and the Blessed Virgin, and was as good as an angel, and sold tarts down by the Rheinkrahn. But her house was very old, and the roof-tiles were broken, and she was too poor to get new ones, and the rain kept coming in, and no Christian soul in Andernach would help her. But the Frau Martha was a good woman, and never did anybody any harm, but went to mass every morning, and sold tarts down by the Rheinkrahn. Now one dark windy night, when all the good Christians in Andernach were asleep in the feathers, Frau Martha, who lay under the roof, heard a great noise over her head, and in her chamber, drip! drip! drip! as if the rain were dropping down through the broken tiles. Dear soul! and, sure enough, it was. And then there was a pounding and hammering overhead, as if somebody were at work on the roof; and she thought it was Pelz-Nickel tearing the tiles off, because she had not been to confession often enough. So she began to pray; and the faster she said her Pater-noster and her Ave-Maria, the faster Pelz-Nickel pounded and pulled; and drip! drip! drip! it went all round her in the dark chamber, till the poor woman was frightened out of her wits, and ran to the window to call for help. Then in a moment all was still, — death-still. But she saw a light streaming through the mist and rain, and a great shadow on the house opposite. And then somebody came down from the top of her house by a ladder, and had a lantern in his hand; and he took the ladder on his shoulder and passed down the street. But she could not see clearly, because the window was streaked with rain. And in the morning the old broken tiles were found scattered about the street, and there were new ones on the roof, and the old house has never leaked to this blessed day.

"As soon as mass was over, Frau Martha told the priest what had happened, and he said it was not Pelz-Nickel, but, without doubt, St. Castor or St. Florian. Then she went to the market and told Frau Bridget all about it; and Frau Bridget said, that, two nights before, Hans Claus, the cooper, had heard a great pounding in his shop, and in the morning found new hoops on all his hogsheads; and that a man with a lantern and a ladder had been seen riding out of town at midnight on a donkey; and that the same night the old windmill, at Kloster St. Thomas, had been mended, and the old gate of the churchyard at Feldkirche made as good as new, though nobody knew how the man got across the river. Then Frau Martha went down to the Rheinkrahn and told all these stories over again; and the old ferryman of Fahr said he could tell something about it; for, the very night that the churchyard-gate was mended, he was lying awake in his bed, because he could not sleep, and he heard a loud knocking at the door, and somebody calling to him to get up and set him over the river. And when he got up, he saw a man down by the river with a lantern and a ladder; but as he was going down to him, the man blew out the light, and it was so dark he could not see who he was; and his boat was old and leaky, and he was afraid to set him over in the dark; but the man said he must be in Ander-

nach that night; and so he set him over. And after they had crossed the river, he watched the man, till he came to an image of the Holy Virgin, and saw him put the ladder against the wall, and go up and light his lamp, and then walk along the street. And in the morning he found his old boat all caulked and tight, and painted red, and he could not for his blessed life tell who did it, unless it were the man with the lantern. Dear soul! how strange it was!

"And so it went on for some time; and whenever the man with the lantern had been seen walking through the street at night, so sure as the morning came, some work had been done for the sake of some good soul; and everybody knew he did it; and yet nobody could find out who he was, nor where he lived; — for, whenever anybody came near him, he blew out his light, turned down another street, and suddenly disappeared, nobody could tell how. And some said it was Rübezahl; and some, Pelz-Nickel; and some, St. Anthony-on-the-Heath.

"Now one stormy night a poor sinful creature was wandering about the streets, with her babe in her arms, and she was hungry, and cold, and no soul in Andernach would take her in. And when she came to the church, where the great crucifix stands, she saw no light in the little chapel at the corner; but she sat down on a stone at the foot of the cross and began to pray, and prayed till she fell asleep, with her poor little babe on her bosom. But she did not sleep long; for a bright light shone full in her face; and when she opened her eyes, she saw a pale man, with a lantern, standing right before her. He was almost naked; and there was blood upon his hands and body, and great tears in his beautiful eyes, and his face was like the face of the Saviour on the cross. Not a single word did he say to the poor woman; but looked at her compassionately, and gave her a loaf of bread, and took the little babe in his arms, and kissed it. Then the mother looked up to the great crucifix, but there was no image there; and she shrieked and fell down as if she were dead. And there she was found with her child; and a few days after they both died, and were buried together in one grave. And nobody would have believed her story, if a woman, who lived at the corner, had not gone to the window when she heard the scream, and seen the figure hang the lantern up in its place, and then set the ladder up against the wall, and go up and nail itself to the cross. Since that night it has never moved again. Ach! Herr Je!"

Such was the legend of the Christ of Andernach, as the old woman in spectacles told it to Flemming. It made a painful impression on his sick and morbid soul; and he felt now for the first time how great is the power of popular superstition.

The post-chaise being already at the door, Flemming was soon on the road to Coblentz, a town which stands upon the Rhine, at the mouth of the Mosel, opposite Ehrenbreitstein. It is by no means a long drive from Andernach to Coblentz; and the only incident which occurred to enliven the way was the appearance of a fat, red-faced man on horseback, trotting slowly towards Andernach. As they met, the mad little postilion gave him a friendly cut with his whip, and broke out into an exclamation, which showed he was from Münster: —

"Jesmariosp! my friend! How is the Man in the Kaufhaus?"

Now to any candid mind this would seem a fair question enough; but not so thought the red-faced man on horseback; for he waxed exceedingly angry, and replied, as the chaise whirled by: —

"The devil take you, and your Westphalian ham, and pumpernickel!"

Flemming called to his servant, and the servant to the postilion, for an explanation of this short dialogue; and the explanation was, that on the belfry of the Kaufhaus in Coblentz is a huge head with a brazen helmet and a beard; and whenever the clock strikes, at each stroke of the hammer, this giant's head opens its great jaws and smites its teeth together, as if, like the brazen head of Friar Bacon, it would say, "Time was; Time is; Time is past." This figure is known through all the country round about as "The Man in the Kaufhaus"; and when a friend in the country meets a friend from Coblentz, instead of saying, "How are all the good people in Coblentz?"—he says, "How is the Man in the Kaufhaus"? Thus the giant has a great part to play in the town. And thus ended the first day of Flemming's Rhine-journey; and the only good deed he had done was to give an alms to a poor beggar woman, who lifted up her trembling hands and exclaimed: —

"Thou blessed babe!"

CHAPTER III.

HOMUNCULUS.

AFTER all, a journey up the Rhine, in the mists and solitude of December, is not so unpleasant as the reader may imagine. You have the whole road and river to yourself. Nobody is on the wing; hardly a single traveller. The ruins are the same; and the river, and the outlines of the hills; and there are few living figures in the landscape to wake you from your musings, distract your thoughts, and cover you with dust.

Thus likewise thought our traveller, as he continued his journey on the morrow. The day is overcast, and the clouds threaten rain or snow. Why does he stop at the little village of Capellen? Because, right above him on the high cliff, the glorious ruin of Stolzenfels is looking at him with its hollow eyes, and beckoning to him with its gigantic finger, as if to say, "Come up hither, and I will tell thee an old tale." Therefore he alights, and goes up the narrow village lane, and up the stone steps, and up the steep pathway, and throws himself into the arms of that ancient ruin, and holds his breath, to hear the quick footsteps of the falling snow, like the footsteps of angels descending upon earth. And that ancient ruin speaks to him with its hollow voice, and says: —

"Beware of dreams! Beware of the illusions of fancy! Beware of the solemn deceivings of thy vast desires! Beneath me flows the Rhine, and, like the stream of Time, it flows amid the ruins of the Past. I see myself therein, and I know that I am old. Thou, too, shalt be old. Be wise in season. Like the stream of thy life runs the stream beneath us. Down from the distant Alps, — out into the wide world, it bursts away, like a youth from the house of his fathers. Broad-breasted and strong, and with earnest endeavors, like manhood, it makes itself a way through these difficult mountain-passes. And at length, in its old age, it falters, and its steps are weary and slow, and it sinks into the sand, and, through its grave, passes into the great ocean, which is its eternity. Thus shall it be with thee.

"In ancient times, there dwelt within these halls a follower of Jesus of Jerusalem, — an Archbishop in the Church of Christ. He gave himself up to dreams; to the illusions of fancy; to the vast desires of the human soul. He sought after the impossible. He sought after the Elixir of Life, — the Philosopher's Stone. The wealth that should have fed the poor was melted in his crucibles. Within these walls the Eagle of the clouds sucked the blood of the Red Lion, and received the spiritual love of the Green Dragon; but, alas! was childless. In solitude and utter silence did the disciples of the Hermetic Philosophy toil from day to day, from night to night. From the place where thou standest, he gazed at evening upon hills, and vales, and waters spread beneath him; and saw how the setting sun had changed them all to gold, by an alchemy more cunning than his own. He saw the world beneath his feet; and said in his heart, that he alone was wise. Alas! he read more willingly in the book of Paracelsus than in the book of Nature; and, believing that 'where reason hath experience, faith hath no mind,' would fain have made unto himself a child, as the Philosopher taught, — a poor homunculus, in a glass bottle. And he died poor and childless!"

Whether it were worth while to climb the Stolzenfels to hear such a homily as this, some persons may perhaps doubt. But Paul Flemming doubted not. He laid the lesson to heart; and it would have saved him many an hour of sorrow, if he had learned that lesson better, and remembered it longer.

In ancient times, there stood in the citadel of Athens three statues of Minerva. The first was of olive-wood, and, according to popular tradition, had fallen from heaven. The second was of bronze, commemorating the victory of Marathon; and the third of gold and ivory, — a great miracle of art, in the age of Pericles.

And thus in the citadel of Time stands Man himself. In childhood, shaped of soft and delicate wood, just fallen from heaven; in manhood, a statue of bronze, commemorating struggle and victory; and, lastly, in the maturity of age, perfectly shaped in gold and ivory, — a miracle of art!

Flemming had already lived through the olive age. He was passing into the age of bronze, into his early manhood; and in his hands the flowers of Paradise were changing to the sword and shield.

And this reminds me that I have not yet described my hero. I will do it now, as he stands looking down on the glorious landscape; — but in few words. Both in person and character he resembled Harold the Fair-Hair of Norway, who is described, in the old Icelandic Death-Song of Regner Hair-Breeches, as " the young chief so proud of his flowing locks; he who spent his mornings among the young maidens; he who loved to converse with the handsome widows." This was an amiable weakness; and it sometimes led him into mischief. Imagination was the ruling power of his mind. His thoughts were twin-born; the thought itself, and its figurative semblance in the outer world. Thus, through the quiet, still waters of his soul each image floated double, " swan and shadow."

These traits of character, a good heart and a poetic imagination, made his life joyous and the world beautiful; till at length Death cut down the sweet blue flower that bloomed beside him, and wounded him with that sharp sickle, so that he bowed his head, and would fain have been bound up in the same sheaf with the sweet blue flower. Then the world seemed to him less beautiful, and life became earnest. It would have been well, if he could have forgotten the past; that he might not so mournfully have lived in it, but might have enjoyed and improved the present. But this his heart refused to do; and ever, as he floated upon the great sea of life, he looked down through the transparent waters, checkered with sunshine and shade, into the vast chambers of the mighty deep in which his happier days had sunk, and wherein they were lying still visible, like golden sands, and precious stones, and pearls; and, half in despair, half in hope, he grasped downward after them again, and drew back his hand, filled only with sea-weed, and dripping with briny tears! And between him and those golden sands a radiant image floated, like the spirit in Dante's Paradise, singing, "Ave Maria!" and while it sang, down-sinking, and slowly vanishing away.

In all things he acted more from impulse than from fixed principle; as is the case with most young men. Indeed, his principles hardly had time to take root; for he pulled them all up, every now and then, as children do the flowers they have planted, — to see if they are growing. Yet there was much in him which was good; for underneath the flowers and greensward of poetry, and the good principles which would have taken root had he given them time, there lay a strong and healthy soil of common sense, — freshened by living springs of feeling, and enriched by many faded hopes, that had fallen upon it like dead leaves.

CHAPTER IV.

THE LANDLADY'S DAUGHTER.

"ALLEZ, Fuchs! allez, lustig!" cried the impatient postilion to his horses, in accents which, like the wild echo of the Lurley Felsen, came first from one side of the river and then from the other, — that is to say, in words alternately French and German. The truth is, he was tired of waiting; and when Flemming had at length resumed his seat in the postchaise, the poor horses had to make up the time he had lost in dreams on the mountain. This is far oftener the case than most people imagine. One half of the world must sweat and groan, that the other half may dream. It would have been a difficult task for the traveller or his postilion to persuade the horses that these dreams were all for their good.

The next stopping-place was the little tavern of the Star, an out-of-the-way corner in the town of Salzig. It stands on the banks of the Rhine; and, directly in front of it, sheer from the water's edge, rise the mountains of Liebenstein and Sternenfels, each with its ruined castle. These are the Brothers of the old tradition, still gazing at each other face to face; and beneath them, in the valley, stands a cloister, — meet emblem of that orphan child they both so passionately loved.

In a small flat-bottomed boat did the landlady's daughter row Flemming "over the Rhinestream, rapid and roaring wide." She was a beautiful girl of sixteen; with black hair, and dark, lovely eyes, and a face that had a story to tell. How different faces are in this particular! Some of them speak not. They are books in which not a line is written, save perhaps a date. Others are great Family Bibles, with both the Old and the New Testament written in them. Others are Mother Goose and nursery tales; others, bad tragedies, or pickle-herring farces; and others, like that of the landlady's daughter at the Star, sweet love-anthologies, and songs of the affections. It was on that account that Flemming said to her, as they glided out into the swift stream,

"My dear child! do you know the story of the Liebenstein?"

"The story of the Liebenstein," she answered, "I knew by heart when I was a little child."

And here her large, dark, passionate eyes looked into Flemming's, and he doubted not that she had learned the story far too soon and far too well. That story he longed to hear, as if it were unknown to him; for he knew that the girl, who had got it by heart when a child, would tell it as it should be told. So he begged her to repeat the story, which she was but too glad to do; for she loved and believed it, as if it had all been written in the Bible. But before she began, she rested a moment on her oars, and, taking the crucifix which hung suspended from her neck, kissed it, and then let it sink down into her bosom, as if it were an anchor she was dropping into her heart. Meanwhile her moist, dark eyes were turned to heaven. Perhaps her soul was walking with the souls of Cunizza, and Rahab, and Mary Magdalen. Or perhaps she was thinking of that nun, of whom St. Gregory says, in his Dialogues, that, having greedily eaten a lettuce in a garden without making the sign of the cross, she found herself soon after possessed with a devil.

The probability, however, is that she was looking at the ruined castles only, and not to heaven, for she soon began her story, and told Flemming how, "a great, great many years ago, an old man lived in the Liebenstein with his two sons; and how both the young men loved the Lady Geraldine, an orphan under their father's care; and how the elder brother went away in despair, and the younger was betrothed to the Lady Geraldine; and how they were as happy as Aschenputtel and the Prince. And then the holy Saint Bernard came and carried away all the young men to the war, just as Napoleon did afterwards; and the young lord went to the Holy Land, and the Lady

Geraldine sat in her tower and wept, and waited for her lover's return; while the old father built the Sternenfels for them to live in when they were married. And when it was finished, the old man died; and the elder brother came back and lived in the Liebenstein, and took care of the gentle lady. Erelong there came news from the Holy Land that the war was over; and the heart of the gentle lady beat with joy, till she heard that her faithless lover was coming back with a Greek wife, — the wicked man! — and then she went into a convent and became a holy nun. So the young lord of Sternenfels came home, and lived in his castle in great splendor with the Greek woman, who was a wicked woman, and did what she ought not to do. But the elder brother was angry for the wrong done the gentle lady, and challenged the lord of Sternenfels to single combat. And while they were fighting with their great swords in the valley of Bornhofen behind the castle, the convent bells began to ring, and the Lady Geraldine came forth with a train of nuns all dressed in white, and made the brothers friends again, and told them she was the bride of Heaven, and happier in her convent than she could have been in the Liebenstein or the Sternenfels. And when the brothers returned, they found that the false Greek wife had gone away with another knight. So they lived together in peace, and were never married. And when they died" —

"Lisbeth! Lisbeth!" cried a sharp voice from the shore; "Lisbeth! where are you taking the gentleman?"

This recalled the poor girl to her senses; and she saw how fast they were floating down stream. For, in telling the story, she had forgotten everything else, and the swift current had swept them down to the tall walnut-trees of Kamp. They landed in front of the Capuchin monastery. Lisbeth led the way through the little village, and, turning to the right, pointed up the romantic, lonely valley which leads to the Liebenstein, and even offered to go with him. But Flemming patted her cheek, and shook his head. He went up the valley alone.

CHAPTER V.

JEAN PAUL, THE ONLY-ONE.

It was already night when Flemming crossed the Roman bridge over the Nahe, and entered the town of Bingen. He stopped at the White Horse; and, before going to bed, looked out into the dim starlight from his window towards the Rhine, and his heart leaped within him to behold the bold outline of the neighboring hills crested with Gothic ruins; — which in the morning proved to be only a high slated roof, with fantastic chimneys.

The morning was bright and frosty; and the river tinged with gay colors by the rising sun. A soft, thin vapor floated in the air. In the sunbeams flashed the hoar-frost like silver stars; and through a long avenue of trees, whose dripping branches bent and scattered pearls before him Paul Flemming journeyed on in triumph.

The man in the play who wished for "some forty pounds of lovely beef, placed in a Mediterranean Sea of brewis," might have seen his ample desires almost realized at the table d'hôte of the Rheinischen Hof, in Mayence, where Flemming dined that day. At the head of the table sat a gentleman with a smooth, broad forehead, and large, intelligent eyes. He was from Baireuth in Franconia; and talked about poetry and Jean Paul to a pale, romantic-looking lady on his right. There was music all dinner-time, at the other end of the hall, — a harp and a horn and a voice, — so that a great part of the fat gentleman's conversation with the pale lady was lost to Flemming, who sat opposite to her, and could look right into her large melancholy eyes. But what he heard so much interested him, — indeed, the very name of the beloved Jean Paul would have been enough for this, —

143

that he ventured to join in the conversation, and asked the German if he had known the poet personally.

"Yes, I knew him well," replied the stranger. "I am a native of Baireuth, where he passed the best years of his life. In my mind, the man and the author are closely united. I never read a page of his writings without hearing his voice, and seeing his form before me. There he sits, with his majestic, mountainous forehead, his mild blue eyes, and finely cut nose and mouth; his massive frame clad loosely and carelessly in an old green frock, from the pockets of which the corners of books project, and perhaps the end of a loaf of bread and the nose of a bottle; a straw hat, lined with green, lying near him; a huge walking stick in his hand, and at his feet a white poodle, with pink eyes, and a string round his neck. You would sooner have taken him for a master-carpenter than for a poet. Is he a favorite author of yours?" Flemming answered in the affirmative.

"But a foreigner must find it exceedingly difficult to understand him," said the gentleman. "It is by no means an easy task for us Germans."

"I have always observed," replied Flemming, "that the true understanding and appreciation of a poet depend more upon individual than upon national character. If there be a sympathy between the minds of writer and reader, the bounds and barriers of a foreign tongue are soon overleaped. If you once understand an author's character, the comprehension of his writings becomes easy."

"Very true," replied the German; "and the character of Richter is too marked to be easily misunderstood. Its prominent traits are tenderness and manliness,—qualities which are seldom found united in so high a degree as in him. Over all he sees, over all he writes, are spread the sunbeams of a cheerful spirit,— the light of inexhaustible human love. Every sound of human joy and of human sorrow finds a deep-resounding echo in his bosom. In every man, he loves his humanity only, not his superiority. The avowed object of all his literary labors was to raise up again the down-sunken faith in God, Virtue, and Immortality;

and, in an egotistical, revolutionary age, to warm again our human sympathies, which have now grown cold. And not less boundless is his love for Nature,—for this outward, beautiful world. He embraces it all in his arms."

"Yes," answered Flemming, almost taking the words out of the stranger's mouth, "for in his mind all things become idealized. He seems to describe himself when he describes the hero of his Titan, as a child, rocking in a high wind upon the branches of a full-blossomed apple-tree, and as its summit, blown abroad by the wind, now sunk him in deep green, and now tossed him aloft in deep blue and glancing sunshine,— in his imagination stood that tree gigantic;—it grew alone in the universe, as if it were the tree of eternal life; its roots struck down into the abyss; the white and red clouds hung as blossoms upon it; the moon as fruit; the little stars sparkled like dew, and Albano reposed in its measureless summit; and a storm swayed the summit out of Day into Night, and out of Night into Day."

"Yet the spirit of love," interrupted the Franconian, "was not weakness, but strength. It was united in him with great manliness. The sword of his spirit had been forged and beaten by poverty. Its temper had been tried by a thirty years' war. It was not broken, not even blunted, but rather strengthened and sharpened, by the blows it gave and received. And, possessing this noble spirit of humanity, endurance, and self-denial, he made literature his profession; as if he had been divinely commissioned to write. He seems to have cared for nothing else, to have thought of nothing else, than living quietly and making books. He says that he felt it his duty, not to enjoy, nor to acquire, but to write; and boasted that he had made as many books as he had lived years."

"And what do you Germans consider the prominent characteristics of his genius?"

"Most undoubtedly, his wild imagination and his playfulness. He throws over all things a strange and magic coloring. You are startled at the boldness and beauty of his figures and illustrations, which are scattered everywhere with a reckless prodigality ; multitudinous, like the blossoms of early summer, and as fragrant and beautiful. With a thousand extravagances are mingled ten thousand beauties of thought and expression, which kindle the reader's imagination, and lead it onward in a bold flight, through the glow of sunrise and sunset, and the dewy coldness and starlight of summer nights. He is difficult to understand, — intricate, — strange, — drawing his illustrations from every by-corner of science, art, and nature, — a comet among the bright stars of German literature. When you read his works, it is as if you were climbing a high mountain, in merry company, to see the sun rise. At times you are enveloped in mist, — the morning wind sweeps by you with a shout, — you hear the far-off muttering thunders. Wide beneath you spreads the landscape, — field, meadow, town, and winding river. The ringing of distant church-bells, or the sound of solemn village clock, reaches you ; — then arises the sweet and manifold fragrance of flowers, — the birds begin to sing, — the vapors roll away, — up comes the glorious sun, — you revel like a lark in the sunshine and bright blue heaven, and all is a delirious dream of soul and sense, — when suddenly a friend at your elbow laughs aloud, and offers you a piece of Bologna sausage. As in real life, so in his writings : the serious and the comic, the sublime and the grotesque, the pathetic and the ludicrous, are mingled together. At times he is sententious, energetic, simple ; then, again, obscure and diffuse. His thoughts are like mummies embalmed in spices, and wrapped about with curious envelopments ; but within these the thoughts themselves are kings. At times glad, beautiful images, airy forms, move by you, graceful, harmonious ; — at times the glaring, wild-looking fancies, chained together by hyphens, brackets, and dashes, brave and base, high and low, all in their motley dresses, go sweeping down the dusty page, like the galley-slaves that sweep the streets of Rome, where you may chance to see the nobleman and the peasant manacled together."

Flemming smiled at the German's warmth, to which the presence of the lady and the Laubenheimer wine seemed each to have contributed something, and then said : —

" Better an outlaw than not free ! — These are his own words. And thus he changes at his will. Like the God Thor, of the old Northern mythology, he now holds forth the seven stars in the bright heaven above us, and now hides himself in clouds, and pounds away with his great hammer."

" And yet this is not affectation in him," rejoined the German. " It is his nature, — it is Jean Paul. And the figures and ornaments of his style, wild, fantastic, and ofttimes startling, like those in Gothic cathedrals, are not merely what they seem, but massive coignes and buttresses, which support the fabric. Remove them, and the roof and walls fall in. And through these gargoyles, these wild faces, these images of beasts and men carved upon spouts and gutters, flow out, like gathered rain, the bright, abundant thoughts that have fallen from heaven. And all he does is done with a kind of serious playfulness. He is a sea-monster, disporting himself on the broad ocean ; his very sport is earnest ; there is something majestic and serious about it. In everything there is strength, a rough good-nature, all sunshine overhead, and underneath the heavy moaning of the sea. Well may he be called ' Jean Paul, the Only-One.' "

With such discourse the hour of dinner passed ; and after dinner Flemming went to the cathedral. They were singing vespers. A beadle, dressed in blue, with a cocked hat, and a crimson sash and collar, was strutting, like a turkey, along the aisles. This important gentleman conducted Flemming through the church, and showed him the choir, with its heavy-sculptured stalls of oak, and the beautiful figures in brown stone over the bishops' tombs. He then led him, by a side-door, into the old and ruined cloisters of St. Willigis. Through the low Gothic arches the sunshine streamed upon the pavement of tombstones, whose images and inscriptions are mostly effaced by the footsteps of many generations. There stands the tomb of Frauenlob, the Minnesinger. His face is sculptured on an entablature in the wall ; a fine, strongly-marked, and serious countenance. Below it is a bas-relief, representing the poet's funeral. He is carried to his grave by ladies, whose praise he sang, and thereby won the name of Frauenlob.

"This, then," said Flemming, "is the grave, not of Praise-God Bare-bones, but of Praise-the-Ladies Meissen, who wrote songs 'somewhat of lust, and somewhat of love.' But where sleeps the dust of his rival and foe, sweet Master Bartholomew Rainbow?"

He meant this for an aside; but the turkey-cock picked it up, and answered: —

"I do not know. He did not belong to this parish."

I will not prolong this journey, for I am weary and way-worn, and would fain be at Heidelberg with my readers and my hero. It was already night when he reached the Manheim gate, and drove down the long Hauptstrasse so slowly, that it seemed to him endless. The shops were lighted on each side of the street, and he saw faces at the windows here and there, and figures passing in the lamplight, visible for a moment, and then swallowed up in the darkness. The thoughts that filled his mind were strange; as are always the thoughts of a traveller who enters for the first time a strange city. This little world had been going on for centuries before he came; and would go on for centuries after he was gone. Of all the thousands who inhabited it, he knew nothing; and what knew they, or thought, of the stranger, who, in that close post-chaise, weary with travel, and chilled by the evening wind, was slowly rumbling over the paved street? Truly, this world can go

on without us, if we would but think so. If it had been a hearse instead of a post-chaise, it would have been all the same to the people of Heidelberg, — though by no means the same to Paul Flemming.

But at the farther end of the city near the Castle and the Carls-Thor, one warm heart was waiting to receive him; and this was the German heart of his friend the Baron of Hohenfels, with whom he was to pass the winter in Heidelberg. No sooner had the carriage stopped at the iron-grated gate, and the postilion blown his horn, to announce the arrival of a traveller, than the Baron was seen among the servants at the door; and, a few moments afterwards, the two long-absent friends were in each other's arms, and Flemming received a kiss upon each cheek, and another on the mouth, as a pledge and seal of the German's friendship. They held each other long by the hand, and looked into each other's face, and saw themselves in each other's eyes, both literally and figuratively; literally, inasmuch as the images were there; and figuratively, inasmuch as each was imagining what the other thought of him, after the lapse of some years. In friendly hopes and questionings and answers, the evening glided away at the supper-table, where many more things were discussed than the roasted hare and the Johannisberger; and they sat late into the night conversing of the thoughts and feelings and delights which fill the hearts of young men who have already enjoyed and suffered, and hoped and been disappointed.

CHAPTER VI.

HEIDELBERG AND THE BARON.

HIGH and hoar on the forehead of the Jettenbühl stands the Castle of Heidelberg. Behind it rise the oak-crested hills of the Geissberg and the Kaiserstuhl; and in front, from the wide terrace of masonry, you can almost throw a stone upon the roofs of the town, so close do they lie beneath. Above this terrace rises the broad front of the chapel of Saint Udalrich. On the left stands the slender octagon tower of the horologe; and on the right, a huge round tower, battered and shattered by the mace of war, shores up with its broad shoulders the beautiful palace and garden-terrace of Elizabeth, wife of the Count Palatine Frederick. In the rear are older palaces and towers, forming a vast, irregular quadrangle;—Rodolph's ancient castle, with its Gothic gloriette and fantastic gables; the Giant's Tower, guarding the drawbridge over the moat; the Rent Tower, with the linden-trees growing on its summit; and the magnificent Rittersaal of Otho-Henry, Count Palatine of the Rhine and Grand Seneschal of the Holy Roman Empire. From the gardens behind the castle, you pass under the archway of the Giant's Tower into the great courtyard. The diverse architecture of different ages strikes the eye, and curious sculptures. In niches on the wall of Saint Udalrich's chapel stand rows of knights in armor, broken and dismembered; and on the front of Otho's Rittersaal, the heroes of Jewish history and classic fable. You enter the open and desolate chambers of the ruin; and on every side are medallions and family arms; the Globe of the Empire and the Golden Fleece, or the Eagle of the Cæsars, resting on the escutcheons of Bavaria and the Palatinate. Over the windows and doorways and chimney-pieces are sculptures and mouldings of exquisite workmanship; and the eye is bewildered by the profusion of caryatides, and arabesques, and rosettes, and fan-like flutings, and garlands of fruits and flowers and acorns, and bullocks' heads with draperies of foliage, and muzzles of

lions, holding rings in their teeth. The cunning hand of Art was busy for six centuries in raising and adorning these walls; the mailed hands of Time and War have defaced and overthrown them in less than two. Next to the Alhambra of Granada, the Castle of Heidelberg is the most magnificent ruin of the Middle Ages.

In the valley below flows the rushing stream of the Neckar. Close from its margin, on the opposite side, rises the Mountain of All-Saints, crowned with the ruins of a convent; and up the valley stretches the mountain-curtain of the Odenwald. So close and many are the hills which eastward shut the valley in, that the river seems a lake. But westward it opens upon the broad plain of the Rhine, like the mouth of a trumpet; and like the blast of a trumpet is at times the wintry wind through this narrow mountain-pass. The blue Alsatian hills rise beyond; and on a platform or strip of level land, between the Neckar and the mountains, right under the castle, stands the town of Heidelberg; as the old song says, "a pleasant town, when it has done raining."

Something of this did Paul Flemming behold, when he rose the next morning and looked from his window. It was a warm, vapory morning, and the struggle was going on between the mist and the rising sun. The sun had taken the hill-tops, but the mist still kept possession of the valley and the town. The steeple of the great church rose through a dense mass of snow-white clouds; and on the hills the dim vapors were rolling across the windows of the ruined castle, like the fiery smoke of a fierce conflagration. It seemed to him an image of the rising of the sun of Truth on a benighted world; its light streamed through the ruins of centuries; and, down in the Valley of Time, the cross on the Christian church caught its rays, though the priests were singing in mist and darkness below.

In the warm breakfast-room he found the

Baron waiting for him. He was lying upon a sofa, in morning gown and purple-velvet slippers, both with flowers upon them. He had a guitar in his hand, and a pipe in his mouth, at the same time smoking, playing, and humming his favorite song from Goethe: —

> " The water rushed, the water swelled,
>   A fisher sat thereby."

Flemming could hardly refrain from laughing at the sight of his friend; and told him it reminded him of a street-musician he once saw in Aix-la-Chapelle, who was playing upon six instruments at once; having a helmet with bells on his head, a Pan's-reed in his cravat, a violin in his hand, a triangle on his knee, cymbals on his heels, and on his back a bass-drum, which he played with his elbows. To tell the truth, the Baron of Hohenfels was rather a miscellaneous youth, rather a universal genius. He pursued all things with eagerness, but for a short time only: music, poetry, painting, pleasure, even the study of the Pandects. His feelings were keenly alive to the enjoyment of life. His great defect was, that he was too much in love with human nature. But by the power of imagination, in him, the bearded goat was changed to a bright Capricornus; — no longer an animal on earth, but a constellation in heaven. An easy and indolent disposition made him gentle and childlike in his maners; and, in short, the beauty of his character, like that of the precious opal, was owing to a defect in its organization. His person was tall and slightly built; his hair light; and his eyes blue, and as beautiful as those of a girl. In the tones of his voice there was something indescribably gentle and winning; and he spoke the German language with the soft, musical accent of his native province of Kurland. In his manners, if he had not " Antinoüs' easy sway," he had at least an easy sway of his own. Such, in few words, was the friend of Flemming.

" And what do you think of Heidelberg and the old castle?" said he, as they seated themselves at the breakfast-table.

" Last night the town seemed very long to me," replied Flemming; " and as to the castle, I have as yet had but a glimpse of it through the mist. They tell me there is nothing finer in its way than this magnificent ruin; and I have no doubt I shall find it so. Only I wish the stone were gray, and not red. But, red or gray, I foresee that I shall waste many a long hour in its desolate halls. Pray, does anybody live there now-a-days?"

" Nobody," answered the Baron, " but the man who shows the Heidelberg Tun, and a Frenchman, who has been there sketching ever since the year eighteen hundred and ten. He has, moreover, written a super-magnificent description of the ruin, in which he says, that during the day only birds of prey disturb it with their piercing cries, and at night, screech-owls, and other fallow deer. You must buy his book and his sketches."

" Yes, the quotation and the tone of your voice will certainly persuade me so to do."

" Take his or none, my friend, for you will find no others. And seriously, his sketches are very good. There is one on the wall there, which is beautiful, save and except that straddle-bug figure among the bushes in the corner."

" But is there no ghost, no haunted chamber in the old castle?" asked Flemming, after casting a hasty glance at the picture.

" Oh, certainly," replied the Baron; " there are two. There is the ghost of the Virgin Mary in Ruprecht's Tower, and the Devil in the Dungeon."

" Ha! that is grand!" exclaimed Flemming, with evident delight. " Tell me the whole story, quickly! I am as curious as a child."

" It is a tale of the times of Louis le Débonnaire," said the Baron, with a smile; " a mouldy tradition of a credulous age. His brother Frederick lived here in the castle with him, and had a flirtation with Leonore von Luzelstein, a lady of the court, whom he afterwards despised, and was consequently most cordially hated by her. From political motives, he was equally hateful to certain petty German tyrants, who in order to effect his ruin accused him of heresy. But his brother Louis would not deliver him up to their fury, and they resolved to effect by stratagem what they could not by intrigue. Accordingly, Leonore von Luzelstein, disguised as the Virgin Mary, and the father confessor of the Elector,

HEIDELBERG.

in the costume of Satan, made their appearance in the Elector's bedchamber at midnight, and frightened him so horribly, that he consented to deliver up his brother into the hands of two Black Knights, who pretended to be ambassadors from the Vehm-Gericht. They proceeded together to Frederick's chamber; where, luckily, old Gemmingen, a brave soldier, kept guard behind the arras. The monk went foremost in his Satanic garb; but no sooner had he set foot in the prince's bedchamber, than the brave Gemmingen drew his sword, and said, quaintly, 'Die, wretch!' and so he died. The rest took to their heels, and were heard of no more. And now the souls of Leonore and the monk haunt the scene of their midnight crime. You will find the story in the Frenchman's book, worked up with a kind of red-morocco and burnt-cork sublimity, and great melodramatic clanking of chains, and hooting of owls, and other fallow deer!"

"After breakfast," said Flemming, "we will go up to the castle. I must get acquainted with this mirror of owls, this modern Till Eulenspiegel. See what a glorious morning we have! It is truly a wondrous winter! what summer sunshine! what soft Venetian fogs! How the wanton, treacherous air coquets with the old graybeard trees! Such weather makes the grass and our beards grow apace! But we have an old saying in English, that winter never rots in the sky. So he will come down at last in his old-fashioned mealy coat. We shall have snow in spring; and the blossoms will be all snow-flakes. And afterwards a summer, which will be no summer, but, as Jean Paul says, only a winter painted green. Is it not so?"

"Unless I am much deceived in the climate of Heidelberg," replied the Baron, "we shall not have to wait long for snow. We have sudden changes here; and I should not marvel much if it snowed before night."

"The greater reason for making good use of the morning sunshine, then. Let us hasten to the castle, after which my heart yearns."

CHAPTER VII.

LIVES OF SCHOLARS.

THE forebodings of the Baron proved true. In the afternoon the weather changed. The western wind began to blow, and drew a cloud-veil over the face of Heaven, as a breath does over the human face in a mirror. Soon the snow began to fall. Athwart the distant landscape it swept like a white mist. The storm-wind came from the Alsatian hills, and struck the dense clouds aslant through the air. And ever faster fell the snow, a roaring torrent from those mountainous clouds. The setting sun glared wildly from the summit of the hills, and sank like a burning ship at sea, wrecked in the tempest. Thus the evening set in; and winter stood at the gate wagging his white and shaggy beard, like an old harper chanting an old rhyme: "How cold it is! how cold it is!"

"I like such a storm as this," said Flemming, who stood at the window, looking out into the tempest and the gathering darkness. "The silent falling of snow is to me one of the most solemn things in nature. The fall of autumnal leaves does not so much affect me. But the driving storm is grand. It startles me; it awakens me. It is wild and woful, like my own soul. I cannot help thinking of the sea; how the waves run and toss their arms about, — and the wind plays on those great sonorous harps, the shrouds and masts of ships. Winter is here in earnest! How the old churl whistles and threshes the snow! Sleet and rain are falling too. Already the trees are bearded with icicles; and the two broad branches of yonder pine look like the white mustache of some old German baron."

"And to-morrow it will look more wintry still," said his friend. "We shall wake up and find that the frost-spirit has been at work all night building Gothic cathedrals on our windows, just as the Devil built the Cathedral of Cologne. So draw the curtains, and come, sit here by the warm fire."

"And now," said Flemming, having done as his friend desired, "tell me something of Hei-delberg and its University. I suppose we shall lead about as solitary and studious a life here as we did of yore in little Göttingen, with nothing to amuse us, save our own day-dreams."

"Pretty much so," replied the Baron; "which cannot fail to please you, since you are in pursuit of tranquillity. As to the University, it is, as you know, one of the oldest in Germany. It was founded in the fourteenth century by the Count Palatine Ruprecht, and had in the first year more than five hundred students, all busily committing to memory, after the old scholastic wise, the rules of grammar versified by Alexander de Villa Dei, and the extracts made by Peter the Spaniard from Michel Psellus's Synopsis of Aristotle's Organon, and the Categories, with Porphyry's Commentaries. Truly, I do not much wonder that Erigena Scotus should have been put to death by his scholars with their penknives. They must have been pushed to the very verge of despair."

"What a strange picture a university presents to the imagination! The lives of scholars in their cloistered stillness; — literary men of retired habits, and professors who study sixteen hours a day, and never see the world but on a Sunday. Nature has, no doubt for some wise purpose, placed in their hearts this love of literary labor and seclusion. Otherwise, who would feed the undying lamp of thought? But for such men as these, a blast of wind through the chinks and crannies of this old world, or the flapping of a conqueror's banner, would blow it out forever. The light of the soul is easily extinguished. And whenever I reflect upon these things, I become aware of the great importance, in a nation's history, of the individual fame of scholars and literary men. I fear that it is far greater than the world is willing to acknowledge; or, perhaps I should say, than the world has thought of acknowledging. Blot out from England's history the names of Chaucer, Shakespeare, Spenser, and Milton only, and how much of her glory would you blot out with them! Take from Italy such names as Dante, Petrarch, Boccaccio, Michael Angelo, and Raphael, and how much would be wanting to the completeness of her glory! How would the history of Spain look, if the leaves were torn out on which are written the names of Cervantes, Lope de Vega, and Calderon? What would be the fame of Portugal, without her Camoens; of France, without her Racine, and Rabelais, and Voltaire; or of Germany, without her Martin Luther, her Goethe, and her Schiller? Nay, what were the nations of old, without their philosophers, poets, and historians? Tell me, do not these men, in all ages and in all places, emblazon with bright colors the armorial bearings of their country? Yes, and far more than this; for in all ages and in all places they give humanity assurance of its greatness, and say, 'Call not this time or people wholly barbarous; for thus much, even then and there, could the human mind achieve!' But the boisterous world has hardly thought of acknowledging all this. Therein it has shown itself somewhat ungrateful. Else, whence the great reproach, the general scorn, the loud derision, with which, to take a familiar example, the monks of the Middle Ages are regarded? That they slept their lives away is most untrue. For in an age when books were few, — so few, so precious, that they were often chained to their oaken shelves with iron chains, like galley-slaves to their benches, — these men, with their laborious hands, copied upon parchment all the lore and wisdom of the past, and transmitted it to us. Perhaps it is not too much to say, that, but for these monks, not one line of the classics would have reached our day. Surely, then, we can pardon something to those superstitious ages, perhaps even the mysticism of the scholastic philosophy; since, after all, we can find no harm in it only the mistaking of the possible for the real, and the high aspirings of the human mind after a long-sought and unknown somewhat. I think the name of Martin Luther, the monk of Wittenberg, alone sufficient to redeem all monkhood from the reproach of laziness. If this will not, perhaps the vast folios of Thomas Aquinas will; or the countless manuscripts,

144

still treasured in old libraries, whose yellow and wrinkled pages remind one of the hands that wrote them and the faces that once bent over them."

"An eloquent homily," said the Baron, laughing; "a most touching appeal in behalf of suffering humanity! For my part, I am no friend of this entire seclusion from the world. It has a very injurious effect on the mind of a scholar. The Chinese proverb is true: a single conversation across the table with a wise man is better than ten years' mere study of books. I have known some of these literary men who thus shut themselves up from the world. Their minds never come in contact with those of their fellow-men. They read little. They think much. They are mere dreamers. They know not what is new nor what is old. They often strike upon trains of thought, which stand written in good authors some century or so back, and are even current in the mouths of men around them. But they know it not; and imagine they are bringing forward something very original, when they publish their thoughts."

"It reminds me," replied Flemming, "of what Dr. Johnson said of Goldsmith, when he proposed to travel abroad in order to bring home improvements: 'He will bring home a wheelbarrow, and call that an improvement.' It is unfortunately the same with some of these scholars."

"And the worst of it is," said the Baron, "that, in solitude, some fixed idea will often take root in the mind, and grow till it overshadow all one's thoughts. To this must all opinions come; no thought can enter there, which shall not be wedded to the fixed idea. There it remains, and grows. It is like the watchman's wife, in the Tower of Waiblingen, who grew to such a size that she could not get down the narrow staircase; and when her husband died his successor was forced to marry the fat widow in the Tower."

"I remember an old English comedy," said Flemming, laughing, "in which a scholar is described as a creature that can strike fire in the morning at his tinder-box, — put on a pair of lined slippers, — sit ruminating till dinner, and then go to his meat when the bell rings;

—one that hath a peculiar gift in a cough and a license to spit;—or, if you will have him defined by negatives, he is one that cannot make a good leg,—one that cannot eat a mess of broth cleanly. What think you of that?"

"That is just as people are always represented in English comedy," said the Baron. "The portrait is overcharged,—caricatured."

"And yet," continued Flemming, "no longer ago than yesterday, in the preface of a work by a Professor of Philosophy in the University of Halle, I read this passage."

He opened a book and read:—

"Here in Halle, where we have no public garden and no Tivoli, no London Exchange, no Paris Chamber of Deputies, no Berlin nor Vienna theatres, no Strasburg Minster nor Salzburg Alps, no Grecian ruins nor fantastic Catholicism,—in fine nothing, which, after one's daily task is finished, can divert and refresh him, without his knowing or caring how,—I consider the sight of a proof-sheet quite as delightful as a walk in the Prater of Vienna. I fill my pipe very quietly, take out my ink-stand and pens, seat myself in the corner of my sofa, read, correct, and now for the first time really set about thinking what I have written. To see this origin of a book, this metamorphosis of manuscript into print, is a delight to which I give myself up entirely. Look you,—this melancholy pleasure, which would have furnished the departed Voss with worthy matter for more than one blessed Idyl (the more so, as on such occasions I am generally arrayed in a morning gown, though, I am sorry to say, not a calamanco one, with great flowers),—this melancholy pleasure has already grown here in Halle to a sweet, pedantic habit. Since I began my hermit's life here, I have been printing; and so long as I remain here, I shall keep on printing. In all probability, I shall die with a proof-sheet in my hand."

"This," said Flemming, closing the book, "is no caricature by a writer of comedy, but a portrait by a man's own hand. We can see by it how easily, under certain circumstances, one may glide into habits of seclusion, and in a kind of undress, slipshod hardihood, with a pipe and a proof-sheet, defy the world. Into

this state scholars have too often fallen; thus giving some ground for the prevalent opinion, that scholarship and rusticity are inseparable. To me, I confess, it is painful to see the scholar and the world assume so often a hostile attitude, and set each other at defiance. Surely, it is a characteristic trait of a great and liberal mind, that it recognizes humanity in all its forms and conditions. I am a student;—and always, when I sit alone at night, I recognize the divinity of the student, as she reveals herself to me in the flame of the midnight lamp. But, because solitude and books are not unpleasant to me,—nay, wished for, sought after, —shall I say to my brother, Thou fool! Shall I take the world by the beard, and say, Thou art old, and mad! Shall I look society in the face, and say, Thou art heartless!—Heartless! Beware of that word! The good Jean Paul says very wisely, that 'Life in every shape should be precious to us, for the same reason that the Turks carefully collect every scrap of paper that comes in their way, because the name of God may be written upon it.' Nothing is more true than this, yet nothing more neglected."

"If it be painful to see this misunderstanding between scholars and the world," said the Baron, "I think it is still more painful to see the private sufferings of authors by profession. How many have languished in poverty, how many died broken-hearted, how many gone mad with over-excitement and disappointed hopes! How instructive and painfully interesting are their lives! with so many weaknesses, so much to pardon, so much to pity, so much to admire! I think he was not so far out of the way who said that next to the Newgate Calendar the Biography of Authors is the most sickening chapter in the history of man."

"It is indeed enough to make one's heart ache!" interrupted Flemming. "Only think of Johnson and Savage, rambling about the streets of London at midnight, without a place to sleep in; Otway starved to death; Collins mad, and howling like a dog, through the aisles of Chichester Cathedral, at the sound of church music! and Goldsmith, strutting up Fleet Street in his peach-blossom coat, to knock a bookseller over the pate with one of his own volumes; and, then, in his poverty, about to marry his landlady in Green Arbor Court."

"A life of sorrow and privation, a hard life indeed, do these poor devil authors have of it," replied the Baron; "and then at last must get them to the workhouse, or creep away into some hospital to die."

"After all," said Flemming, with a sigh, "poverty is not a crime."

"But something worse," interrupted the Baron; "as Dufresny said, when he married his laundress, because he could not pay her bill. He was the author, as you know, of the opera of Lot, at whose representation the great pun was made: — I say the great pun, as we say the great Tun of Heidelberg. As one of the performers was singing the line, '*L'amour a vaincu Loth,*' (*vingt culottes,*) a voice from the pit cried out, '*Qu'il en donne une à l'auteur!*'"

Flemming laughed at the unseasonable jest; and then, after a short pause, continued: —

"And yet, if you look closely at the causes of these calamities of authors, you will find that many of them spring from false and exaggerated ideas of poetry and the poetic character; and from disdain of common sense, upon which all character worth having is founded. This comes from keeping aloof from the world, apart from our fellow-men; disdain-

ful of society, as frivolous. By too much sitting still the body becomes unhealthy, and soon the mind. This is Nature's law. She will never see her children wronged. If the mind, which rules the body, ever forgets itself so far as to trample upon its slave, the slave is never generous enough to forgive the injury, but will rise and smite its oppressor. Thus has many a monarch mind been dethroned."

"After all," said the Baron, "we must pardon much to men of genius. A delicate organization renders them keenly susceptible to pain and pleasure. And then they idealize everything; and, in the moonlight of fancy, even the deformity of vice seems beautiful."

"And this you think should be forgiven?"

"At all events, it is forgiven. The world loves a spice of wickedness. Talk as you will about principle, impulse is more attractive, even when it goes too far. The passions of youth, like unhooded hawks, fly high, with musical bells upon their jesses; and we forget the cruelty of the sport in the dauntless bearing of the gallant bird."

"And thus do the world and society corrupt the scholar!" exclaimed Flemming.

Here the Baron rang, and ordered a bottle of Prince Metternich. He then very slowly filled his pipe, and began to smoke. Flemming was lost in a day-dream.

CHAPTER VIII.

LITERARY FAME.

Time has a Doomsday-Book, upon whose pages he is continually recording illustrious names. But as often as a new name is written there, an old one disappears. Only a few stand in illuminated characters, never to be effaced. These are the high nobility of Nature, — Lords of the Public Domain of Thought. Posterity shall never question their titles. But those whose fame lives only in the indiscreet opinion of unwise men, must soon be as well forgotten as if they had never been. To this great oblivion must most men come. It is better, therefore, that they should soon make up their minds to this, — well knowing that, as

their bodies must erelong be resolved into dust again, and their graves tell no tales of them, so must their names likewise be utterly forgotten, and their most cherished thoughts, purposes, and opinions have no longer an individual being among men, but be resolved and incorporated into the universe of thought. If, then, the imagination can trace the noble dust of heroes, till we find it stopping a beer-barrel, and know that

"Imperial Cæsar, dead and turned to clay,
May stop a hole to keep the wind away," —

not less can it trace the noble thoughts of great

men, till it finds them mouldered into the common dust of conversation, and used to stop men's mouths, and patch up theories, to keep out the flaws of opinion. Such, for example, are all popular adages and wise proverbs, which are now resolved into the common mass of thought; their authors forgotten, and having no more an individual being among men.

It is better, therefore, that men should soon make up their minds to be forgotten, and look about them, or within them, for some higher motive, in what they do, than the approbation of men, which is fame, — namely, their duty; that they should be constantly and quietly at work, each in his sphere, regardless of effects, and leaving their fame to take care of itself. Difficult must this indeed be, in our imperfection; impossible, perhaps, to achieve it wholly. Yet the resolute, the indomitable will of man can achieve much, — at times, even this victory over himself; being persuaded that fame comes only when deserved, and then is as inevitable as destiny, for it is destiny.

It has become a common saying that men of genius are always in advance of their age; which is true. There is something equally true, yet not so common; namely, that of these men of genius, the best and bravest are in advance not only of their own age, but of every age. As the German prose-poet says, every possible future is behind them. We cannot suppose that a period of time will ever arrive, when the world, or any considerable portion of it, shall have come up abreast with these great minds, so as fully to comprehend them.

And, oh, how majestically they walk in history! some like the sun, "with all his travelling glories round him;" others wrapped in gloom, yet glorious as a night with stars. Through the else silent darkness of the past, the spirit hears their slow and solemn footsteps. Onward they pass, like those hoary elders seen in the vision of an earthly paradise, attendant angels bearing golden lights before them, and, above and behind, the whole air painted with seven listed colors, as from the trail of pennons!

And yet, on earth, these men were not happy, — not all happy, in the outward circumstance of their lives. They were in want, and in pain, and familiar with prison-bars, and the damp, weeping walls of dungeons! Oh, I have looked with wonder upon those who, in sorrow and privation, and bodily discomfort, and sickness, which is the shadow of death, have worked right on to the accomplishment of their great purposes; toiling much, enduring much, fulfilling much; — and then, with shattered nerves, and sinews all unstrung, have laid themselves down in the grave, and slept the sleep of death, — and the world talks of them, while they sleep!

It would seem, indeed, as if all their sufferings had but sanctified them; as if the death-angel, in passing, had touched them with the hem of his garment, and made them holy; as if the hand of disease had been stretched out over them only to make the sign of the cross upon their souls! And as in the sun's eclipse we can behold the great stars shining in the heavens, so in this life-eclipse have these men beheld the lights of the great eternity, burning solemnly and forever!

This was Flemming's reverie. It was broken by the voice of the Baron, suddenly exclaiming: —

"An angel is flying over the house! — Here, in this goblet, fragrant as the honey of Hymettus, fragrant as the wild-flowers in the Angel's Meadow, I drink to the divinity of thy dreams."

"This is all sunshine," said Flemming, as he drank. "The wine of the Prince, and the Prince of wines. By the way, did you ever read that brilliant Italian dithyrambic, Redi's Bacchus in Tuscany? an ode which seems to have been poured out of the author's soul, as from a golden pitcher,

'Filled with the wine
Of the vine
Benign,
That flames so red in Sansovine.'

He calls the Montepulciano the king of all wines."

"Prince Metternich," said the Baron, "is greater than any king in Italy; and I wonder that this precious wine has never inspired a German poet to write a Bacchus on the Rhine. Many little songs we have on this theme, but none very extraordinary. The best are Max Schenkendorf's Song of the Rhine, and the Song of Rhine Wine, by Claudius, a poet who never drank Rhenish without sugar. We will drink for him a blessing on the Rhine."

And again the crystal lips of the goblets kissed each other, with a musical chime, as of evening bells at vintage-time from the villages on the Rhine. Of a truth, I do not much wonder that the German poet Schiller loved to write by candle-light with a bottle of Rhine-wine upon the table. Nor do I wonder at the worthy schoolmaster, Roger Ascham, when he says, in one of his letters from Germany to Mr. John Raven, of John's College: "Tell Mr. Maden I will drink with him now a carouse of wine; and would to God he had a vessel of Rhenish wine; and perchance, when I come to Cambridge, I will so provide here, that every year I will have a little piece of Rhenish wine." Nor, in fine, do I wonder at the German emperor of whom he speaks in another letter to the same John Raven, and says, "The emperor drank the best that I ever saw; he had his head in the glass five times as long as any of us, and never drank less than a good quart at once of Rhenish wine."

"But to resume our old theme of scholars and their whereabout," said the Baron, with an unsual glow, caught, no doubt, from the golden sunshine, imprisoned, like the student Anselmus, in the glass bottle; "where should the scholar live? In solitude, or in society? in the green stillness of the country, where he can hear the heart of Nature beat, or in the dark, gray town, where he can hear and feel the throbbing heart of man? I will make answer for him, and say, in the dark, gray town. Oh, they do greatly err who think that the stars are all the poetry which cities have; and therefore that the poet's only dwelling should be in sylvan solitudes, under the green roof of trees. Beautiful, no doubt, are all the forms of Nature, when transfigured by the miraculous power of poetry; hamlets and harvest-fields, and nut-brown waters, flowing ever under the forest, vast and shadowy, with all the sights and sounds of rural life. But after all, what are these but the decorations and painted scenery in the great theatre of human life? What are they but the coarse materials of the poet's song? Glorious indeed is the world of God around us, but more glorious the world of God within us. There lies the Land of Song; there lies the poet's native land. The river of life, that flows through streets tumultuous, bearing along so many gallant hearts, so many wrecks of humanity;—the many homes and households, each a little world in itself, revolving round its fireside, as a central sun; all forms of human joy and suffering, brought into that narrow compass;—and to be in this, and be a part of this; acting, thinking, rejoicing, sorrowing, with his fellow-men;—such, such should be the poet's life. If he would describe the world, he should live in the world. The mind of the scholar, if you would have it large and liberal, should come in contact with other minds. It is better that his armor should be somewhat bruised by rude encounters even, than hang forever rusting on the wall. Nor will his themes be few or trivial, because apparently shut in between the walls of houses, and having merely the decorations of street scenery. A ruined character is as picturesque as a ruined castle. There are dark abysses and yawning gulfs in the human heart, which can be rendered passable only by bridging them over with iron nerves and sinews, as Challey bridged the Sarine in Switzerland, and Telford the sea between Anglesea and England, with chain bridges. These are the great themes of human thought; not green grass, and flowers, and moonlight. Besides, the mere external forms of Nature we make our own, and carry with us everywhere, by the power of memory."

"I fear, however," interrupted Flemming, "that in towns the soul of man grows proud. He needs at times to be sent forth, like the Assyrian monarch, into green fields, 'a wondrous wretch and weedless,' to eat green herbs, and be wakened and chastised by the rain shower and winter's bitter weather. Moreover, in cities there is danger of the soul's becoming wed to pleasure, and forgetful of its high vocation. There have been souls dedicated to heaven from childhood, and guarded by good angels as sweet seclusions for holy thoughts, and prayers, and all good purposes; wherein pious wishes dwelt like nuns, and every image was a saint; and yet in life's vicissitudes, by the treachery of occasion, by the thronging passions of great cities, have become soiled and sinful. They resemble those convents on the river Rhine, which have been changed to taverns; from whose chambers the pious inmates have long departed, and in whose cloisters the footsteps of travellers have effaced the images of buried saints, and whose walls are written over with ribaldry and the names of strangers, and resound no more with holy hymns, but with revelry and loud voices."

"Both town and country have their dangers," said the Baron; "and therefore, wherever the scholar lives, he must never forget his high vocation. Other artists give themselves up wholly to the study of their art. It becomes with them almost religion. For the most part, and in their youth at least, they dwell in lands where the whole atmosphere of the soul is beauty; ladened with it, as the air may be with vapor, till their very nature is saturated with the genius of their art. Such, for example, is the artist's life in Italy."

"I agree with you," exclaimed Flemming; "and such should be the poet's everywhere; for he has his Rome, his Florence, his whole glowing Italy, within the four walls of his library. He has in his books the ruins of an antique world, — and the glories of a modern one, — his Apollo and Transfiguration. He must neither forget nor undervalue his vocation; but thank God that he is a poet; and everywhere be true to himself, and to 'the vision and the faculty divine' he recognizes within him."

"But, at any rate, a town life is most eventful," continued the Baron. "The men who make, or take, the lives of poets and scholars, always complain that these lives are barren of incidents. Hardly a literary biography begins without some such apology, unwisely made. I confess, however, that it is not made without some show of truth, if by incidents we mean only those startling events which suddenly turn aside the stream of time, and

change the world's history in an hour. There is certainly a uniformity, pleasing or unpleasing, in literary life, which for the most part makes to-day seem twin-born with yesterday. But if by incidents you mean events in the history of the human mind, (and why not?) noiseless events, that do not scar the forehead of the world as battles do, yet change it not the less, then surely the lives of literary men are most eventful. The complaint and the apology are both foolish. I do not see why a successful book is not as great an event as a successful campaign; only different in kind, and not easily compared."

"Indeed," interrupted Flemming, "in no sense is the complaint strictly true, though at times apparently so. Events enough there are, were they all set down. A life that is worth writing at all is worth writing minutely. Besides, all literary men have not lived in silence and solitude; — not all in stillness, not all in shadow. For many have lived in troubled times, in the rude and adverse fortunes of the state and age, and could say, with Wallenstein,

' Our life was but a battle and a march;
    And, like the wind's blast, never resting, homeless,
    We stormed across the war-convulsed earth.'

Many such examples has history recorded, — Dante, Cervantes, Byron, and others; men of iron, — men who have dared to breast the strong breath of public opinion, and, like spectre-ships, come sailing right against the wind. Others have been puffed out by the first adverse wind that blew; disgraced and sorrowful, because they could not please others. Had they been men, they would have made these disappointments their best friends, and learned from them the needful lesson of self-reliance."

"To confess the truth," added the Baron, "the lives of literary men, with their hopes and disappointments, and quarrels and calamities, present a melancholy picture of man's strength and weakness. On that very account the scholar can make them profitable for encouragement, consolation, warning."

"And after all," continued Flemming, " perhaps the greatest lesson which the lives of literary men teach us is told in a single word: Wait!—Every man must patiently bide his time. He must wait. More particularly in lands like my native land, where the pulse of life beats with such feverish and impatient throbs, is the lesson needful. Our national character wants the dignity of repose. We seem to live in the midst of a battle,—there is such a din, such a hurrying to and fro. In the streets of a crowded city it is difficult to walk slowly. You feel the rushing of the crowd and rush with it onward. In the press of our life it is difficult to be calm. In this stress of wind and tide, all professions seem to drag their anchors, and are swept out into the main. The voices of the Present say, 'Come!' But the voices of the Past say, 'Wait!' With calm and solemn footsteps the rising tide bears against the rushing torrent up stream, and pushes back the hurrying waters. With no less calm and solemn footsteps, nor less certainty, does a great mind bear up against public opinion, and push back its hurrying stream. Therefore should every man wait,—should bide his time. Not in listless idleness,—not in useless pastime,—not in querulous dejection,—but in constant, steady, cheerful endeavors, always willing and fulfilling, and accomplishing his task, that, when the occasion comes, he may be equal to the occasion. And if it never comes, what matters it? What matters it to the world, whether I, or you, or another man did such a deed, or wrote such a book, so be it the deed and book were well done? It is the part of an indiscreet and troublesome ambition to care too much about fame,—about what the world says of us;—to be always looking into the faces of others for approval; to be always anxious for the effect of what we do and say; to be always shouting to hear the echo of our own voices. If you look about you, you will see men who are wearing life away in feverish anxiety of fame, and the last we shall ever hear of them will be the funeral bell that tolls them to their early graves! Unhappy men, and unsuccessful! because their purpose is, not to accomplish well their task, but to clutch the 'trick and fantasy of fame'; and they go to their graves with purposes unaccomplished and wishes unfulfilled. Better for them, and for the world in their example, had they known how to wait! Believe me, the talent of success is nothing more than doing what you can do well; and doing well whatever you do,—without a thought of fame. If it come at all, it will come because it is deserved, not because it is sought after. And, moreover, there will be no misgivings, no disappointment, no hasty, feverish, exhausting excitement."

Thus endeth the First Book of Hyperion. I make no record of the winter. Paul Flemming buried himself in books,—in old, dusty books. He worked his way diligently through the ancient poetic lore of Germany, from Frankish Legends of Saint George, and Saxon Rhyme-Chronicles, and Nibelungen-Lieds, and Helden-Buchs, and Songs of the Minnesingers and Meistersingers, and Ships of Fools, and Reynard the Foxes, and Death-Dances, and Lamentations of Damned Souls, into the bright, sunny land of harvests, where, amid the golden grain and the blue corn-flowers, walk the modern bards, and sing.

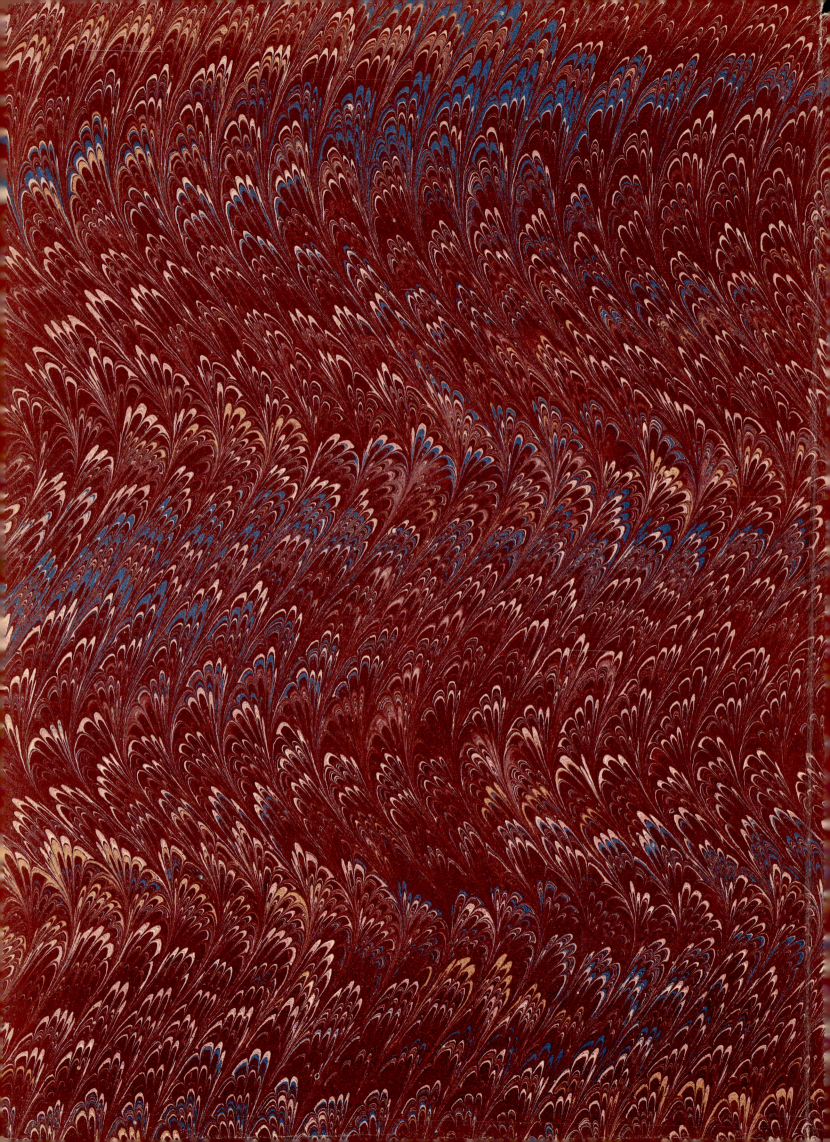